D0310915

State-Local Tax Equity

State-Local Tax Equity

An Empirical Analysis of the Fifty States

Donald Phares
University of Missouri–St. Louis

Lexington Books
D.C. Heath and Company
Lexington, Massachusetts
Toronto London

Library of Congress Cataloging in Publication Data

Phares, Donald.
State-local tax equity.

Bibliography: p.
1. Taxation, State. 2. Local taxation–United States. I. Title.
HJ2385.P5 336.2'00973 72-13400
ISBN 0-669-86108-1

Published simultaneously in Canada.

Printed in the United States of America.

International Standard Book Number: 0-669-86108-1

Library of Congress Catalog Card Number: 72-13400

"To Those who make it all worth while:
Chris, Scott, Mark and Sean."

Contents

List of Tables

Preface

The fiscal pressures emerging in the state-local sector are widely analyzed from many points of view. An extensive literature has developed on the determinants of state-local fiscal activity, and more recently a new literature on fiscal disparities has emphasized still another dimension of the state-local fiscal dilemma.

At the present, however, the body of literature on the burden of state-local taxation is limited in one crucial respect. While there does exist substantial literature on the comparative burden of state-local taxation, it is aggregate in nature and gives no explicit recognition to the distributional dimension of burden. The weakness lies in the fact that more detailed knowledge is required on the incidence configuration of each specific state-local tax and total taxes for each state. It is the contention of this study that more explicit knowledge on the distribution of the state-local tax burden is necessary for an effective public policy, both state-local and federal.

The level of tax burden in a particular state, the regressivity of various forms of taxation and the total tax system, variation across states and income groups, and specific features of a system's tax structure designed to cope with regressivity and extreme burden all have important implications for equity (however defined) and the capacity of state-local systems to meet the demands for public goods and services.

The following study is designed to elaborate on these aspects of state-local taxation. It is not intended to replace studies such as those done by the Advisory Commission on Intergovernmental Relations or the indices of tax effort of the National Education Association but rather to complement them by providing empirical content to the incidence dimension of state-local taxation.

My debt in preparing this study accrues to many people. My work with Roy Bahl provided the genesis for the study and much assistance during the early stages of gestation. My greatest debt is to Seymour Sacks who was always willing to spend time as a "sounding block" and provide comments and suggestions for improvement. The many hours spent in discussion with him were invaluable.

I would also like to thank the Center of Community and Metropolitan Studies at the University of Missouri-St. Louis and its director, Norton Long, for the time and assistance necessary for the completion of the manuscript. In particular I would like to thank Mmes. Evastein King, LaVerne Cadamey, and Thessalonia Bunton for their diligent preparation of the manuscript and Ms. Nena Groskind for her editorial assistance.

Responsibility for the final product, however, remains with the author and all shortcomings must accrue thereto.

State-Local Tax Equity

1 Introduction: Purposes, Achievements, and Caveats

At present, state-local fiscal activity occupies a focal point in the public forum. Discussion ranges from the cries of agony of taxpayers to the day-by-day financial plight of public officials to the research concerns of academia. The emerging fiscal tension has focused attention on the problem of financing the state-local public sector. Growth in the number of studies on revenue sources, debt-financing, federal and state aid, and expenditure patterns is a good proxy for the increasing intensity of concern. More recently, attention has shifted to the comparative position of local governments and the nature and extent of disparities in tax base, expenditure level, tax capacity, and tax effort.[1] Thus there now exists a new literature on disparities in local fiscal activity and the tax base available to finance public goods. This book is intended to supplement existing literature by examining interstate variations in fiscal characteristics.

It is imperative for the formulation of responsible public policy that the fiscal milieu of the state-local sector be properly understood. If the American federal system is to survive as a form of governmental organization, its constituent units must be viable fiscal entities. A brief journey through the pages of Senate hearings, popular magazines, local newspapers, and academic research will attest to the demand for such knowledge. The need is especially acute at an empirical level.

Despite the rising level of anxiety over state and local fiscal matters on the part of taxpayers and government officials, there remains a paucity of empirical research on the distribution of the costs of the state-local public sector, state by state. This gap results from a concentration of existing research at one or the other of two extremes. On the one hand, there is a group of studies examining the cost of public goods at an aggregate level (i.e., "all government" or the federal, state, or local governments as distinct sectors) a type of analysis which, while useful for some purposes, is potentially deceptive when operating in the context of the state-local sector, where extreme variation in public policy is a predominant feature. At the other extreme is more limited research on particular states. Once again, such a focus may be useful for specific purposes, but the results are of questionable value in generalizing about fiscal activity in other systems.

In light of the fiscal plight of the state-local sector, it seems appropriate to examine empirically each of these fifty governmental systems. This makes it possible either to focus attention at the level of one individual system or to shift to interstate comparisons. By undertaking such a study, the variation across systems that is methodologically "hidden" by aggregate sector analysis or "ignored" by individual state analysis is made explicit, providing information that is necessary and long overdue.

Scope of the Study

The scope of past studies on the distribution of the costs of the public sector has been limited to either entire governmental sectors or individual states,[a] leaving a wide range of activity within the state-local sector that has not been given sufficient statistical scrutiny. This study will attempt to fill that gap by focusing on the question of tax incidence/tax burden for each state-local system. In line with this goal, each of the fifty state-local tax systems, as well as the characteristics of specific taxes used within those systems, will be examined. To address the question of tax incidence/tax burden, effective rates of taxation are estimated; burden is defined as taxes paid relative to income. To examine the incidence of public sector costs, the income distribution is divided into nine discrete intervals ranging from $0-1,999 to $15,000 and over. Effective rates are estimated for each state by type of tax and income class.

The end product of this empirical analysis is a set of effective tax-rate data matrices, one for each tax. In addition, estimates are made of the incidence of taxation using alternative shifting-incidence assumptions. This produces a set of twenty-two matrices of effective tax rates which provide the data for the statistical analysis in Chapters 5 and 6. The effective rate matrices are provided in Appendix D.

Outline of the Study: Major Purposes

The purpose of this study, broadly defined, is to examine the level and distribution of the costs of public goods for each of the fifty states. This is accomplished by developing a model to estimate the claim of the public sector on private resources. Effective rates of taxation are computed as an approximation to this claim. To do this, the model incorporates, on a state-by-state basis, variations in income, major provisions of the tax system, and theoretical-empirical knowledge of the shifting-incidence of taxation. In addition to these considerations, a model dealing with the state-local sector must also specify the flow of taxes among fiscal systems. Thus the basic incidence model defined in Chapter 3 is modified in Chapter 4 to allow for the spatial flow of taxes among governmental systems.

A second purpose of this study is to examine empirically the distributional impact of the costs of the public sector. The findings for each specific tax are

[a]This will be documented in Chapter 2.

detailed in Chapter 5. Effective tax rates are estimated for each type of tax, and the variation in these rates across states for each tax is computed. This provides a tax-by-tax picture of tax incidence/tax burden. When the mean (level of tax burden) and coefficient of variation (variation across systems) for each tax by income class are computed for those states actually using the tax,[b] it is found that there are substantial differences across systems in both the level and variation of burden for specific taxes and comparatively, across various types of taxation. Differences in state-local tax policy manifested as differences in tax incidence/tax burden are documented and their nature and extent approximated.

To facilitate state-by-state analysis, three statistical techniques are applied to the data on effective rates of taxation derived from the model developed in Chapters 3 and 4 (see Appendix D). Each of these techniques deals with a different facet of the tax structure. The first—regression analysis—examines the pattern of effective tax rates as it varies with income. The results, reported in Chapter 6, indicate the nature and variation in tax incidence (i.e., regressive, proportional, progressive) and provide sufficient data to classify states according to their overall pattern of incidence. The second technique—factor analysis—is used to construct indices of tax burden for each system. These indices summarize not only the level of burden but also the manner in which it is distributed to various income groups. The third technique—the Gini Ratio of Concentration—examines inequality in the distribution of tax payments. The results indicate how taxes are allocated by tax-paying units (families) or by income shares. These three statistical techniques permit the impact of taxation to be scrutinized from several points of view, providing knowledge of the regressivity-progressivity of tax structures, the burden of taxation as it varies by state, and the degree of inequality in the allocation of tax payments among family units and income shares.

Finally, the output of the statistical analysis will be related to existing tax policy, and suggestions for change will be made. Inferences about the fiscal relation among levels of government are also possible. The question of "equity" in taxation comes immediately to mind and is one of the major focuses of the study. By examining each state-local system and the characteristics of their tax structure, much can be inferred about the end result of different systems of taxes (e.g., Delaware versus Washington), permitting some conclusions about "desirable" versus "undesirable" tax structure composition. In addition, equity for the state-local sector is heavily dependent upon how the costs of providing public goods will be shared among the federal, state, and local governments.

[b]The mean and coefficient of variation are purposely computed for only those systems that actually use the tax. Thus for the personal income tax the sample size for computing these statistics is the thirty-seven states that had a personal income tax in effect. This shows the level and variance in actual rather than potential use if some systems do not use a certain type of taxation.

Continued dependence on property taxation at the local level raises interesting questions of federal and state aid to local government, the rearrangement of expenditure responsibility and general governmental reorganization. For example, what is the rationale for shifting welfare costs to the federal government and education costs to the state?

Another factor which must be considered is the impact of the local sector within each of the fifty systems. It is this sector that has shouldered much of the fiscal burden of the process of urbanization inherent in our rural-to-urban population migration. Also, the majority of the U.S. population now lives in one of the nation's Standard Metropolitan Statistical Areas. The distribution of the costs of public goods in the local sector, resulting from its heavy dependence on the property tax, has important implications for its capacity to keep pace with a rising level of demand for public goods and services, local financing of education, alternative forms of "fiscal federalism," local government reorganization schemes, and recent court decisions on the constitutionality of financing education with the property tax. These issues will be discussed in Chapters 7 and 8.

Some Caveats

No pretense is made concerning the comprehensiveness of the material to follow. The extreme variation that characterizes state and local taxation policy is sufficient to stymie any attempt at developing a model specified fully enough to cover all possible nuances. But this probably would not be a worthwhile expenditure of time and effort. Discerning patterns of fiscal behavior and developing generalizations concerning taxation at the state-local level seem much more reasonable and profitable endeavors. The ability to describe the incidence pattern and degree of variation across governmental units of a certain tax, or to show that certain systems are progressive, proportional, or regressive and that they vary in their pattern of incidence, represents a relevant and important contribution to the understanding and design of public policy both within a given state and for the fiscal relation among sectors of the federal system. Detailed provisions for change in any particular government's tax policy must necessarily be based on close scrutiny of the unit in question—a scrutiny this study is not intended to provide. It is designed, rather, to delineate the comparative position of each system vis-à-vis the incidence and burden of their tax structures and specific tax instruments.

There are a few caveats that must be made explicit before the reader continues. First, the focus is explicitly on the tax side of the budget. A fully specified model would examine the incidence of expenditures as well. While some attempts have been made to carry out such research for entire governmental sectors, much of the comment on such endeavors has not been overly optimistic.[2] The incidence of public expenditures is a question that remains plagued by serious conceptual and methodological confusion.[c] Second, no consideration is given to the possibility of a declining marginal utility of income. Thus the question of whether an effective tax rate of 0.05 for the $0-1,999 income class represents the same burden as a 0.05 rate for the over $15,000 class is not answered. Third, no attention is given to the excess burden of taxation. The focus is on defining what the actual incidence and burden of taxation is rather than how some hypothetical modification might shift toward a more Pareto optimal position.[d] Let it be noted, however, that often the first step in reaching "where we would like to be" is an understanding of "where we are" and how to define policy so that we are able to move between the two positions. Fourth, the study looks at the incidence of taxation without attempting to delineate the full ramification of tax policy. Incidence and burden of taxation represent one aspect of fiscal activity most closely related to the distribution function of government. Problems of allocation and stabilization are not dealt with here.[3] For example, the effect on resource allocation of a certain tax is not dealt with. Finally, even though the state-local sector has been disaggregated into its constituent units, there remains considerable variation within each of these systems that is not dealt with. Variation in local government property taxation policy can only be approximated given the thousands of local governments that have the constitutional authority to levy such a tax. The model defined for this study deals with each state-local system but not individual local governments within systems.

Major Accomplishments

With the purposes and limitations of the study spelled out, a brief statement of achievements is in order. Its major contribution lies in a disaggregation of the state-local sector. To date, no study has examined tax incidence and tax burden, state-by-state, with the detail to follow.[e] Such disaggregation permits statistical analysis of the variation across governmental units in the incidence and burden of entire systems of taxes as well as specific taxes. Two of the statistical techniques employed have not as yet been applied to problems of tax incidence/tax burden—factor analysis and the Gini Ratio of Concentration. It is found that both have a great deal to contribute to the understanding of these

[c]For example, one need only look as far as the joint consumption of public goods and their incidence or how to determine the value of public sector output to get a feel for the problems involved in estimating expenditure incidence. At an empirical level, the paucity of data further aggravates the situation.

[d]Pareto optimality is, simple stated, a point from which any movement will make someone worse off.

[e]Chapter 2 summarizes the body of tax-expenditure incidence and shows quite clearly the gap in existing research.

phenomena. In fact, factor analysis is proven to be extremely sensitive to variations in both the level and incidence of tax burdens, offering a powerful technique not yet applied to problems of tax policy. Finally, in the course of the empirical analysis, a detailed set of effective tax rates by type of tax, state, and income class is estimated. These are provided in Appendix D to permit the reader to examine a particular state or set of states in more detail or to carry out further statistical analysis. It is felt that the study offers a genesis for further work in state-local taxation leading eventually to some examination of the total fiscal impact of the state-local budget for each of the fifty governmental systems.

2 Who Pays State-Local Taxes?

The burden of taxation is an area of inquiry that has long been of concern to students of public finance. Since the emergence of public finance as a distinct branch of economics, its students have devoted much time and conceptual effort to determining the incidence of taxation and, more recently, the magnitude of the tax burden. For policy reasons, analysis has focused on the incidence of taxation rather than on its impact, the analytical concern being who actually pays the taxes rather than who has the legal liability for payment.

The analysis of shifting and incidence encompasses a substantial segment of earlier public finance literature. Given various assumptions concerning market structure, price elasticity, cost conditions, and type of taxes, economists are able to isolate the incidence of a tax with varying degrees of success. The analytical framework is generally partial equilibrium, and in this format solutions to the ultimate incidence question are not attempted.

A major problem to be recognized, however, is the general equilibrium nature of incidence. The forces that influence shifting are numerous and highly interrelated. All ramifications of a tax levy can be traced only when recognition is given to every adjustment that is elicited in response to a tax. When certain assumptions are made, e.g., concerning market structure, and everything else is held under *ceteris paribus*, the incidence of a tax can be determined. However, a conceptually complete solution is one that permits the full specification of all adjustment processes.

At an empirical level, a general equilibrium model of incidence is not manageable or conceptually well-defined, especially when the focus is each tax for each state-local system.[a] An empirical solution must utilize the "best" available theory on the shifting and incidence of specific taxes balanced with unavoidable empirical constraints. Any study (including this one) must make use of such assumptions while attempting to account for as much of the variation in state-local tax policy as is empirically practicable.[1]

A tax burden study is, in essence, an empirical manifestation of certain shifting and incidence assumptions; such a study does not test such assumptions but rather uses them in estimating burden. It goes beyond the findings of

[a]A general equilibrium analysis would require a set of equations similar in form to a Walrasian solution for general equilibrium but substantially complicated by problems of imperfect market structure, varying elasticities of supply and demand, types of taxes used and characteristics of governmental systems. This is not to mention problems inherent in the nature of public goods.

incidence theory, however, by estimating the magnitude as well as the incidence of the burden. To stipulate that taxes upon corporations are shifted 50 percent to stockholders does little more than indicate the direction of incidence. Since a crucial policy consideration is the magnitude of the burden, the next logical step is to utilize existing knowledge to determine the dollar magnitude of burdens. As a pioneering tax study emphasizes: "There is much qualitative theory on where taxes fall and on their eventual effect on the economy, but very little is known quantitatively in terms of dollar aggregates."[2]

To investigate the impact of taxation, analysis is focused on the distribution of taxes and income by income groups. Burden is estimated by relating taxes paid to income for a given class. This ratio—effective rate of taxation—indicates the claim on private income that is exerted by public sector tax policy. It is an average for a class and does not attempt to deal with excess burden, the incidence of public sector expenditures, or variations in the marginal utility of money.[3]

Past studies on the distribution of tax burdens have been focused at two almost polar opposite positions. Most empirical research has dealt with aggregate tax burdens at the federal, state-local, or "all government" level, the objective being to determine the tax burden for an entire governmental sector of the economy. At the other extreme are studies concerned with taxation in one particular state-local system.

The balance of this chapter will serve two purposes. First, it will trace the historical development in analysis, technique, and empirical feasibility of tax burden studies. Second, it will emphasize the polarity that has developed in the literature by indicating the total lack of attention to variations in the distributional aspects of tax burdens across states.[b]

Aggregate Studies: Distribution of Tax Burdens

There were several studies during the late 1930s and early 1940s that provided the impetus for more detailed empirical investigation of the distributive impact of taxation. The first, by Newcomer, examined the burden of taxation on twenty hypothetical families of various occupations and incomes in New York and Illinois.[4] Due to the limited focus of the study, the results were only tentatively amenable to a more general definition of national patterns. While this study coped with numerous theoretical problems relevant to shifting and incidence, provided estimates using alternative assumptions, and utilized the most refined data available (on income, consumption patterns, taxes, etc.), the results were extremely vulnerable due to its limited scope.[5]

[b]Explicit discussion of the allocation of taxes by income class will be presented in Chapter 3. The purpose of this chapter is to relate the historical context and relevance of the present study.

The first study to deal with the aggregate distribution of tax burdens was that of the Temporary National Economic Committee (TNEC) for the period 1938-39.[6] While the available data were little better than for the Newcomer analysis, the focus was national and the results were more generally indicative of aggregate patterns. In a follow-up study, Helen Tarasov responded to many criticisms of the TNEC study by introducing refinements in the techniques used to allocate taxes and in the data on aggregate income. The result was an updated, refined version of the TNEC study purged of many of its methodological and empirical deficiencies.[7]

The major contribution of these early studies lies in their attempt to examine the aggregate distribution of tax burdens by developing a model that related shifting and incidence theory to available data on income and consumption patterns. In terms of earlier attempts, the TNEC-Tarasov studies offered considerable improvement in the representativeness of the results.

Following the Tarasov work came a series of studies concerned with the distribution of aggregate tax burdens. The most important of these is that by Musgrave, et al., for the year 1948.[8] This represents the most meticulous investigation of tax incidence that had been undertaken to that date and provides a conceptual and statistical focal point for subsequent analysis. The rationale of the study, as Musgrave points out, is:

> The question who pays the taxes must be answered if taxes are to be raised in accordance with the public's ideas of distributional justice and the maintenance of sound economic conditions.[9]

As is readily admitted by the authors, the study makes use of some "grossly simplifying assumptions" about incidence. Nonetheless, it has assumed a classic position in the literature because of its great attention to detail and precise theoretical specification of the problem. Effective rate estimates are given for all levels of government and several alternative assumptions concerning shifting and incidence are employed to provide a range of plausible distributions.

The research by Musgrave, et al. provided the genesis for a number of studies focused on aggregate tax incidence. Reverberating through academic journals during the early 1950s was a lengthy debate on the theoretical and empirical nuances of tax burden analysis. Much of the debate took place between Musgrave and Rufus Tucker with the 1948 Musgrave study as the focus.

Tucker took issue with this study because of its exclusion of certain categories of income from the base for calculating effective tax rates. He states:

> The effect of ignoring nonmoney income was to make the income of the lowest bracket about two thirds as large as it really was, and therefore to make the apparent tax burden about three halves as large as it really was.[10]

He proceeded to recompute tax burdens for 1948 using an income base which included certain nonmonetary and imputed income components. He summarizes his refinements on the Musgrave, et al. study as follows:

The net effect . . . is enough to vitiate his principal conclusion, regarding the high rate of taxation on persons with incomes under $1,000 and the 'U-shaped' curve of tax rates in our present system as a whole.[11]

Tucker also suggested minor refinements in shifting and incidence assumptions, but these admittedly did not significantly alter Musgrave's findings. The major source of variation results directly from the base chosen for calculating effective rates. The variation that emerges in the final distribution is most significant for the lowest income classes where nonmonetary and imputed items are of greatest relative importance.

The Tucker-Musgrave debate was brought to focus at a round-table discussion held at the 1952 National Tax Association conference.[12] The result was agreement on the source of variation in the distribution of tax burdens across studies, but not on the correct base to be used in the calculation of effective rates.

Still another facet was added to the income base controversy by George Bishop. Using Department of Commerce data for 1958, Bishop noted that the gap between gross national product and personal income was $83 billion. He then argued:

It can hardly be concluded that no part of the tax burden falls on this sizable amount of 'product' for which there are no corresponding income payments to individuals.[13]

Accordingly, Bishop argued for the use of net national product (NNP) as a more appropriate base for computing effective rates of taxation.[c]

Aggregate Studies: Distribution of Tax Burdens and Expenditure Benefits

One inherent weakness in aggregate tax burden studies is their focus on taxation in isolation. This facet of public sector activity can be properly evaluated only in light of the benefits derived from government expenditure policy. As Musgrave points out:

Another defect of this simplified approach is that it is based on a concept of absolute incidence which is open to considerable theoretical objection. Rather we ought to think in terms of a combined incidence of public expenditures and taxes. . . .[14]

While analysis can focus legitimately on each component of a public budget, an analytically complete picture emerges only when the entire budget (taxes and expenditures) is given explicit consideration. This involves empirical estimation of the benefits of public sector expenditures by income class.

[c]The income base controversy will be elaborated upon in Chapter 3.

One of the first studies to relate the burdens and benefits of public sector activity was performed by Adler.[15] He was concerned with the redistribution of income that occurred between 1938-39 and 1946-47. Accordingly, his analysis dealt with the distribution of both taxes and expenditures and the net fiscal influence of the public sector budget. While his model benefited from past work, virtually no statistical or conceptual analysis was then available on the incidence of public expenditures.

Recognizing that this was a weak conceptual foundation on which to base a study of the distribution of government expenditure benefits, Adler offered a rationale based more on politics than economics:

> Statesmen and politicians show full awareness of the incidence of benefits of government expenditures. . . . There is, therefore, a strong presumption in favor of the economist's attempt to allocate the benefits of government services to distinct income classes, geographical areas, or occupational groups.[16]

His results are presented in aggregate form for total government—federal, state, and local. The weakness of dealing with a composite government category lies in the distortion introduced by not giving account to the variation in redistributive impact by level of government. While this is recognized by Adler, no attempt is made to provide disaggregate estimates.[17]

The most significant contribution of the Adler study is not so much the precision of his results as a shift in conceptual emphasis. Adler attempts to define an aggregate picture of the fiscal impact of government and estimate the redistribution that occurred between 1938-39 and 1946-47. This is the first such attempt to deal explicitly with the benefits of government expenditures and is open to considerable criticism, especially concerning the incidence of certain expenditure categories. However, the genesis is provided for more refined subsequent analysis.

Almost cotemporal with the Adler study was one by Tucker, also dealing with the incidence of government expenditure benefits. Noting the almost total lack of empirical research on the incidence of public expenditure benefits, he attempted to reach some general conclusions concerning their effects.[18]

Tucker's calculation of tax burdens rests almost entirely on his past research. He goes further, however, by relating this distribution to one estimated for government expenditure benefits, aggregated for all levels of government. He emphasizes that some types of expenditures may actually be harmful to certain categories of citizens or "positively injurious to the nation as a whole." Despite this, the assumption is made that *every* dollar of expenditure "represents a dollar's worth of benefit to someone."[19]

Using expenditure data for 1948, Tucker isolates some \$30.2 billion that can not be identified as benefiting any specific group of citizens, \$19.6 from the federal government and \$10.6 from state and local governments. The decision was made to allocate this \$30.2 billion (55 percent of total government expenditures in 1948) on four alternative bases, all of which assume proportionality.[20] Such an assumption, taken alone, is sufficient to raise doubts about the results, except as a highly tentative indication of the incidence of government benefits. Tucker sums up his study by stating:

> Rough as they are [the allocators used] they do establish the fact that insofar as the benefits of allocable government expenditures are concerned, the consumer units under $4,000 got a larger share than would correspond to their incomes and those over $4,000 a smaller one.[21]

The next major empirical investigation of the distribution of burdens and benefits of government activity was that by W. Irwin Gillespie.[22] Acutely aware of the severe gap in the literature on the distribution of government expenditure benefits, Gillespie developed data and a methodology to permit a first approximation to expenditure incidence. The analysis commences by noting several possible assumptions concerning the impact of a public sector on the private economy. He defines incidence in terms of a change in relative income position due to public sector budget policy.[23] The empirical calculations assume three dimensions: (1) measurement of an income base, (2) calculation of tax incidence and (3) calculation of expenditure incidence. By combining these three dimensions, using alternative assumptions, Gillespie arrives at ten possible "budget experiments," each of which makes a particular assumption about the treatment of income (Y), taxes (T), transfer payments (R) and government expenditures on goods and services (B).[24] His empirical results are based on two of these budget assumptions. They are:

1. $ER = \dfrac{T}{Y}$

2. $ER = \dfrac{T}{Y + B + R - T}$

Y = Broad income

$(Y + B + R - T)$ = Adjusted broad income

ER = Effective rate

Gillespie readily admits that his study adds nothing to the extant body of tax incidence theory. His contribution lies in estimating the distribution of government expenditure benefits and the net redistributive impact of combined tax and expenditure policy.

Gillespie's study is meticulous in the detail of allocating public expenditures by income class. However, careful attention to detail does not overcome the problems inherent in estimating the impact of public expenditures. As Brazer has aptly noted:

> He [Gillespie] finds himself compelled to accept so many 'simplifying' assumptions that the over-all results may be worthless, or worse than worthless if anyone should look to them for policy guidelines.[25]

The most recent study on fiscal incidence is that of the Tax Foundation.[26] Under the aegis of George Bishop, the study concentrates upon providing broad estimates of the total tax burden and expenditure benefits by level of government. While the basic methodology does not differ substantially from Gillespie's, there are several significant refinements.

First, and perhaps most consequential for the results, the analysis benefits from the availability of much more detailed data on consumer expenditures and income. The availability of data compiled by the Bureau of Labor Statistics (BLS) permits substantial improvement over allocators used in past studies.[27] The statistical base of the BLS survey is a larger national sample and accordingly provides a much more accurate definition of consumption and income patterns. Second, a preliminary attempt was made to determine changes in the pattern of redistribution. While 1961 was the year chosen for most critical analysis, fiscal incidence estimates were also computed for 1965. The results are highly tentative, however, since no attempt was made to allow for changes in the distribution of income between 1961 and 1965.[28] Third, the study used net national product (NNP) as an income base. This differs from earlier studies by the inclusion of indirect business taxes as an imputed component of income to individuals, some $48 billion in 1961. As stated in the report:

> In peacetime, it seems more reasonable to assume that the tax burden comes out of national output over and above what is required to replace capital equipment. Consequently, we take net national product (NNP) as the most appropriate base against which to measure effective rates of the total tax burden.[29]

Finally, the study necessarily benefited from refinements in methodology and technique developed in earlier studies.

The findings of the report provide a detailed set of data on tax incidence, expenditure incidence, and the net fiscal impact of public sector activity. The results are general in nature but this conforms with the stated purpose of the study.

State Studies: Tax Burden In a Given State-Local System

The final category of tax burden studies deals with public sector activity in one particular state-local system. The focus of these studies is an almost polar opposite to the focus of those dealing with aggregate public sector activity.

While there have been numerous studies on the structure and characteristics of a particular state-local tax system, most of them either ignore the question of tax burden or treat it superficially.[30] Their concern is with the general structure of the tax system, trends in revenue, expenditure and debt composition, and direct implications for potential legislation. Fortunately, there are three notable exceptions to the above type of study, each dealing explicitly (at least in part) with the distribution of the tax burden. These studies were done for Michigan, Minnesota, and Wisconsin and represent detailed analyses of the distribution of tax burdens within a given state-local system.

The Michigan study, under the direction of Harvey Brazer, was part of a much more comprehensive analysis of the fiscal structure of Michigan.[31] In this study, Musgrave and Daicoff attempt to delineate the incidence of taxes collected in Michigan, recognizing the almost total lack of precedent for such a study and stating the caveat that the results "reflect conclusions arrived at on the basis of theoretical reasoning and certain assumptions concerning the shifting of taxes, applied in some cases with the aid of rather insufficient data."[32]

The assumptions concerning tax incidence do not differ substantially from earlier studies. Much of the data on consumption patterns, and so forth, are derived from the Time-Life study or the University of Michigan Survey Research Center. In this respect, the study suffers from most of the data weaknesses discussed previously. The results represent a first attempt to uncover the distribution of tax burdens for a given state-local system. Two major reservations are noted:

> First, our allocation of the tax burden between major economic groups is based largely upon theoretical assumptions as to incidence, and not upon empirical findings. The second lies in the imperfect nature of the economic data used in translating our incidence hypotheses into an estimate of the total tax burden borne by Michigan residents and distributing it among Michigan income groups.[33]

In addition to looking at the pattern of tax burdens, Musgrave and Daicoff provide estimates "of a highly tentative sort" concerning the incidence of Michigan state-local expenditures. This is the first such attempt to investigate the combined tax and expenditure incidence of a single state, thus allowing some conclusions to be reached concerning the net fiscal impact of public sector activity.

A unique feature of the Michigan study is its treatment of Michigan vis-à-vis the balance of the national economy. It is assumed that Michigan acts as an independent decision-making unit making unilateral fiscal decisions. An "open" economy is the milieu in which Michigan functions and incidence is handled accordingly.[d]

The second study of tax incidence for a particular state is that for Wisconsin done under the direction of Harold Groves.[34] The major concern of this study was the incidence of taxation in Wisconsin. The analysis differs methodologically from the Michigan study by the assumption that Wisconsin operates in a "closed" economy, i.e., Wisconsin is not treated in a national context but rather as it relates to surrounding states—Illinois, Indiana, Iowa, Michigan, Minnesota, and Ohio.

The openness of the economy is approximated by relating Wisconsin to its neighboring states, the implication being that Wisconsin's fiscal decisions are not

---

[d]This assumption has implications for the geographical incidence of taxation. Discussion of the importing and exporting of taxes will be deferred to Chapter 4.

unilateral but rather respond to decisions made in its "fiscal community." In effect, the Wisconsin economy is treated as open with respect to its fiscal community but closed with respect to the nation as a whole. Recognition is given to the exporting of taxes, but aside from the federal offset tax-exporting is handled in the context of a closed economy.[35]

In the Wisconsin study, two alternatives are presented for the treatment of exporting and importing of taxes. Case I assumes that exported and imported taxes just offset each other, which in effect assumes away the problem. Case II allows for the exporting of taxes (about 21 percent of total taxes) but does not deal with the importation of taxes into Wisconsin. This represents an improvement over the Michigan study where analysis is performed only in terms of the burden of Michigan taxes upon Michigan residents.[36]

Methodologically, a case can be developed for either approach. Chapter 4 will present an argument for treatment of state-local taxes in the context of an open economy and the investigation of the tax burden on residents of a state from all sources of taxation. Such an approach gives explicit recognition to the open nature of the economy in which states function.

The most recent individual state study was done for Minnesota by O.H. Brownlee.[37] The emphasis, as in the Michigan study, is on both tax and expenditure incidence and the net fiscal impact of the state-local budget. The reader is appropriately warned about the "crude estimate of the distribution of the benefits of public services. . . ." Also, the problem of evaluating government expenditures at other than cost is recognized, and wherever possible incidence is based upon alternative assumptions that provide the reader with a "range of plausible values and the author's judgment of the most probable values."

While the Brownlee study benefits from refinements in earlier tax burden studies, it inherits many of their problems. The best data on consumption patterns at the time of Brownlee's study were still the Time-Life and Survey Research Center series. In addition, the conceptual problems involved in allocating the benefits of government expenditures, while recognized, remained no less formidable. For example, all government services are evaluated at cost and treated as benefiting either persons or property. Governmental services are then allocated using population, personal services, and income or expenditure series for property-related services.[e] This method provides, at best, a first approximation to the actual distribution of benefits derived from public spending.

Finally, the phenomenon of tax-exporting is recognized but not treated in detail. Explicit provision is made for the federal offset as a form of exporting,

[e]The problem of evaluating public services lacks conceptual clarity due to the absence of a market price analog for the public sector. As has traditionally been the case, valuation is set at cost, when in fact the "benefits" of certain expenditures could legitimately be viewed as negative, i.e., the net result of public sector expenditures is to leave certain individuals on a lower indifference curve. As is the case with all benefit studies, there seems to be no empirically tractable alternative.

but, concerning the exporting of taxes to residents of other states, Brownlee states, "Although accurate estimates of such contributions by nonresidents are difficult to obtain, estimates have been made and are taken into account wherever feasible in the analysis."[38] The phenomenon of tax-importing is not dealt with at all.

Summary

The purpose of the above discussion was twofold. First, the historical development in technique, methodology, and data availability was traced, and the variation in the focus of tax burden and benefit studies was made explicit. Initially, analysis emphasized the aggregate distribution of tax burdens for various levels of government (e.g., federal, state, local). The redistributive effects of the public sector were examined solely in terms of tax policy. Analysis was later broadened to include both taxation and expenditure policy, thus permitting discussion of the total impact of the public sector. A limited number of studies were concerned with the burden of taxation within one state-local system. The second purpose was to demonstrate that there has emerged a gap in the literature causing a serious lack of attention to the nature of interstate variations. It is this void in the literature that provides the genesis of this study.

With the historical and methodological background properly detailed, the analysis of the present study can be defined and related to the existing body of research on the burden of public sector taxation. The chapters to follow will serve the purpose of filling the void in the existing literature concerning the tax burden within each state-local system and comparatively across all fifty systems.

3 A Model for Estimating the Distribution of Tax Burdens

An empirical investigation of interstate variations in the distribution of tax burdens utilizes many of the assumptions that underlie traditional studies of aggregate tax burden. This chapter will discuss those assumptions and indicate refinements to account for the focus of this study—the fifty state-local systems. With a basic model developed, attention can be turned to the spatial aspects of tax incidence. Geographical incidence, a consideration of crucial importance for interstate variations, will be the topic of Chapter 4.

The Setting of Analysis

Any study of the burden of taxation must begin with a delineation of the shifting and incidence of various types of taxes. Predicated upon certain assumptions, inferences about the incidence of various taxes can be drawn. This permits taxes to be allocated to various income groups in accordance with existing consensus.

The forces acting to influence shifting are numerous and interact in a highly complex fashion to determine the degree and direction of shifting that obtains. While the assumptions necessary to permit an analytical determination of incidence set the framework as partial rather than general equilibrium, the general nature of the final solution must be recognized. Partial equilibrium facilitates examination of a specific area of interest, holding everything else under *ceteris paribus*; however, the problem remains that the final solution reflects forces that can not be so held. A methodology that permits the holding of all other forces constant except the one under examination is convenient and necessary from a pedagogical point of view. It is at the same time incomplete from a conceptual point of view. The framework must be made explicit to avoid any confusion in interpretation of the empirical results.

The rationale of partial equilibrium is that it enables one to deal conceptually with the adjustments elicited following an alteration in tax or expenditure policy. A distinction can be made, for example, between changes in the distribution of income as opposed to a change in the level of income. However as Musgrave notes, in a general equilibrium setting, "such distinctions [i.e., various lines of adjustment] are meaningless and untenable. . . . "[1]

The shifting of taxes is a phenomenon resulting from market and/or political conditions that permit a tax to be transferred from its initial point of impact to some other point in the economy. Incidence, as it has been traditionally defined, refers to the final resting place of the tax and the resulting burden imposed.[2] Musgrave takes exception to this point of view due to the ambiguity involved in defining incidence as the final or ultimate resting place of a tax. He suggests an alternative definition of incidence that examines the distribution of income—in a Lorenz curve sense—by income size class.[3]

This modification of the definition of incidence is a reflection of Musgrave's emphasis upon differential as opposed to absolute incidence. Following Wicksell, Musgrave opts for the use of differential analysis to permit isolation of the effects that result from changes in tax or expenditure policy or a budgetary surplus or deficit. Incidence is accordingly defined in terms of a change in the distribution of income resulting from an alteration of tax policy.

The application of differential incidence, however, shifts analysis back into the arena of general equilibrium. Determination of differential incidence necessarily involves considerations that extend beyond the initial impact of the tax. As Shoup has noted in commenting on differential incidence:

> No techniques have been suggested, however, short of general equilibrium analysis, for ascertaining the increase in the rate of one tax . . . that will be the resource equivalent of a stated decrease in the rate of some other tax. . . .[4]

While the process of shifting and final incidence relates to the movement of taxes from the point of impact to the group that bears the burden, the effects of taxation policy can be approximated by using several alternative conceptual devices. Each of these methods exerts different demands on a model designed to quantify the burden of public sector taxation policy.

The model developed here relies upon partial equilibrium analysis of shifting and incidence, expressing the impact of the public sector in terms of absolute rather than differential incidence. The effective rates, therefore, provide an approximation to the impact of taxation on various income groups but do not attempt to specify the full ramifications of public sector activity.

It must also be noted explicitly that the estimates made in following chapters do not in any way attempt to deal with the excess burden of a tax or system of taxes. The estimates are based strictly upon what is, and do not attempt to show what might be, given some hypothetical alteration of the tax structure toward a more Pareto optimal configuration.

The purpose of this section has been to specify the framework for the analysis to follow. Perusal of the literature on shifting and incidence serves to emphasize the complexity of the task at hand—providing empirical content to the question "who pays the taxes?" The forces acting to determine shifting are numerous and are completely specified only in a general equilibrium setting. The dictates of a study on the distribution of tax burdens require, however, that the problem be empirically tractable. While general equilibrium analysis may, under certain rigorous assumptions, be empirically manageable for a specific tax, such a framework is not amenable to inquiry into the state-local tax structure for all states.

Accordingly, a model must be developed using partial equilibrium which necessarily disregards some of the forms of adjustment that may be elicited in response to tax policy. Use of such analysis will permit some general conclusions to be reached concerning the distribution of tax burdens by income class-results which, at present, seem to be an acceptable goal.

The Allocation of Taxes by Income Class

A major task facing a study of the distribution of tax burdens is relating the theoretical analysis on shifting and incidence to the empirical allocation of various types of taxes by income class. Given the findings of shifting and incidence theory, a methodology must be developed to permit the allocation of various types of taxes by income class. This involves the selection of statistical series that reflect the incidence pattern of each state-local tax. Allocators are chosen to reflect the incidence of a tax. Each tax is then allocated by income class on the basis of each class's percentage of the allocator series. This produces a distribution of the tax in accordance with an analytically determined pattern of incidence.

The entire range of tax burden studies discussed in Chapter 2 use exactly such a methodology. Given the extant body of partial equilibrium analysis on tax-shifting, certain assumptions are made concerning incidence. These assumptions are then used to allocate taxes by income class. The effective rates (burden) are computed by relating the distribution of taxes to the distribution of income.

The resulting effective rates must not be construed, however, as empirical estimates (in an econometric or statistical sense) of the incidence of taxation. The distribution is entirely a reflection of the reality of the shifting and incidence assumptions, and the accuracy of the allocator series in reflecting the incidence of various taxes. Given partial equilibrium analysis of tax shifting, certain assumptions concerning the incidence of various taxes can be deduced. Based on these assumptions, the effective rates can be estimated. Any conclusions drawn from the results must be interpreted in light of the underlying assumptions concerning incidence.[5]

The specific assumptions employed in a tax burden study have substantial import for the results. Accordingly, they must reflect theoretical considerations (and empirical evidence, where available) and must be made explicit to the reader. The assumptions do not purport to represent the entire adjustment resulting from the imposition of a tax; however, they do reduce the task to empirically tractable proportions.

The following sections will discuss the assumptions employed in this study and the allocation techniques chosen. Chapter 4 will complete the development of the model by examining the spatial aspects of tax incidence.

Personal Income Tax

The state individual income tax is a broad-based tax levied within a political jurisdiction large enough to require substantial mobility to permit avoidance. In addition, there is no market mechanism available to the individual to permit shifting of the tax. Accordingly, past studies have all assumed that the tax rests with the individual upon whom the statutory liability is imposed. That assumption will not be altered in this study, but an alternative method of allocation will be suggested.

In past studies, a distinction has been made between federal and state income taxes by allocating the state component on the basis of state income tax yields. This often involved use of a proxy state distribution to allocate all state income taxes. For example, the annual distribution of Wisconsin state income tax yields was used by both Musgrave and Bishop to allocate aggregate state income tax payments by income class.[6]

While this method is an improvement over allocation by series such as total personal income taxes (federal and state), it does make the rather heroic assumption that aggregate state income taxes are distributed in the same way as state income taxes in Wisconsin. While such an assumption is perhaps tenable in the aggregate, it certainly is not when the focus of analysis is each state-local system and variation across systems.

To eliminate the error resulting from such a method of allocation, an alternative procedure was devised to estimate the distribution of state-local income tax payments for each state. The rationale is that the personal income tax is the major progressive influence in the state-local tax system. If the tax is not allocated in a manner that reflects this influence, the resulting effective rates carry considerably less import. In addition, the pattern of progressity-regressity that emerges, both for the income tax and the total tax system, will be less reflective of the true pattern.

Using Bureau of Labor Statistics (BLS) data, average income was computed for each income class for each state. This figure is average money income before taxes for the average tax-paying unit in each class, for each state. It was assumed to be representative of the members of the class (in an average sense), recognizing the often extreme variation that exists within a given class. These statistics were used as the base for calculating a distribution of tax payments to be used as an allocator for the state income tax.

To obtain a distribution of income taxes, the aggregate state income tax was allocated on the basis of tax payments for each income class in each state. Given average income for a cell, a distribution of tax payments was calculated for each state as follows. First, the level of personal exemption for a joint return was determined. Second, the exemption for dependents was calculated by taking average family size in excess of 2.0 (husband and wife) and multiplying it by exemption per dependent. Finally, it was assumed that the standard deduction was used and this amount was determined. These three items were added and their total subtracted from the average income figure to arrive at taxable income. The tax bill for each cell was then calculated using tax rates applicable to each state. The computations are summarized symbolically as follows.[7]

$$TI = GI - [P + D + S]$$
$$TAX = (TI)(R)$$
$$D = (F - 2.0)(E)$$
$$S = (GI)(SD) \text{ where } S \leqslant MAX$$

GI = Average gross income ($)
TI = Taxable income ($)
TAX = Tax payment ($)
R = Tax rate (%)
P = Personal exemption ($)
D = Dependent exemption ($)
S = Standard deduction ($)
F = Average family size (#)
SD = Standard deduction, rate (%)
MAX = Maximum allowable standard deduction ($)
E = Exemption per dependent ($)

The resulting tax payments were interpreted as an average and weighted by tax-paying units to get class totals for each state. Total income tax for each state was then allocated on the basis of each class's proportion of total tax payments.

The above method is a substantial improvement over the representative state method employed by Musgrave-Daicoff and Bishop. It gives explicit recognition to the variation present in the features of the income tax in each state by accounting for differences in deductions, exemptions, and tax rates. Even more crucial, it permits the model to account for sources of variation across states.

Corporate Income Tax

The incidence of the corporate income tax has been the subject of more analysis than any other tax. For a long period of time it was held that shifting, both short- and long-run, was not possible, and the tax was borne by the owners of the firm in the form of reduced returns.[8]

More recently, analysis underlying the no-shifting dictum has been exposed to much more rigorous theoretical and empirical investigation. The result has been the emergence of a three-sided dispute concerning the shifting of corporate income taxes. The three forces emerge as follows: (1) those who maintain that little or none of the tax is shifted, (2) those who feel that varying and often indeterminate amounts are shifted, and (3) those who feel rather strongly that most, if not all the tax, can be shifted in the long run (and some who accept short-run shifting as well).

In addition to rigorous analytical investigation, the incidence of this tax has been the subject of considerable empirical analysis. Recently, several major studies have emerged on the incidence of the corporate income tax. The results of these studies offer support to almost polar opposite conclusions.[9]

Separate studies by Harberger and by Cragg, et al., both reach the conclusion that while in the long run the tax will be reflected in the price of the product, this does not necessarily imply the tax is borne by the consumer. Part of the burden is borne by capital in the form of lower returns. The results of Harberger's study indicate that nearly 100 percent of the burden of the tax rests with owners of capital.

Cragg, et al., viewing with great skepticism the results of the controversial Krzyzaniak-Musgrave (K-M) model, make an attempt to correct some of its statistical and theoretical deficiencies, and their empirical results tend to confirm Harberger's findings. They state:

> Instead of implying the more than 100 per-cent shifting of the corporation tax which K-M found, our estimates imply that capital bears approximately 100 per-cent of the burden of the tax.[10]

Perhaps the most controversial study on the incidence of the corporate tax is that by Musgrave and Krzyzaniak (K-M).[11] Their results contradict all other empirical findings, and the study accordingly, has been the focus of much controversy and criticism. The essence of the K-M results is that the corporate income tax is shifted forward more than 100 percent, thereby actually benefiting the owners of capital.[12] The paradox emerges that any increase in tax results in a price increase *more than sufficient* to offset the tax.

The implications of such findings, if accepted, are quite serious. For example:

> Indeed, it is certainly not far from the truth to say that if we accept the Krzyzaniak-Musgrave results at face value, we must also accept the task of rebuilding the foundations of the theory of the behavior of the firm.

or:

> The finding of short-run shifting transcends in importance the relatively narrow question of who pays the corporate tax since it conjures up a strange new world in which neoclassical theories of the firm, the competitive structure, and the marginal cost-marginal revenue equilibrium are relegated to the scrap heap.[13]

Needless to say, the K-M study, while pioneering in its econometric investigation of corporate tax-shifting, has produced results that remain the source of rather intense controversy and skepticism.

The empirical studies discussed above indicate a possible range of shifting between 100 percent to owners of capital and 100 percent or more to consumers. This study will not add more contradictions to the somewhat contradictory body of knowledge that already exists but will instead make use of these tentative results. The assumption adopted is that one-half the tax is borne by consumers in the form of increased prices and one-half by owners of capital in the form of reduced returns. Such an assumption has already been used in studies by Tucker, Bishop, and the Tax Foundation and—given the lack of consensus—it is probably a reasonable position. Until the incidence question has been settled on an empirical basis, there will be no justification for lending full support to either extreme. The data used to allocate the tax are total current consumption expenditures (for forward shifting) and dividend receipts (for the burden on capital). Alternative estimates have been made (e.g., on the basis of full forward shifting) to permit comparison with other findings on incidence. The standard case, however, is one-half shifting to consumers and one-half shifting to owners of capital.

Property Tax

The property tax is the most difficult of state-local taxes to allocate by income class, both conceptually and empirically. The preeminent use of property-taxing power by local governments has resulted in an extreme proliferation of taxing units, rates, classes of property, and assessment practices. Such variety makes it hard to think of the property tax except as its base is defined in terms of property. The differences have become so great that the property tax actually resembles many taxes depending upon where and on what it is levied. As Netzer has commented:

> It is an old institution and it is actually not a single national tax but an incredibly complex collection of taxes with literally thousands of local variations.[14]

About 90 percent of all local governments (excluding special districts) have the legal authority to levy property taxes. This results in thousands of variations in form and administration.

To permit the property tax to be allocated by income class for individual states, some simplifying assumption is necessary to cope with this incredible variation. An allocation technique employed in several aggregate studies can be adopted to the present analysis. Perusal of data on locally-assessed, taxable, real property indicates that, for each state taken individually, single family houses account for approximately 50 percent of assessed value; the balance is accounted for by commercial, industrial, land acreage and farms.

Using this information, it was decided to adopt a methodology suggested by

Bishop for the allocation of property taxes by income class. The allocation "reflects the fact that roughly half of the property tax is levied on business and is . . . assumed to be shifted forward to consumers; the other half is assumed to fall on home owners."[15]

Since about 50 percent of assessed value represents single family houses, it is assumed that the burden of this component rests with the homeowner. This portion of the tax is assumed not to be shifted and is allocated on the basis of housing expenditures. The other 50 percent falls on business and the assumption is made that it is fully shifted forward in higher prices. This portion is allocated on the basis of consumption expenditures. While this method undoubtedly introduces some distortion in a few states where the business-nonbusiness balance differs from 50-50, it is not felt to present any severe problems for the final results. Accordingly, the property tax is allocated one-half on the basis of consumption expenditures and one-half on the basis of expenditures for housing.

General Sales Tax

The general sales tax is assumed to be fully shifted forward to the consumer. Since it is a broad-based tax, the case for its shifting is even more tenable than that for a more narrowly-based, specific sales tax.[16] The general sales tax therefore is allocated on the basis of consumption expenditures, with one refinement. As the Tax Foundation has noted:

> The portion of sales and excise taxes allocated on total consumption expenditures . . . probably *overstates* the degree of regression because no account is taken of those states where the sales tax exemptions include food and other items relatively important in the budgets of low income families.[17]

To account for the influence of exempted items on the regressivity of the general sales tax, an allocator was constructed based on expenditures for current consumption net of exempted items. This adjusts the effective rates for the influence of items exempted from general sales taxation and accounts for their impact on regressivity. In addition, it has the desirable effect of incorporating in the estimating procedure the differential provisions that exist across states. Table 3-1 illustrates the varied treatment of items exempted from general sales taxation.

Selective Sales Taxes

For purposes of analysis, selective sales taxes are categorized as in Table 3-2. Each tax is not treated separately; rather, certain of the less significant selective

Table 3-1
General Sales Tax Exemptions

State	Food	Clothing	Medicine
California	X		X
Connecticut	X	X	X
Florida	X		X
Maine	X		X
Maryland	X		X
Michigan			50% of Drugs
North Carolina			X
North Dakota			X
Ohio	X		X
Pennsylvania	X	X	X
Rhode Island	X		X
Texas	X		X

Motor Fuel[a] exempted in all states.
Services[b] exempted in all states.

[a]Motor fuel is generally not subject to sales taxation.

[b]Some services are taxed in some states but most states exempt services from taxation.

Source: ACIR, TAX OVERLAPPING IN THE UNITED STATES 1961 (Washington, D.C.: Advisory Commission, 1961), pp. 115-119. The data are for 1962.

Table 3-2
Selective Sales Taxes as a Percentage of Total Tax Revenue

Tax		Percentage
Alcohol		1.8
Tobacco		2.7
Motor fuel		8.9
Public utility		1.8
Other selective sales		2.7
Insurance	1.4	
Amusement	0.1	
Pari-mutuel	0.7	
Other and unallocable	0.5	
	2.7	
Total Selective Sales		17.9

Source: United States Bureau of the Census, CENSUS OF GOVERNMENTS: 1962, Vol. IV, No. 4, Compendium of Government Finances (Washington, D.C.: United States Government Printing Office, 1964), Table 28, p. 48. The data are for 1962.

sales taxes are aggregated into a composite "other" category. While this produces some minor distortions in states for which these taxes are of above average importance, in the aggregate, none of these distortions are of great significance. Table 3-2 illustrates the relative importance of these taxes.

The burden of sales taxation is one of the many unsettled conceptual issues in incidence theory. Arguments have been presented for points of view ranging from full backward to full forward shifting to incidence equivalent to a proportional-rate income tax. John Due, however, gives a persuasive case for forward shifting:

> A major unresolved controversy in the field of public finance is that of whether or not consumers 'bear' sales taxes.
>
> . . . .
>
> The conclusion reached is that, except under very restrictive assumptions, the traditional view of sales tax incidence—that it is distributed in relation to consumer spending—is correct.[18]

This is generally the assumption made in past studies, and there seems to be no compelling reason to alter it now. Accordingly, selective sales taxes are allocated by income class on the basis of the class's relative consumption of the taxed commodity. The incidence of the tax rests fully on the consumer of the taxed commodity. Due argues that this is, in fact, the intent of sales tax legislation, and that other adjustments (especially monetary) will be made to permit such shifting to occur.[19]

The statistical series used to allocate selective sales taxes are as follows:[20]

Tax	Allocator
Alcohol	Alcoholic beverage consumption
Tobacco	Tobacco consumption
Motor fuel	Automobile operation expenditures
Public utility	Gas and electricity expenditures
Other selective sales	Consumption expenditures

Death and Gift Taxes

Most tax burden studies have assumed that the burden of death and gift taxes rests on the highest income class. There are two reasons for continued adherence to this assumption. First, as Musgrave has stated: "In view of the high level of exemptions permitted under both Federal and state succession taxes, it . . . [seems] reasonable to assume that all but a negligible part of the yield should be imputed to income recipients in the top bracket."[21] Secondly, an inheritance or gift of even relatively small magnitude can considerably increase before-tax income. Thus it is most likely that the recipient unit will be moved to a higher income class by the bequest. These two considerations are sufficient to indicate that allocation of death and gift taxes to the highest income class will not produce severe distortion.

All Other Taxes

The "all other" category is a composite including various taxes of relatively minor importance in the state-local revenue structure. The composition is indicated in Table 3-3.

The most important of these taxes is motor vehicle licenses. It is the only tax in the all other category that is of any consequence for all states. Nonetheless, it remains a relatively minor source of revenue in the aggregate.

The only other taxes in this composite category of relative importance are so for only certain states. They are:

State	Tax	Percentage of Tax Revenue[22]	
New Mexico	Severance	11.7	
Louisiana	Severance	23.0	
Texas	Severance	10.1	
Oklahoma	Severance	7.5	
Delaware	Other and unallocable	13.8	(corporate franchise tax)
Nevada	Other and unallocable	12.3	(gambling and related taxes)

Table 3-3
All Other Taxes as a Percentage of Total Tax Revenue

Tax		Percentage
Motor vehicle licenses		4.0
Severance		1.1
Licenses		1.5
Motor vehicle operator	0.3	
Alcoholic beverage	0.2	
Hunting and fishing	0.3	
Miscellaneous	0.7	
Other and Unallocable		3.4
Total		10.0

Source: United States Bureau of the Census, CENSUS OF GOVERNMENTS: 1962, Vol. IV, No. 4, Compendium of Government Finances (Washington, D.C.: United States Government Printing Office, 1964), Table 28, p. 49. The data are for 1962.

It is evident that severance taxes are of considerable importance in Louisiana, New Mexico, and Texas, as are corporate franchise taxes in Delaware, and gambling related taxes in Nevada. While some of the taxes included in "all other" are important sources of revenue for a few specific states, they remain relatively unimportant for the majority of states. In addition, the burden of the taxes in these states is, for the most part, exported to residents of other states. (This is discussed more fully in Chapter 4.) The actual burden remaining with the residents of the taxing state is therefore considerably reduced.

The substantial increase in calculation required to treat each tax separately for each state, rather severe data problems, and the relative unimportance of these taxes all contribute to the decision to allocate them in the aggregate. It is not felt that the results would be made substantially more realistic by separate treatment. Accordingly, the "all other" category is allocated in proportion to total current consumption. The implicit incidence assumption is that the burden of these taxes rests with consumers in proportion to consumption expenditures.

Direct-Indirect Taxes and the Shifting Process

The classification of taxes into direct and indirect is, at best, a confusing endeavor. Analytically, direct taxes are those that can not be shifted from point of legal impact. Indirect taxes are shifted through market price (either resource or product) to some other group in the economy. This distinction would appear to be quite clear. However, the actual taxonomy employed, which is often at variance with analytical considerations, has been tempered by administrative and social accounting demands.[23] In addition, final incidence is an empirical question to be handled in a manner similar to analysis of the corporate income tax.

The assumption concerning the shifting of general and selective sales taxes underlying this study is that they are borne in relation to consumption expenditures. This implies that the burden is fully shifted to consumers in the form of higher prices. While this is a standard assumption concerning the incidence of these taxes, it is not always the most satisfactory.

The changes elicited in response to the imposition of a tax might well entail adjustments in factor income (wages and/or profits). The exact nature of final incidence depends upon numerous factors and could quite possibly entail decreased profits for producers and/or wages for workers.

The assumption of forward shifting is an empirical convenience used to make the estimation of burden manageable. While much of the conceptual analysis relevant to this area of shifting and incidence theory supports forward shifting, there emerges no unanimity of opinion. The existence of backward shifting and reduced profits must be recognized as distinct possibilities.

The Income Base for Effective Rates

The selection of an income base to be used in calculating effective rates of taxation is an analytical problem that awaits solution. There is considerable divergence of opinion over which is the correct base, and the final choice must ultimately be tempered by purpose and professional judgment.

The focus of discord centers on the inclusion of various categories of imputed and nonmonetary income in the base. Tucker argues that these sources should be defined as income since they are of great relative importance for the lower income classes. Inclusion of such items would serve to lessen the tax burden in the lower income classes to a much greater extent than in the middle and upper classes, thereby lessening the degree of regression for the tax system as a whole.[24]

Musgrave's position is that any attempt to include imputed and/or nonmonetary elements in the income base causes severe conceptual problems concerning the definition of income. If an attempt is made to impute nonmonetary items, such as wages in kind or home grown food, he asks "why not also include the services of housewives?" Thus the point is made! Once one ventures beyond the use of money income, there exists no clearly defined logic for the inclusion or exclusion of a wide range of imputed and nonmonetary forms of income, ranging from home grown food to the value of leisure time.[25]

Another problem related to the use of a broader base is the influence that these additional sources of income have upon income groupings. If the base is modified to be more inclusive, it is highly likely—especially in the lower income classes—that the added income will move some persons into a higher class. If this phenomenon is not accounted for by adjusting the classes accordingly, the estimates of burden will be biased—the net effect being to substantially lower the effective rate. The statistical problems involved in correcting the income classes to account for the additional income components are formidable and any adjustments will be crude, at best. The influence of imputed income on the upward shift of taxpayers was apparently not allowed for by either Musgrave or Tucker in their studies. As Colm and Wald note: ". . . nonmonetary and imputed income were lumped together with money income in each class, and effective rates were recomputed."[26]

The Musgrave-Tucker debate over the income base remains unresolved. In point of fact, the debate seems not so much a dispute as a variance in purpose. Each of the writers is attempting to measure a distinct type of tax burden. Accordingly, their results, when interpreted in light of the purpose, need not necessarily contradict each other.

Musgrave measures the burden of taxation as it relates to the legal definition of income for tax purposes, using money income as the base for effective rates.[27] Since the policy operation of the public sector influences mainly monetary components of income (the nonmonetary components remain relatively insulated from direct policy manipulation), Musgrave's results show the burden as it relates to the income base most amenable to policy manipulation.[a]

Tucker's use of a broader income base is an attempt to relate the burden to a measure of the economic well-being of the taxpayer. The base is not that legally defined for tax purposes but includes additional nonmonetary and imputed items in an effort to more clearly define economic well-being. The logical extension of the Tucker measure is somewhat ambiguous but would seem to relate to an individual's level of satisfaction, e.g., an indifference curve mapping. The burden can be related to the process of adjustment in response to a tax and to the final position of the taxpayer on a post-tax indifference curve. While this is a conceptually clear indication of economic well-being, it is empirically intractable.

The crux of the income debate revolves around the distinction between income as defined for taxation and income reflecting economic well-being. The two approaches, however, measure two distinct types of burden. The former defines burden in relation to income for tax purposes (policy-oriented) and the latter relates burden to the economic position of the taxpayer. The crucial factor is proper interpretation of the effective rates and incidence pattern, not the choice of some base as being sacrosanct or ultimately correct.

Effective rates calculated from money income will produce a much less progressive distribution (especially in the lower income classes) than obtains from a broader base. Or with a regressive tax, the regressivity will be considerably greater with money than with broad income.

The distinction between money income and broader base also has important implications for the types of families under investigation. The broader definition is clearly more relevant to rural families since a large portion of their income is likely to be derived from nonmonetary sources. For urban families, however, the tax burden is more clearly related to money income since nonmonetary components are relatively insignificant. The logical implication, of course, is that separate analyses should be performed for rural and urban families since their income bases clearly differ in composition.[28]

In addition to the Musgrave and Tucker approaches, Bishop has presented yet another alternative. In his study of the distribution of tax burdens for 1958, he argued for the use of net national product (NNP) as a base for effective rates. This, he felt, would avoid the fluctuation that occurs in the definition of national income resulting from a change in the balance between indirect and direct taxes.[29] He was concerned with certain inconsistencies that result from

---

[a]In a study concerned with the entire budget, interpretation is substantially altered. However, when dealing with the taxation side of the budget, analysis is abstracted from the effects of expenditure policy. Attention is focused instead upon distributional changes elicited by taxation. The income that is most subject to tax policy manipulation is money income.

the use of national income but do not arise when NNP is used. His case centers on the inclusion of indirect taxes as a form of imputed income. Bishop argues that indirect taxes represent income of individuals that, through collective action, has been diverted to governmental use. He states: "The essence of the argument . . . is that indirect taxes are a form of undistributed 'income' collectively allocated to governmental uses."[30]

Such a definition of income is at variance with national income convention. The Department of Commerce makes the implicit assumption that indirect taxes are shifted forward and reflected only as changes in market price. For this reason, and due to the unavailability of net national product data by states, this measure was not considered an empirically viable alternative.

Table A-1 in Appendix A shows the difference between personal income excluding capital gains (Department of Commerce definition) and net national product (NNP). The personal income definition used by the Department of Commerce excludes capital gains but does include certain types of imputed and nonmonetary income. The gap between the personal income measure used in this study and NNP is more significant—some $58.0 billion in 1961. The money income definition used by the Bureau of Labor Statistics (BLS) is also shown. It is the least inclusive measure of income and differs from NNP by $126.8 billion and personal income (Department of Commerce) by $68.8 billion.

The personal income base used here was selected from among these alternatives for the following reasons. First, the BLS money income base was felt to be too narrow due to its exclusion of some major components of income (amounting to some $78.8 billion). Second, personal income includes several forms of imputed, nonmonetary, and other income. Exclusion of these items from the income base alters both the level and incidence of burden in a misleading manner. Finally, personal income data by state are published on a regular basis by the Department of Commerce.[31]

The personal income data used here are aggregate for the state. Appendix A discusses the method used to construct a distribution of personal income for each state. This provides the income data used in calculating effective rates.

Summary

The preceding sections have focused on the basic model for estimation of tax burdens. After a discussion of shifting and incidence theory, attention was turned to the empirical implementation of this theory for the distribution of state-local taxes. A detailed discussion of the incidence assumptions and allocation techniques used in the current study indicated how taxes were distributed by income class. In addition, suggestions were made to obtain a more representative allocation of personal income and general sales taxes. This was done to give explicit acknowledgment to the variation that exists across the tax structures of the fifty state-local systems. Finally, the income base controversy was defined, and the income base chosen for this study was elaborated upon.

With this discussion behind, inquiry can be shifted to a dimension of tax burden analysis not directly relevant to aggregate studies—the geographical incidence of taxation. Since states operate in an open economy, incidence is spatial as well as interpersonal. Exporting and importing of taxes must be given explicit recognition in a model focused upon interstate variations in tax burdens. Chapter 4 will deal with this phenomenon. After the spatial dimensions of tax incidence have been delineated, the model can be utilized to examine empirically the characteristics of the fifty state-local tax systems. Chapters 5 and 6 will provide empirical content to the model developed in Chapters 3 and 4.

4 Spatial Incidence and State-Local Taxation

The preceding chapter has provided detail on the model used to calculate the distribution of state tax burdens. Refinements were incorporated, where relevant, to adjust for the disaggregate focus of the study—the fifty states. There remains, however, another critical dimension not dealt with in previous chapters.

A state-local system operates in the context of an open economy. State boundaries, while effective in defining legal, institutional, budgetary, and fiscal variations, do not serve as effective barriers against the flow of tax burdens and expenditure benefits. Accordingly, in a study of the distribution of tax burdens for state-local systems, explicit account must be given to this geographical flow of taxes. The approach assumed here is to investigate the burden of taxes at their final spatial resting place, not just the burden of taxes actually levied within each particular state—i.e., geographical incidence rather than impact.[a] The discussion to follow will develop an empirical approximation to the dollar magnitude of the flow of taxes into (importing) and out of (exporting) state-local systems. Using this information, the empirical results will more accurately depict the burden of taxation—level and distribution—both within and across states.

The existing body of literature on the geographical incidence of taxation is sadly lacking. As McLure notes, "although there is an extensive literature on the subject of incidence, most of it is in the context of a closed economy, so that all statutory taxpayers and ultimate bearers of the taxes are residents of the taxing region."[1] This remains true despite the fact that a major trait of a state is the openness of its economy. Any assumption that taxes levied in a state impose a burden only within that state and that these taxes represent the only tax burden on its residents, is conceptually simplistic and empirically untenable, especially when the focus of analysis is interstate comparisons. Taxes levied in any given state-local system can have repercussions throughout the entire economy and become manifest as a burden on residents of other states. The task at hand, therefore, assumes three distinct dimensions. First, the exporting of taxes must be determined by state and type of tax; second, the amount of taxes imported into each state must be estimated; finally, the effect of exporting-importing upon the level and distribution of tax burdens must be incorporated into the model before computing incidence.[2]

Only when the model gives explicit account to this flow of tax burdens among states in the form of exported and imported taxes will the resulting

[a]The question of final geographical incidence is akin to ultimate incidence in an interpersonal sense; it cannot be determined except in a general equilibrium model.

effective rates be indicative of the true pattern. More importantly, exporting-importing has a substantial impact upon interstate variations in the burden of taxation, and—as will be shown—the variation across states is considerable.

States that are in a position to export a substantial part of their taxes, e.g., Nevada's gambling taxes, or Delaware's corporate franchise tax, impose a much lower level of burden on their residents than would be indicated by analysis done on a geographical impact basis. The burden structure is altered by the geographical flow of taxes. Table 4-1 summarizes the magnitude and relative importance of this flow for the study year. In effect, part of the cost of providing public goods in a particular state is borne by residents of other states. This is not meant to imply that states institute tax policies with the explicit intent of exporting the burden. It is only meant to imply that certain types of taxes are much more amenable to exporting.

Historical Treatment of Geographical Incidence

The phenomenon of geographical incidence has been treated analytically in two distinct ways in past studies of single states. It must be recognized, however, that the focus of these studies was different from that of the present analysis.[b]

The first method, called the "Michigan approach," results from the work of Richard Musgrave and Darwin Daicoff. The assumption was made in their study that taxes levied in all other states are of no consequence to the state under analysis.[3] In effect, these taxes are assumed to be beyond the control of the state and, accordingly, only the tax policy of a given state is considered. The state is viewed as acting unilaterally in its fiscal decisions, not in response to forces operating in other governmental systems.

The second approach, called the "Wisconsin approach," results from the study WISCONSIN'S STATE AND LOCAL TAX BURDEN done under the aegis of Harold Groves.[4] In this study, taxes in Wisconsin are treated in relation to the taxes levied in neighboring states. It is assumed that states do not operate unilaterally in making fiscal decisions but rather are influenced by circumstances existing in other states. Thus each of these distinct conceptual approaches to tax incidence makes an alternative assumption concerning the nature of the economy in which state-local systems operate. The Michigan approach assumes an open economy where fiscal decisions are unilateral, the Wisconsin approach a type of closed economy where decisions are made in relation to other states in an interdependent fashion.

The Minnesota Study, under O.H. Brownlee, accounts for the exporting of taxes through the federal offset and higher prices reflecting the tax.[5] No attempt

[b]Exporting and importing taxes are strictly speaking, not relevant to aggregate studies. Geographical incidence arises as a major consideration when the unit of analysis is one particular state or all of the fifty state-local systems individually.

Table 4-1
Dimensions of Geographical Incidence

State	Total Exported Taxes ($ Millions)	Exported Taxes as a Percentage of Total Taxes	Total Imported Taxes ($ Millions)	Imported Taxes as a Percentage of Total[a] Taxes	Total Federal Offset ($ Millions)
Alabama	$ 89.52	20.5	$ 72.0	17.2	$ 28.46
Alaska	9.85	18.8	6.8	13.8	3.61
Arizona	82.98	25.3	37.3	13.2	23.98
Arkansas	53.51	21.0	36.8	15.5	13.94
California	1,013.15	19.7	539.1	11.6	492.21
Colorado	92.28	19.4	53.6	12.3	43.65
Connecticut	137.48	20.1	93.0	14.6	53.35
Delaware	41.20	36.7	14.2	16.7	2.00
Florida	215.45	20.3	134.5	13.7	45.36
Georgia	120.46	19.2	90.4	15.1	42.49
Hawaii	38.22	22.0	17.3	11.3	13.93
Idaho	28.23	20.7	18.9	14.9	6.99
Illinois	519.45	21.1	324.7	14.3	149.99
Indiana	164.53	17.3	136.1	14.8	22.78
Iowa	116.81	18.3	74.1	12.5	30.93
Kansas	101.64	19.6	60.9	12.8	29.67
Kentucky	93.82	20.1	69.4	15.7	30.21
Louisiana	174.92	26.7	75.1	13.5	15.57
Maine	31.16	15.8	25.7	13.4	7.56
Maryland	151.32	21.2	96.7	14.7	82.44
Massachusetts	250.39	17.6	170.8	12.7	125.42
Michigan	367.86	19.4	234.3	13.3	121.83

Table 4-1 (cont.)
Dimensions of Geographical Incidence

State	Total Exported Taxes ($ Millions)	Exported Taxes as a Percentage of Total Taxes	Total Imported Taxes ($ Millions)	Imported Taxes as a Percentage of Total[a] Taxes	Total Federal Offset ($ Millions)
Minnesota	166.76	19.2	92.5	11.7	68.33
Mississippi	64.94	20.5	39.4	13.5	15.77
Missouri	144.07	17.6	119.3	15.0	59.43
Montana	35.49	21.9	19.4	13.3	5.89
Nebraska	46.55	17.2	37.3	14.3	7.28
Nevada	46.64	49.0	10.0	17.1	3.79
New Hampshire	22.84	18.2	18.4	15.2	5.16
New Jersey	293.73	19.4	222.2	15.5	113.63
New Mexico	41.56	22.2	25.7	15.0	7.51
New York	1,112.11	20.4	585.3	11.9	634.30
North Carolina	152.92	20.7	98.8	14.4	68.25
North Dakota	25.23	18.7	14.7	11.8	5.10
Ohio	368.32	18.6	292.1	15.4	104.94
Oklahoma	103.08	22.5	60.9	14.6	26.67
Oregon	83.58	20.0	56.7	14.5	41.45
Pennsylvania	434.42	18.6	356.7	15.8	147.47
Rhode Island	41.89	22.2	26.3	15.2	13.31
South Carolina	64.46	19.5	48.3	15.4	22.62
South Dakota	26.17	17.2	15.8	11.1	3.81
Tennessee	108.83	20.6	81.4	16.3	31.82
Texas	516.37	27.9	250.6	15.8	56.22

Utah	42.87	20.9	35.7	18.0	15.73
Vermont	14.64	15.9	10.5	11.9	5.85
Vriginia	108.49	17.4	101.9	16.5	48.46
Washington	125.33	16.5	92.5	12.7	36.46
West Virginia	64.65	21.1	44.7	15.6	6.74
Wisconsin	171.52	17.6	114.0	12.4	102.22
Wyoming	20.65	25.2	10.5	14.6	20.36
All States	8,342.00	21.0	5,296.0	14.2	3,046.00

[a]Total defined after geographical incidence, i.e., [Total–(Exporting-Importing)].

Source: Charles McLure, "An Analysis of Regional Tax Incidence"; Benjamin Bridges, Jr., "Deductibility of State and Local Nonbusiness Taxes under the Federal Individual Income Tax," NATIONAL TAX JOURNAL 19 (March 1966): 1-17. The data are for 1962.

is made, however, to estimate the impact of taxes imported into Minnesota upon the tax burden for residents of the state. The results of the analysis understate the burden on Minnesota residents by an amount which is a function of the degree to which exported and imported taxes do not offset each other.

Musgrave and Daicoff account for the exporting of taxes and its influence upon the burden of taxation in Michigan by noting:

So far we have noted that Michigan residents will be relieved of that portion of the tax shifted to the outside of the State through price and income changes. But, in addition, the tax burden on Michigan residents is reduced in all cases where payments of Michigan taxes lead to a reduction of their federal tax liabilities.[6]

They estimate $374 million, about 21 percent of Michigan taxes in 1956, were exported. The calculation of the effective rates for Michigan accounts for this exporting, but as in the Minnesota study the problem of tax-importing is not given explicit attention. This results from the methodology of the study which limits analysis to the burden of taxes actually levied in Michigan.

The Wisconsin study also accounts for the exporting of taxes. It is estimated that more than 20 percent of Wisconsin's taxes were exported to the federal government or out-of-state consumers in 1956 ($156 out of $727 million).[7] However, as in the other state studies, tax-importing is dismissed on the assumption that imported and exported taxes are offsetting: ". . . in the absence of reliable export-import data, it is best to assume that they are offsetting and that Wisconsin residents bear the burden of Wisconsin-imposed taxes."[8]

The only model which makes empirical adjustments for the geographical flow of taxes, both in and out of an area, was developed by Hirsch, et al. in a study of the external costs and benefits of providing education in Clayton, Missouri.[9] The Hirsch study was concerned with the analysis of a small municipality and the flow of costs and benefits arising from the provision of education in this community. In examining the cost flows, a spatial tax incidence model was developed to deal with the spillin and spillout of taxes relevant to the financing of education. The methodology of the Hirsch study is much the same as here only the focus differs. Hirsch was not concerned with the flow of taxes among all local governments but rather with their flow according to the following scheme.

Spatial Incidence for Hirsch Study

Area	Spillout	Spillin	Net Spillover
Rest of St. Louis County			
City of St. Louis			
Rest of SMSA		(dollar tax flows)	
Rest of Missouri			
Rest of United States			

The focus is explicitly upon Clayton; other geographical areas are incorporated to make the results for Clayton more representative.

Thus far, in all studies with the state as unit of analysis, incidence estimates do not properly reflect the burden of taxation since that part of the burden imported from other states is not considered. While in the context of one particular state, such a methodology may be acceptable; when all states are considered and the focus is interstate variations, attention must be given to the impact of both exporting and importing.

Estimates of the magnitude of imported taxes by state are shown to be a significant factor in the tax structure of all state-local systems; Table 4-1 indicates that this category of (implicit) taxation averages 14.2 percent, with a range between 18.0 and 11.1 percent of total taxes. In addition, it is found that exporting and importing *do not* offset each other as often assumed in prior models. This finding is not surprising since there is no a priori reason to assume that they should.

The following sections will discuss the extent of importing and exporting in the state-local systems and the incorporation of such estimates into a model for calculating the distribution of tax burdens.

The Scope of Exporting-Importing

The importance of tax-exporting for the state-local fiscal system is evident from an examination of the data in Table 4-1. Based on McLure's estimates, exported taxes represented about 21 percent of total state-local tax revenue, some $8.3 billion out of $42 billion for the study year.[10] The impact of exported taxes upon the geographical distribution of tax burdens is considerable. One-fifth of the total burden of state-local taxes is exported from the state in which levied to rest upon residents of other states. The final spatial incidence of these taxes has substantial impact on the burden of taxation in any given system and on the variation across systems.

The percentage of total taxes exported ranges from a high of 49.0 in Nevada (due to the importance of gambling and related taxes) to a low of 15.8 in New Hampshire. In the aggregate, the variation across states is considerable. Exporting of specific taxes exhibits still greater variation. The average amount exported ranges from a high of 44.7 percent of corporate taxes (with a range from 80.6 percent in Delaware to 32.7 percent in South Dakota) to 6.2 percent of miscellaneous taxes (with a range from 64.8 percent in Nevada to less than 0.1 percent for states such as Alaska, Iowa, Kansas, etc.). This range in the amount of specific taxes exported is a major source of interstate variation in tax burdens. It is summarized in Table 4-2.

The coefficient of variation for the percentage of specific taxes exported further accentuates the variation across states. Taxes such as severance, recrea-

Table 4-2
Range and Coefficient of Variation[a] for Percentage of State-Local Tax Revenue Exported, by Type of Tax

Tax	Range High	Range Low	Coefficient of Variation
Corporate income	80.6	32.7	.160
Individual income	29.5	14.6	.221
Property	25.1	11.5	.219
General sales	32.5	0.0[b]	.273
Selective sales:			
Alcohol	51.7	0.0	.749
Tobacco	35.9	2.1	.650
Motor fuel	31.1	16.9	.132
Public utility	81.2	0.0[b]	1.191
Insurance	61.8	28.1	.208
Recreation	59.9	0.0[b]	1.422
Death and gift	91.6	0.0[b]	.632
Motor vehicle license	41.1	15.4	.170
Severance	76.9	0.0[b]	1.263
Miscellaneous	64.8	0.0[b]	1.734
Total Exported	49.0	15.8	.253

[a]For state actually using the tax.

[b]Exported tax less than 0.1 percent of total tax revenue.

Source: Computed from data in McLure, "An Analysis" (see note 1). The data are for 1962.

tion, public utility, and alcohol exhibit a high degree of variation across states, while corporate income, motor fuel, motor vehicle license, individual income, and property taxes cluster around the mean value.

It becomes evident that not only is there considerable variation across states in the relative importance of exporting various types of taxes, but there is also considerable divergence by type of tax. While there is some variation in the relative exporting of each type of tax, there are some forms of taxation that are much more amenable to exporting, for example, gambling taxes in Nevada or severance taxes in Texas. It is exactly this type of variance in the use and relative importance of specific exported taxes that is crucial to obtaining a representative distribution of effective rates by state.

The estimated $8.3 billion of state-local taxes exported (see Table 4-1) represents a geographical shifting of the burden of taxation to residents of other systems. For example, taxes levied in Michigan upon various phases of automobile production are reflected in higher prices for the finished product. The burden of these taxes is shifted partially to residents of other states; it is borne by Michigan residents only in proportion to their consumption of automobiles produced in Michigan. In a similar manner, Michigan residents bear the burden of taxes levied in other states and reflected in higher prices paid for goods consumed by Michigan residents.

Exported taxes, however, must become manifest as a burden somewhere in the economy. That burden can be separated into two distinct parts; (1) the burden that remains within the state-local system and (2) the burden shifted to the federal revenue structure in the form of reduced tax yields. The latter results from provisions of federal tax law that permit the deduction of state-local taxes in determining federal tax liability.[11] The task becomes one of isolating that portion of exported taxes borne by the federal revenue structure. The balance represents the burden of exported taxes remaining with residents of the state-local system.[c] This element can be treated as a separate category of taxation (a composite of various types of imported taxes) and its incidence calculated as with other taxes.

Bridges has estimated the cost to the federal government of state-local nonbusiness tax deductions by state for the study year.[12] His estimates are based, however, on 1964 federal tax law and revised 1965 rates. To adapt his estimates to the present study, his state-by-state data were: (1) adjusted to account for states that did not use general sales or income taxes in 1962 and (2) prorated to the level of 1962 costs under 1962 law. The total cost of nonbusiness tax deductions is estimated as $2.73 billion; this is disaggregated by type of tax and by state.

The cost of business tax deductions is based on McLure's data on the percentage of locally borne state corporate income taxes.[13] The dollar amount of corporate taxes borne locally was then computed using these data. Assuming a 50 percent federal tax rate, one-half of state corporate income taxes is shifted to the federal revenue structure as reduced federal tax yields. The total cost of these provisions is estimated at $316 million.

Given these estimates of the cost of business and nonbusiness tax deductions to the federal revenue structure, state-by-state and tax-by-tax adjustments can be made so that the effective rates reflect the impact of federal tax law on state-local tax incidence. The total amount of state-local taxes borne by the federal government through the deductibility provisions of federal tax law is $3.046 billion (see Table 4-1). The balance of exported taxes is manifest as a burden on residents of state-local systems in the form of various state-local taxes imported from other states.

Having isolated the burden of exported taxes remaining with residents of the state-local system from that borne by the federal government, the aggregate

---

[c]A point of clarification is perhaps necessary. The burden being considered here is only that of state-local taxation. It is, of course, residents of state-local systems that ultimately bear the burden of *all* taxation.

dollar amount of imported taxes ($5.3 billion) must be allocated to each state. This allocation must be done on a basis that reflects the relative importation of taxes into each state. Since this is a conglomerate category reflecting the importing of various types of taxes, it is felt that allocation on the basis of consumption expenditures best reflects the relative importation of taxes. Taxes exported, exclusive of the federal offset, are for the most part exported in the form of higher prices. It is felt that consumption is a good proxy for the importation of these taxes since it reflects the price effect of taxes inherent in the consumption of imported goods and services. Accordingly, the aggregate dollar amount of imported taxes is allocated among states on the basis of a state's proportion of total national consumption expenditures. The dollar amount of taxes imported into each state (allocated as discussed above) is shown in Table 4-1. It is this amount that must be distributed by income class to make exhaustive the estimation of total tax incidence.

Table 4-1 provides data by state on each component of geographical tax flows. Exported taxes, imported taxes, and total federal offset are indicated along with the relative importance of exported and imported taxes. The data reflect the methodology developed in this chapter for incorporating spatial tax flows into an incidence model. With the estimation of imported taxes and their distribution by income class, the burden of taxation for the state-local system is exhaustive and the interstate pattern is reflective of the variation that

Geographical Incidence and the Burden of Taxation

The burden of taxation on the residents of a given state is lessened to the extent that taxes levied within the state are exported to residents of other states. In an analogous manner, this burden is increased to the extent that residents of a given state bear the burden of taxes levied in other states. The question of burden thus becomes considerably more complex in the context of an open economy where taxes are not confined to the state in which levied. Spatial flows must be incorporated to adjust for this flow of burdens in and out of state-local systems. More importantly, unless such flows are accounted for explicitly, the variation across states will be distorted to the extent that: (1) imported and exported taxes do not exactly cancel each other and (2) the federal revenue structure absorbs some of the burden in reduced tax yields.

Making use of McLure's estimates on exporting, the dollar amount of exported taxes can be determined for each type of tax for each state. The dollar amount of exported taxes borne by the federal revenue structure can be estimated as outlined earlier. The difference between these two magnitudes defines aggregate imported taxes, that is, taxes imported into a state from other states.

This data must then be incorporated into a tax incidence model to account for the flow of tax burdens in and out of state-local systems. To accomplish this, the dollar amount of each specific tax exported is netted out of the total for each tax for each state. This provides an estimate of the amount of a tax whose incidence remains within the confines of the state in which levied. This dollar amount for each tax, allocated as indicated in Chapter 3, provides a preliminary estimate of the distribution of tax burdens for each state.

Exported taxes, however, become manifest as a burden either on residents of a state-local system or on the federal revenue structure in the form of reduced tax yields. Of the exported taxes, $5.3 billion represent a direct burden on residents of the state-local system in the form of imported state-local taxes. The balance, some $3.0 billion, is absorbed by the federal government and, assuming constant yield, retaxed against the citizenry in accordance with the federal tax structure.

The final task in completing the model is the allocation of imported state-local taxes by income class. This provides an exhaustive classification of taxes on which to base the calculation of state-local tax incidence. Imported taxes—which represent a composite of several types of taxes—are allocated by income class on the basis of total current consumption. The taxes included in the imported category are those that have been exported through the market in the form of a higher price. It is assumed that consumption expenditures reflect this price effect and the relative consumption pattern and thus provide an acceptable proxy for the incidence of imported taxes. The distribution of tax burdens that emerges—after exporting and importing—accounts for both the interpersonal and geographical incidence of taxation. In addition, the effective rates reflect the variation that exists across state-local systems vis-à-vis the impact of spatial tax flows.

Summary

Past literature on tax burdens has given little or no attention to the phenomenon of spatial tax flows among governmental units and between levels of government. While this may not be cause for serious distortion in aggregate studies dealing with entire governmental sectors, it is a source of potentially serious distortion when examining the fifty state-local systems. Since the focus of this study is each state-local system, spatial tax flows must be properly weighted for the empirical analysis to carry any validity.

It has been estimated that the geographical flow of state-local taxes among governmental systems amounted to some $8.3 billion or 21 percent of total state-local tax revenue for the study year. Of equal consequence for empirical analysis is the fact that the variation across the fifty states is quite extreme. Not only is the magnitude of the tax flows substantial but the degree of variance across states is also considerable. Coefficients of variation as high as 1.4 and 1.7 are found for the percentage of certain taxes exported.

The purpose of this chapter has been first to define the need for incorporating the impact of spatial tax flows and second to provide estimates of the magnitudes involved. With this accomplished, the model developed in Chapter 3 can be refined to adjust for geographical incidence. The empirical results to follow in Chapters 5 and 6 reflect the standard incidence assumptions delineated in the previous chapter and the spatial incidence estimates developed in this chapter. These results reflect not only the level of the tax burden within a given state but also the relative positions of states vis-à-vis the burden of specific taxes and the total system of taxes. This makes possible a comparative analysis of tax burdens for all states.

5 The Nature of Individual State-Local Taxes

The existing literature on state-local incidence distorts the actual pattern in two distinct ways: (1) by assuming an aggregate distribution to be representative of the component systems or (2) by attributing to all states a pattern similar to one particular state. Either method introduces potentially severe distortion by lending credence to data as being somehow representative.

Even a cursory examination of the features of state-local taxation (e.g., rates, deductibility features, exemptions and reliance on çertain types of taxation) points unequivocally to its most outstanding feature—extreme variability.[1] It is this variability that lessens the representativeness of any aggregate or specific state study. The variation across states dictates that each state's peculiar features be permitted to influence the construction of a representative distribution for any single tax or total taxes. Only when such a methodology is followed will the resulting distribution of effective rates be indicative—in a statistical sense—of the level and incidence of tax burdens existing in a state.

Empirical implementation of the model developed in Chapters 3 and 4 results in a (50 x 9) matrix of effective rates for each tax and total taxes (50 states, 9 income classes). As is immediately obvious, any analysis except that relating to a given state must rely upon some form of statistical summarization to define general patterns and relationships. The most logical choice in this context is the arithmetic mean as a measure of the average level of effective rate for a given income class and the coefficient of variation to indicate the degree of dispersion. Used in conjunction, these two measures summarize both the level and variation of effective rates in each income class and the average incidence pattern for individual taxes and the total tax structure. Tables 5-1 and 5-2 show the means and coefficients of variation calculated from the estimates of effective rates by state. The statistics are computed using only those states in which the tax is actually levied (e.g., thirty-seven states for the individual income tax); this indicates variation in actual rather than potential use.

Table 5-1 shows quite clearly that the tax with the highest effective rate is the property tax. The range is from 5.9 in the lowest class to 2.1 in the highest. The only other tax approaching this level is the general sales tax with a range between 2.1 and 0.8. The level of the property and general sales taxes reflects their importance in the state-local revenue structure. For the study year, property taxes accounted for 45.9 percent of total state-local tax revenue, with a high of 70.5 percent in Nebraska. General sales taxes accounted for an average of 14.6 percent of state-local tax revenue. The range is less severe, however; Hawaii raised a high of 37.9 percent, Oregon a low of 0.5 percent.

Table 5-1
Means of Effective Rates for State and Local Taxes

Tax	$0-1,999	2,000-2,999	3,000-3,999	4,000-4,999	5,000-5,999	6,000-7,499	7,500-9,999	10,000-14,999	Over 15,000	Number of States
Corporate Income										
All consumption	0.388	0.326	0.310	0.279	0.262	0.250	0.232	0.212	0.153	36
½ consumption, ½ dividends[a]	0.234	0.199	0.221	0.168	0.170	0.157	0.165	0.225	0.566	36
All Sales and Gross Receipts	3.998	3.458	3.495	3.221	2.976	2.794	2.580	2.300	1.505	50
General Sales and Gross Receipts	2.152	1.773	1.690	1.528	1.425	1.363	1.272	1.172	0.861	41
Selective Sales and Gross Receipts	2.233	2.005	2.109	1.969	1.808	1.676	1.557	1.339	0.798	50
Alcohol	0.183	0.163	0.183	0.179	0.158	0.180	0.168	0.193	0.148	50
Tobacco	0.514	0.439	0.404	0.356	0.311	0.280	0.234	0.162	0.087	48
Public utility										
Telephone and telegraph	0.244	0.194	0.177	0.157	0.148	0.143	0.126	0.110	0.074	46
Gas and electric[a]	0.338	0.252	0.202	0.170	0.155	0.138	0.116	0.095	0.061	46
Motor fuel	0.902	0.902	1.081	.1.048	0.980	0.881	0.834	0.717	0.377	50
Other selective sales	0.325	0.287	0.271	0.245	0.229	0.219	0.203	0.186	0.134	50
Property										
All housing	6.280	5.143	4.410	3.998	3.750	3.520	3.156	2.820	2.193	50
½ housing, ½ consumption[a]	5.950	4.899	4.370	3.977	3.713	3.520	3.211	2.901	2.176	50
All consumption	5.620	4.655	4.331	3.957	3.675	3.511	3.265	2.982	2.159	50
½ property taxes, ½ consumption	5.412	4.386	3.658	3.370	3.409	3.597	3.368	3.174	2.649	50
Personal Income	0.061	0.106	0.221	0.310	0.403	0.540	0.736	1.043	1.821	37
Death and Gift	–	–	–	–	–	–	–	–	0.475	49
All Other	1.394	1.152	1.087	0.984	0.010	0.879	0.816	0.744	0.534	50
Imported	2.015	1.677	1.578	1.432	1.337	1.276	1.186	1.083	0.780	50
Total Taxes	13.572	11.408	10.853	9.966	9.366	8.977	8.456	7.962	7.214	50
Total Taxes Net of Property Tax	7.622	6.508	6.482	5.988	5.654	5.461	5.245	5.061	5.039	50

[a]Alternative used in calculating total burden.

Table 5-2
Coefficients of Variation of Effective Rates for State and Local Taxes

Tax	$0-1,999	2,000-2,999	3,000-3,999	4,000-4,999	5,000-5,999	6,000-7,499	7,500-9,999	10,000-14,999	Over 15,000	Number of States
Corporation Income										
All consumption	.446	.454	.450	.451	.452	.451	.451	.455	.468	36
½ consumption, ½ dividends[a]	.462	.468	.503	.468	.467	.429	.434	.480	.546	36
All Sales and Gross Receipts	.420	.361	.360	.342	.346	.359	.350	.363	.388	50
General Sales and Gross Receipts	.598	.540	.548	.537	.530	.542	.529	.516	.507	41
Selective Sales and Gross Receipts	.250	.229	.229	.219	.227	.256	.221	.248	.273	50
Alcohol	.586	.657	.674	.652	.601	.632	.609	.684	.814	50
Tobacco	.362	.362	.343	.340	.340	.335	.330	.343	.358	48
Public utility										
Telephone and telegraph	.967	.949	.944	.938	.938	.943	.942	.940	.949	46
Gas and Electric[a]	.966	.961	.957	.963	.962	.955	.956	.953	.952	46
Motor Fuel	.353	.287	.278	.257	.268	.303	.248	.254	.239	50
Other selective sales	.886	.836	.844	.836	.828	.847	.835	.827	.830	50
Property										
All Housing	.415	.399	.358	.373	.362	.359	.338	.338	.371	50
½ Housing, ½ consumption[a]	.400	.386	.352	.368	.355	.356	.345	.347	.368	50
All consumption	.385	.372	.346	.362	.349	.353	.353	.355	.371	50
½ property taxes, ½ consumption	.440	.420	.378	.381	.359	.350	.340	.336	.320	50
Personal Income	3.455	1.708	1.082	.863	.791	.698	.654	.609	.526	37
Death and Gift	–	–	–	–	–	–	–	–	.811	49
All Other	.445	.410	.423	.413	.413	.422	.415	.410	.405	50
Imported	.110	.073	.078	.071	.073	.077	.073	.074	.083	50
Total Taxes	.183	.139	.113	.117	.105	.108	.100	.103	.198	50
Total Taxes Net of Property Tax	.249	.204	.215	.194	.196	.199	.191	.207	.284	50

[a]Alternative used in calculating total burden.

Imported taxes—a category reflecting taxes imported from other states—falls next in relative importance. The exact implication of tax revenue derived from residents of other states is not obvious. The estimates undertaken in this study, while tentative in nature, provide an approximation of the relative importance of this revenue source. The preliminary indication, however, is that the relative importance is not insignificant. The U.S. average for 1962 was 12.6 percent of total state-local tax revenue.

The total tax effective rate, on the average, ranges from 13.5 in the lowest income class to 7.2 in the highest. This represents the interaction of each specific tax to produce the total effective rate. A simple adjustment of this data permits an approximation of the separate contributions of the state and the local sectors. By examining the effective rates of all taxes except the property tax, a close approximation to the state component of total burden can be obtained. The difference between the incidence pattern of total burden and burden net of property taxes indicates the influence of local sector taxation policy. Such a taxonomy provides a convenient method for making inferences concerning the regressivity of each governmental sector.

As mentioned earlier, the impact of the property tax is pronounced. The effective rates range between 5.9 and 2.1 on the average, accounting for between one-half the total effective rate in the lowest class and one-third in the highest. No other single tax has such a pronounced impact on both the level of burden and the incidence pattern. It is the most predominant influence in the state-local tax structure. Table 5-1 gives the average effective rates for total taxes both including and excluding the property tax. This provides an approximation to the burden of each governmental sector.

While the level of effective rate for a tax is dependent upon its relative importance in a system of taxes, the distributional pattern depends upon the incidence of the tax on specific income classes. Even though two taxes have the same relative importance in a particular tax system (e.g., individual income is 12.0 percent and general sales and gross receipts are 13.8 percent of total tax revenue in Colorado), the incidence pattern can be vastly different.

The distributional pattern of a specific tax depends upon the incidence of the tax, but the incidence of total taxes is a reflection of the interaction of each separate tax—both level and distribution. The characteristics of the incidence pattern and the level of effective rate in any given income class depend upon the influence of each specific type of tax. Examination of the total burden of state-local taxation requires aggregation across taxes for each state. The results reflect both the importance of the tax and its incidence weighted in relation to all other sources of tax revenue.

The configuration of the total burden is dependent upon many forces interacting to produce the final distribution. Attention must first be turned to the characteristics of each specific tax. This emphasizes the contribution of each tax to the level and distributional pattern of total burden. Examination of the features of the total tax structure will be dealt with in Chapter 6.

Corporate Income Tax

The average distribution of effective rates for the corporate income tax (one-half consumption, one-half dividends) exhibits a pattern that cannot be categorized unequivocally. A clear range of progression is indicated above $6,000; the effective rates increase from 0.15 to 0.57. The pattern less than $6,000 is less obvious and there is no regularity whatsoever (see Table 5-1). The data in Appendix D show that the same situation holds for individual states; a progressive influence is present above $6,000. The level of burden, of course, varies with the relative importance of the tax in each state.

The progression at the upper end of the income range results from the burden of the tax resting partially upon holders of equity. To the extent that the tax does fall on equity, the distribution is increasingly progressive. That portion of the tax that can be shifted to the consumer in the form of higher prices is borne in proportion to consumption. This tends to produce a mild regressive influence below $6,000. It is somewhat surprising to find such progressivity in the corporate income tax. Aside from individual income, it is the only tax that exhibits any range of progression. The influence of this progressivity upon the total burden configuration, while mitigated somewhat by its relative unimportance in the tax system, is clearly toward lessened regressivity.

The lack of unanimity underlying the theory of corporate tax-shifting makes any estimate somewhat tentative. It is evident, however, that the greater the incidence of the tax on equity holdings, the greater the progressive influence on the total structure. The incidence assumption used in this study represents a median position between two seemingly unrealistic extremes—burden all on consumption or all on equity. A realistic approach assumes a matter of degree between the extremes, not the choice of one over the other.[a]

Table 5-2 shows the coefficients of variation by income class for the corporate income tax. The range is between 0.42 and 0.54, indicating the presence of substantial dispersion. The greatest degree of variation is present in the two highest classes and would seem to result from variations in the distribution of equity holdings combined with the relative importance of the tax. The main point, however, is the existence of considerable variation in effective rates across states. While part of the variation results from differences in the distribution of income and the series used for allocation, a considerable amount is related to differences in taxation policy and the exportability of the tax.

The provisions for the taxation of corporate income show considerable "political disagreement" across states concerning the role of the tax and its specific features.[2] In addition, the extent of exporting of the corporate tax also

[a]It is highly probable that the balance between consumption and equity as bearing the incidence of the corporate income tax will vary across states. Factors such as the scope of industry in the state, i.e., national or local, and the elasticity of demand facing the industry will influence the tradeoff between incidence on consumption and equity.

varies across states. While the coefficient of variation for exported taxes as a percentage of total tax revenue is low (0.160), this variation interacts with other forces to produce the effective rates summarized in Table 5-1.

General Sales Tax

The distributional pattern of the general sales tax is clearly regressive, on the average. The effective rates decline steadily from 2.1 in the lowest class to 0.8 in the highest. This could be anticipated a priori since the consensus on incidence is that it falls in proportion to consumption expenditures. However, there is an additional influence that operates to alter this pattern—overt state policy to exempt certain items from the tax base. By the exclusion of certain categories of items from the tax base, the incidence pattern can be altered. It has been found in this study that certain exemptions serve to lessen—not eliminate—overall regressivity. This is not a surprising fact in and of itself and has been subject to alternative forms of empirical verification.[3] The exemptions do alter the incidence pattern in the exempting state and accordingly the variation across states and the incidence pattern for the total tax system.

States with no exemptions and a heavy reliance on the general sales tax, such as Hawaii and Washington (37.9 and 37.8 percent of total state-local tax revenue respectively in 1962), exhibit high levels of burden combined with a marked degree of regression. For example, the effective rates in Hawaii range from 6.4 to 2.1. Were food to be exempted in Hawaii, the incidence pattern would be altered in favor of less regression. The level would also be affected to the extent that the decreased yield due to food exemption was not offset by higher rates sufficient to maintain a constant yield.[4] On the other hand, Connecticut and Pennsylvania—states that exempt food, clothing, and medicine from the tax base—exhibit a less marked degree of regression. In both states, the pattern approximates proportionality for the middle income range.[5]

Thus, in states that have actually implemented policy to exempt certain items from general sales taxation, the effect has been to move toward a more equitable distribution of the burden. While the implication of exemptions (especially food) for the pattern of incidence is clear, the effect of changes in yield due to the exemption is not. In the face of new exemption provisions, the decreased yield of the general sales tax would require increased reliance on present taxes or the adoption of new revenue sources. The change in the tax structure due to the exemption provisions depends upon the distributional pattern of the tax(es) used to maintain constant yield. For example, if the decrease in yield due to the exemption of food was recouped by increased reliance on a progressive individual income tax, the net effect would be less regression for the system as a whole. An alternative form of taxation, if it were highly regressive, could negate the intended policy effects.

The relative importance of the general sales tax for the state-local tax system (an average of 14.6 percent of total taxes with a high of 37.9 percent in Hawaii) marks it as a major regressive influence. The role of exemptions lessens the severity of the regression in a few states but not markedly on the average.

The variation across states in the burden of general sales taxation is considerable; the coefficients of variation range from a high of 0.59 in the lowest class to 0.51 in the over $15,000 class (see Table 5-2). The higher degree of variation in the less than $2,000 class is a reflection of varying provisions for exempted items. It is also a reflection of differences across states in the relative importance of the tax.

At this point, it is interesting to speculate about inclusion in the tax base of a class of consumption that is increasing in importance and yet remains untaxed in most states—services. While a few states do tax some services, most states generally exclude them from the base of general sales taxation.[b] In a paper presented at the 1969 National Tax Association, Professor David Davies presented some empirical findings on the inclusion/exclusion of services from the general sales tax base. Using several types of services and measures of income, he concludes: "It appears, on the basis of the evidence presented and analyzed here, that including or excluding services has no significant effect on the equity indices."[6]

Based on Davies' findings, the cause of equity does not seem to be advanced by the inclusion of services in the tax base; the cause of yield would, of course, be substantially benefited. These findings seem at variance with a priori reasoning that might go, "since services are relatively more important in individual budgets as income increases, inclusion of services in the base would introduce a progressive influence." Davies' findings have important implications for state policy aimed at ameliorating the regressivity of general sales taxation.

Selective Sales Taxes

Selective sales taxes generally exhibit a regressive incidence similar to the general sales tax. The figures for total selective sales taxes show a regressive pattern with only one instance of inversion in the $2,000-$3,999 range (see Table 5-1). However, the nature of incidence should be related to the rationale underlying certain of the selective sales taxes. Generally, a taxonomy can be made into sumptuary and benefit taxes, alcohol and tobacco falling in the former and

[b]The major exception is Hawaii which subjects all services to general sales taxation.

motor fuel in the latter. The other selective sales taxes are not so clearly categorized and while not sumptuary in nature, do possess some element of *quid pro quo.*[c]

Alcohol and tobacco taxes can be considered sumptuary in nature, with the tax representing an attempt on the part of society to curtail the consumption of socially unmeritorious goods.[d] If one accepts a collective policy decision to curtail consumption, the regressivity of the tax does not raise as serious equity considerations as do, for example, the property and general sales taxes. Since presumably the social costs are greater than the private costs, the tax is introduced to decrease consumption and close the social-private cost gap. The regression of the tax can be rationalized on this basis and the additional burden on lower classes reflects their willingness to compensate for the social costs of consumption.[7] If acceptance is made of the sumptuary nature of the tax, then the regressivity-equity problem does not loom so prevalent. The heavier burden on lower classes reflects their preference to consume the good and pay the costs involved, social as well as private.

While the regressivity of tobacco taxes is quite evident (the effective rates decline steadily from 0.51 to 0.08) such is not the case with alcohol. On the average, it appears to be more nearly proportional than regressive; the effective rates remain in the 0.17 to 0.18 range across the entire income range. The low effective rates for both the tobacco and alcohol taxes serve to mitigate its incidence. They are simply too small in magnitude to be of any great influence on the total effective rate. In only one instance out of 450,(50 states, 9 income classes) does the effective rate for either reach 1.0 (Louisiana in the less than $2,000 class).

The situation for the other selective sales taxes is not so evident. Their regressivity cannot be rationalized on the basis of collective decision-making. Both public utility and other selective sales taxes exhibit regressivity. If the taxes do bear an obvious relation to benefits received, then the tax serves the purpose of imposing the costs on the recipients of the benefits on a *quid pro quo* basis; the tax becomes an indirect form of price. There are serious questions to be raised, however, concerning the *quid pro quo* nature of these taxes.

The motor fuel tax seems to bear the closest relation to *quid pro quo* of any selective sales tax. Taxes on motor fuels are at least partially related to the benefits (direct or indirect) derived from the consumption of highways. The

[c]Using the taxonomy indicated, 50 percent of selective sales taxes were benefit 30 percent sumptuary in 1962. The balance represented other selective sales taxes. In order to empirically determine whether a tax is sumptuary, in both effect and intent, knowledge of the demand curve by state (for, e.g., alcohol and tobacco) would be required. If the tax yield began to decline after a certain degree of taxation and the rate was not altered to maintain constant yield, then the tax is sumptuary both in effect and intent.

[d]An unmeritorious good can be viewed as the converse of Musgrave's merit good where the externalities are negative and society acts collectively to limit consumption or gain compensation for the excess of social over private costs.

pattern, while regressive above $4,000, exhibits a slight progressive-proportional pattern in the lowest three classes. Once again, the equity argument may be tempered with the closer proximity of taxes to benefits, assuming one accepts the benefit principle of taxation. As Due has noted, final judgments on equity are heavily value laden:

> Questions of equity are of necessity ones involving value judgments and no scientific approach to the definition of equity is possible. Standards of equity for taxation are determined solely by consensus of thought in a particular society; the tendency to attach scientific validity to standards of equity is unfortunate.[8]

The variation in effective rates of selective sales taxation is considerable, both across states for a given income class and for various types of taxes. While tobacco and motor fuel taxes exhibit a relatively low degree of variation across states by income class (coefficients of variation of 0.33-0.36 for tobacco and 0.25-0.35 for motor fuel), public utility, alcohol, and other selective sales exhibit much more variation (0.95-0.96, 0.58-0.81, and 0.83-0.89 respectively). This variation is reflective of the degree of similarity in characteristics of the tax systems. The provisions affecting the level of burden show much more consensus across states for motor fuel and tobacco than for alcohol and public utilities. The implication seems to be that, despite interstate differences in the specific provisions of a tax, the political implementation of the tax produces, *de facto*, a certain amount of agreement concerning its impact on income groups. Certain taxes are less susceptible to extreme variation in the level of burden across states than others.[9]

Property Tax

The property tax is the most important revenue source for the state-local system. In 1962 nearly 46 percent of tax revenue was derived from this tax: the high was 71 percent in Nebraska, the low 16 percent in Hawaii. Nearly all (97 percent) of property tax revenue was collected locally and it represented 88 percent of total local tax revenue. This tax is uniquely local in two ways: (1) it is almost 100 percent locally raised and (2) it is the main source of local revenue. Accordingly, examination of the impact of the property tax provides an acceptable approximation to the impact of local sector taxation policy. Its influence—both level and incidence—reflects local sector activity. In a few states, some distortion is introduced by making property taxation synonomous with the local sector. However, the national average of the property tax as a percentage of total local taxes (87.7 percent) strongly supports this assumption.

Perusal of the frequency distribution presented in Table 5-3 emphasizes the strengths and weaknesses inherent in such an approach.

Table 5-3
Property Tax Frequency Dsitribution

Property Tax as a Percentage of Total Local Tax Revenue	Number of States
95-99 %	17
90-94	14
80-89	9
70-79	8
below 70	2
	50

Source: Derived from U.S. Department of Commerce, CENSUS OF GOVERNMENTS: 1962, Compendium of Government Finance, (Washington, D.C.: Government Printing Office, 1964), p. 45.

In seventeen states the property tax represented virtually 100 percent of local tax revenue, the small balance being other and unallocable. In forty states property taxes accounted for 80 percent or more of local tax revenue, the remainder being selective sales and other and unallocable. In only ten states does property tax revenue decline to less than 80 percent of local taxes. The two extreme low cases are Alabama and Hawaii where the percentages are 46 and 67 respectively. Hawaii and Alabama are states in which local responsibility for raising revenue is very low; local tax assignment ratios are 0.24 and 0.30, respectively, compared to a national average of 0.45.[10] The assignment for taxation in these states is predominantly at the state level resulting in a decreased reliance on the property tax as a revenue source.

In only two states—Pennsylvania and Kentucky—is decreased local reliance on the property tax paralleled by a substantial use of local income taxes; for the study year, local income taxes accounted for 14 percent and 15 percent of local tax revenue in Pennsylvania and Kentucky respectively. Of the ten states with property taxes less than 80 percent of local tax revenue, sales and gross receipts account for the majority of the nonproperty tax revenue. The case in favor of equating property taxes with local taxes, while not perfect, does have a high degree of credence in at least 80 percent of the states. In addition, nonproperty tax revenue is not substantially comprised of local income taxes, i.e., a regressive tax has not been partially replaced with one that is proportional-progressive.

Not surprisingly, it was found that the incidence of the property tax (one-half housing, one-half consumption) is regressive. Netzer concluded the same in his study in which he found both the residential and nonresidential components of the tax to be regressive relative to money income.[11] The effective rates are found to decline steadily from 5.95 in the lowest class to 2.17 over $15,000. The regressivity is most pronounced at each end of the income distribution. In the range $4,000-$7,499, the pattern becomes nearly proportional; less than $4,000 and above $7,500 the incidence is more regressive.

In the lowest classes, the property tax accounts for over 40 percent of the total burden of state-local taxation; this declines to 30 percent over $15,000. Its influence is not as positive distributionally as might be desired. As Netzer has commented:

> It [the property tax] is a generally inferior tax instrument, although not the worst of all possible taxes. But an inferior tax becomes a monstrous one if applied at high enough rates.[12]

Examination of state-by-state data on effective rates indicates the level of burden is markedly above average in those states where the property tax plays a crucial role in local finance, e.g., Massachusetts, Minnesota, California, and South Dakota. The level of the property tax burden in a given state—relative to the average— is directly related to local assignment for taxation, a major determinant of the relative magnitude of the effective rate vis-à-vis other states. Using the tax assignment ratio, states with above average effective rates (e.g., New Jersey, California, Massachusetts, New Hampshire, etc.) exhibit high local tax assignment (0.71, 0.54, 0.61, and 0.63 respectively).[13] On the low side, states such as Delaware, Hawaii, West Virginia, and South Carolina with below average effective rates have a low local tax assignment (0.22, 0.24, 0.31, and 0.26 respectively). The assignment of tax-raising responsibility to the local sector means increased reliance on the property tax in most states and, accordingly, a higher level of burden and more regressive influence on the total tax structure.

Variation in the level of burden across states is summarized in Table 5-2. Generally, there is less dispersion across states for the property tax than for most other taxes; the coefficients of variation range between 0.40 and 0.35.[e]

The property tax is the major source of revenue for state-local governments. The implication of the aggregate dimensions of this tax are impressive enough. However, its impact on the configuration of the tax in specific states is also of major import. This will be made explicit in Chapter 6.

[e]While the variation across states may be small, the variation within states, across local governments, is much more severe. A major problem with a study focused on states as units is that variation across local governments cannot be completely reflected. Data for the state present an average picture. The distortion—potentially greatest in the case of the property tax—must be made explicit.

Individual Income Tax

The individual income tax is the only state-local tax that is unequivocally progressive. For the study year, thirty-seven states used this tax, and it accounted for 7.3 percent of total state-local tax revenue; the high was 30.8 percent in Delaware.[14] The progressivity of the tax is obvious. The pattern of effective rates, on the average, ranges from 0.06 in the lowest class to 1.82 in the over $15,000 class, with a steady increase as income rises. However, its impact on the total tax structure is weighted by its importance vis-à-vis other sources of tax revenue, for example, property and general sales. In a few states (Delaware, New York, Oregon, and Hawaii) the progressive influence is reinforced by a heavy weighting in the tax system. This serves to mitigate the regressivity of other taxes and influences the total burden toward proportionality or less regressivity.

The average level of effective rate is quite low at the left end of the income distribution and increases sharply in the upper three classes (over $7,500), reaching a peak of 1.8 in the highest. In some states, however, the burden on the upper income classes is much more pronounced, for example, 3.9 in Wisconsin and 3.3 in Kentucky. This exerts a significant progressive impact in these states.

The most striking feature of the individual income tax, aside from its progressivity, is the extreme degree of variation in the level of burden both across states for a given income class and across income classes. The lowest class has a coefficient of variation of 3.45; this declines sharply to 0.53. There are two distinct types of variation: (1) that within a given class across states and (2) differences in the degree of variation across states as income increases, i.e., across income classes. Variation within a class represents the simultaneous interaction of many forces such as the distribution of income and the rate structure. The change in the degree of variation across classes reflects these forces and also the wide range of provisions for exemptions, deductions, and definition of tax base across states.[15]

The greatest degree of variance is present in the lowest income class where exemptions and deductions differ considerably. For example, Mississippi's $7,000 exemption for a joint return combined with a standard deduction of 10 percent results in the elimination of any burden on income up to $10,000. Only over $10,000 is there a burden present. This marks the tax as being a strongly progressive influence on the distribution of the total tax burden in Mississippi. The highly progressive incidence pattern is mitigated by the fact that the tax accounts for only 2.6 percent of state-local tax revenue.

The variation across classes and states is considerable but decreases sharply as the exemption and deduction features become less important relative to income. The coefficients of variation of 3.45 and 1.71 in the lowest two classes reflect the differential impact of specific state deduction and exemption provisions and their relative importance for these groups. In the over $15,000 class, the index of variation declines to 0.53. This reflects a lessened relative importance for specific exemption and deduction provisions vis-à-vis income.

Death and Gift Taxes

The burden of the death and gift tax falls entirely on the highest income class (see Chapter 3). While the tax is not of great relative importance in the state-local tax structure (national average is 1.3 percent, with a range between 3.4 percent in Connecticut and 0.1 percent in Nebraska) it does exert a progressive influence in the over $15,000 class.

The average effective rate is 0.48 and accordingly the progressive impact is slight. More interesting, however, is the range across states. To the extent that the tax is borne by the highest income class, a progressive influence exists. The greater the yield of the tax in a given state, the more marked this influence. Maine with an effective rate of 1.8 and Alaska with 0.2 define the extremes.

Variation in the level of burden across states is considerable; the coefficient of variation is 0.81. The Advisory Commission best explains the reason for this finding:

> There are important variations in virtually every structural feature of the States' taxes [death and gift]—in definitions of the gross tax base, in the deductions and exemptions as well as in rates and payment provisions.[16]

The variance in provisions of the tax across states reflects the differential response of the political decision-making mechanism in each state to the implementation and gradual alteration of the tax. The net result is indicated by differences in effective rates.

Imported Taxes

Taxes imported into a state can be viewed as the cost to residents of a given state for the support of public sector activity in other states. Due to the openness of the economy and the geographical flow of state-local taxes among states, some element of imported taxes is implicit as a burden on residents of each state; the analysis here was performed to make this burden explicit by setting up a specific category for imported taxes. The net burden, after exporting and importing have been accounted for, is a function of the geographical flow of state-local tax burdens among states and to the federal government.

To the extent that exported taxes exceed imported taxes in the aggregate, the burden of state-local taxation is lessened (this was estimated as some $3.0 billion for 1962). Some portion of taxes exported does not become manifest as a burden on residents of states in the form of state-local taxation. The federal government absorbs part of the burden through the deductibility features of federal tax law.[f]

To the extent that exported exceed imported taxes for individual states, the total burden is lessened for that state. The net effect is determined by the relative magnitude of exported and imported taxes. The most beneficial situation would be one in which a high proportion of taxes is exported and a low proportion imported. The burden of the provision of public goods and services is, in effect, shifted to the federal government and residents of other states. Exporting and importing are actually phenomena acting simultaneously to rearrange state-local taxation on two distinct planes; (1) geographically by state and (2) by level of government, i.e., state-local to federal.

The distributional pattern of imported taxes is regressive with the effective rates declining steadily from 2.0 in the lowest income class to 0.8 in the over $15,000 class. In addition, the level of burden ranks this tax in importance with the general sales tax. As a category of taxation, it must be considered second to the property tax in its impact upon the total tax burden.

While imported taxes are comprised of various types of taxes exported from other states, they are imported predominantly in the form of prices. The burden, therefore, tends to be regressive since the tax is reflected in higher prices for consumption goods. While exporting of a specific tax may result in a decrease in the level of burden for a progressive tax such as the individual income tax, the importing of taxes results in an additional regressive influence. The net effect of the export-import phenomenon (to the extent that public services in other states are paid for by residents of a specific state) is that the burden is borne in a highly regressive manner. Since importing is manifest as higher prices, the burden falls in relation to consumption.

There is also some preliminary evidence to indicate that taxes more amenable to exporting tend to be those with more progressive incidence such as individual and corporate income and the death and gift tax. Exporting and importing therefore have implications for the distributional pattern of the total state-local tax burden. This will be examined in some detail in Chapter 6 when attention is turned to the characteristics of the total tax structure.

The degree of variation in the burden of imported taxes is in marked contrast to other forms of state-local taxation. The coefficients of variation range from a high of 0.11 to a low of 0.07. As a type of (implicit) taxation, imported taxes exhibit a low degree of variation in effective rates, differences in the incidence pattern being remarkably small over all states. This low degree of variation holds

[f]The burden is, of course, ultimately borne by residents of the state-local systems through the federal sector. It is reasonable to assume, however, that it is distributed in a more progressive manner due to the marginal rate structure of federal taxation.

true in spite of the considerable variation across states in both imported and exported taxes.

Summary

This chapter has discussed in detail the structure of each major state-local tax. The purpose was to uncover differentials in the level and distribution of effective rates for each tax. Separate estimates were made by type of tax and these data were used to estimate the tax burden of each state's tax structure. Estimates were also made of the extent of variation in effective rates for each type of tax by income class. The development of these effective rate data makes it possible to incorporate interstate variations in state-local tax policy in the estimates of incidence for the total tax system.

It was found that the major influence on the state-local system is the property tax. Not only is it of high relative importance, but it is also extremely regressive. Most other taxes were also found to be regressive with the exception of the individual income tax and the death and gift tax's effect on the highest income class. Imported taxes were found significant both in relative importance and as a regressive influence.

The variation in effective rates of specific taxes was found to be substantial in certain instances and subject to rather extreme variation by type of tax and income class. The range for the coefficients of variation is from a high of 3.45 for the individual income tax to a low of 0.07 for imported taxes. These differentials (summarized in Table 5-2) emphasize the nuances in taxation policy across governmental systems. It is exactly this variation that must be reflected in the incidence estimates for them to have empirical credence. The model developed in Chapters 3 and 4 was designed with this purpose in mind.

Data on effective tax rates summarized in Tables 5-1 and 5-2 and discussed in this chapter were developed to assist in understanding how all of the taxes in a system interrelate to produce an overall tax burden. This information will be used in the next chapter to examine the characteristics of each state's entire tax structure.

The Structure of the State-Local Tax System

The progressivity-regressivity of a tax is only of significance when it is related to its importance in a system of taxes. Thus the question of equity must deal with taxes as they comprise a system, not just as they stand alone. The concern is how individual taxes interrelate to produce a total tax burden.[1] The last chapter discussed the incidence of specific taxes and the variation and relative impact of each. Such an orientation, however, presents a disaggregate view of tax burden. Additional knowledge is needed on the effect of each tax when combined with others to produce a tax system.

While the level of effective rate and incidence of each tax is crucial in determining the configuration of the total burden, it is the total tax structure that must withstand attack—e.g., on equity or burden grounds. It is often stated that state-local taxes are highly regressive in a particular state or that the burden of taxation is greater in State X than in State Y. This is more often the case than indictment of one tax as possessing a particular pattern of incidence or level of burden. Also, tax burden is more properly viewed as a total claim on private resources. Effective design of policy requires an understanding of the entire tax system as well as each specific tax.

Extant literature on tax burdens is considerable. Chapter 2 served to make this point. At the same time this literature deals exclusively with either aggregate taxation or taxation in one state. It is the contention of this study that such results are deceptive in that they do not give explicit recognition to extreme variation across states in the burden of specific taxes and features of tax systems. The degree of variation indicated in Table 5-2 understates the actual amount.[a] These differences across states in rates, provisions for deductions and exemptions, exporting-importing, relative importance of various taxes in the system, and so forth, make any empirical results obtained from individual state or aggregate studies much less tenable.

To discern the structure of a state's tax system, data on effective rates for each tax must be aggregated into a distribution reflecting total burden. With such data, attention can be shifted from the characteristics of each tax to the configuration of a system of taxes, remembering of course that this represents an interaction of both the level of burden and incidence pattern of each component tax.

The empirical analysis to follow will focus on each state to permit classifica-

[a]This is so since it is impossible to incorporate all of the variation in state-local tax systems into a single model. Data availability alone stymies such an attempt.

tion and comparative analysis. States will be grouped according to the characteristics of their tax systems. A second level of analysis will isolate the influence of the local sector. This will be accomplished by examining the total burden of the tax system net of property taxes for each state. This offers a good approximation to the influence of local sector tax policy and permits analysis to determine the characteristics of those systems in which local tax assignment is above average.[2] Finally, the influence of geographical incidence will be made explicit. The end result is a better understanding of how each tax interacts to produce total burden (Chapter 5) and how differential interaction produces state-local tax systems with varying configurations (Chapter 6).

The Regression Model

The first technique to be employed—regression analysis—is selected to deal with a classic problem in public finance-measuring the regressivity of a tax or system of taxes.[3] Regression analysis is applied to the total effective rate to define a classification of states according to incidence. Using data on total effective rates, regression analysis offers a relatively simple, yet efficient, technique for examining changes in the effective rate of taxation (taxes paid as a percentage of income) as income varies. If the rates increase as income increases, increase as income decreases, or remain a relatively constant proportion of income, then the system can be classified as progressive, regressive, or proportional.[4]

A least squares regression relating average income to effective tax rate by income class provides a line of average relationship between income and the burden of taxation; such a relationship can be estimated for each state. The coefficient of the independent variable indicates the average change in the burden of taxation per unit change in income. As the coefficient is greater than, equal to, or less than 0.0, the tax system is progressive, proportional, or regressive.[b]

The model for estimating the distributional configuration of each state-local tax structure is indicated in equation (1).

$$ER_{ij} = a_j + b_j(\overline{Y}_{ij}) \tag{1}$$

$$ER_{ij} = (T_{ij}/Y_{ij})$$

$\overline{Y}_{ij}$ = average income $\qquad i$ = 1,2, . . . , 9 (income classes)

T_{ij} = aggregate taxes $\qquad j$ = 1,2, . . . , 50 (states)

Y_{ij} = aggregate income

[b]The analysis is applied to the entire system of taxes in an attempt to discern the structure of the system. The same analysis is equally applicable to each specific tax but has not been done here.

There are nine observations for each regression, one per income class. The analysis is done on a state-by-state basis. The results of the analysis permit states to be classified according to the estimated value for b_j. The null hypothesis is:

$$H_0 : b_j = 0.0$$

with alternative hypotheses,

$$H_1 : b_j > 0.0$$
$$H_2 : b_j < 0.0$$

Hypothesis H_0 implies proportionality, H_1 progressivity, and H_2 regressivity. Tests of significance are applied to b_j and used to determine whether H_0, H_1 or H_2 is satisfied. The 0.05 level is chosen as cutoff value for significance, not because of its sanctity, but rather because it affords adequate protection against rejection of a correct hypothesis. Tables 6-1 and 6-2 summarize the results of the regression analyses applied to each state before and after adjusting for geographical incidence. Tables 6-3 and 6-4 summarize the results using total state-local tax burden net of the property tax. This latter set of analyses isolates the influence of the local sector.

Examination of these results permits inferences to be drawn concerning: (1) the average incidence configuration of each state, (2) the influence of exporting-importing on this configuration and (3) the influence that the local sector exerts upon the total state-local tax system. The analysis in all cases is done for each state.

Regression Analysis of State-Local Tax Structures

The empirical results of the regression analyses reveal some interesting findings. It is often accepted that state and local taxes are regressive, with the exception of the income tax. Chapter 5 has provided results that tend to substantiate this in relation to specific taxes. The configuration of a system of taxes in any state, however, represents the interaction of each specific tax in a manner unique to a given state, the final result being weighted by the level and incidence of each tax comprising the system.

While past studies have, in fact, indicated regressivity for state-local tax systems (see Chapter 2), they have dealt with aggregate state-local taxation.[5] The danger in such an approach lies in the implication that each state is regressive. It is, of course, quite possible for an aggregate or average distribution to exhibit one pattern and its components to be markedly different.

Empirical findings of this study reveal that there are several proportional states and one that is nearly progressive. When the influence of the local sector (i.e., property taxation) is eliminated, it is found that on the average ten states are progressive and twenty-one proportional (see Table 6-3).

The first stage of analysis (unadjusted for geographical incidence) shows one state, Delaware, as progressive and sixteen others proportional (see Table 6-1). One-third of the states have tax structure that deviate from the "conventional wisdom" of aggregate analysis. Delaware, for example, can be accounted for by a high relative reliance on income taxes (30.8 percent individual, 6.5 percent corporate) combined with relatively low reliance on property taxation (20.5 percent—second lowest to Hawaii). This reflects low local tax assignment (0.22—lowest of all states). The other nonregressive states are not so neatly categorized as Delaware. The final configuration reflects in a more complex manner hinted at in Chapter 5 the interaction of all taxes simultaneously, both the level of burden and distributional impact.

When exporting-importing is taken into account, the classification of states changes in an interesting way. It was suggested earlier that the amenability to exporting of various taxes can have a pronounced differential impact across states on the incidence of total taxes. Perusal of data on spatial tax flows strongly suggests the existence of greater exporting for the more progressive taxes such as corporate and individual income and death and gift taxes. This influences the incidence configuration toward increased regressivity. If taxes exported are those that possess some degree of progression, then the larger the proportion of these taxes exported, the greater the regressive influence. When this is viewed in conjunction with regressive incidence for imported taxes, the impact on a state's total burden configuration is considerable.

When compared to Table 6-1, Table 6-2 emphasizes the regressive influence of spatial incidence; no states are progressive and the number proportional has declined from sixteen to eleven. Delaware, for example, which was progressive before exporting-importing, becomes proportional after adjusting for spatial incidence. State-by-state data on exporting indicate that there is an above average degree of exporting for corporate and individual income taxes in Delaware. The net effect has been to lessen the progressive influence on the tax structure to such an extent that the total configuration changes from progressive to proportional. A similar type of interaction has resulted in the tax structures of Arkansas, Massachusetts, Mississippi, Missouri, and Pennsylvania being transformed from proportionality to regressivity. Comparison of Tables 6-1 and 6-2 shows explicitly changes in the taxonomy of states. The rankings next to each state provide some indication of shifts in relative position.[c]

The taxonomy of states in Tables 6-1 and 6-2 reflects the interaction of numerous forces in a highly complex manner, that is, all of the factors discussed

[c]These rankings need to be interpreted with caution. There is no unequivocal way to rank the results of a series of regression analyses applied across distinct units (states). The method used here is to rank on the basis of the values for b_j when a 0.05 test indicated that either H_1 or H_2 was satisfied, i.e., rank states within each group on the basis of the value for b_j.

Table 6-1
Regression Analysis Taxonomy of State-Local Tax Structure, Total Taxes—Unexported[a]

Progressive ($n = 1$)		$H_1: b_j > 0.0$			
Delaware					
Proportional ($n = 16$)		$H_0: b_j = 0.0$			
Arkansas		Montana			
Colorado		New York			
Idaho		North Carolina			
Kentucky		Oregon			
Massachusetts		Pennsylvania			
Minnesota		South Carolina			
Mississippi		Vermont			
Missouri		Wisconsin			
Regressive ($n = 33$)		$H_2: b_j < 0.0$			
Alabama	3	Kansas	23	Ohio	29
Alaska	7	Louisiana	8	Oklahoma	4
Arizona	25	Maine	13	Rhode Island	12[b]
California	18	Maryland	6	South Dakota	24
Connecticut	12[b]	Michigan	30	Tennessee	5
Florida	15	Nebraska	21	Texas	16
Georgia	2	Nevada	22	Utah	20
Hawaii	14	New Hampshire	11	Virginia	1
Illinois	27	New Jersey	19	Washington	31
Indiana	26	New Mexico	28	West Virginia	10
Iowa	17	North Dakota	9	Wyoming	32

[a]The number beside the state name is its rank within hypothesis H_1 or H_2; Low = 1, High = n.

[b]Tied ranking.

Source: Taxonomy based on estimated values for b_j in equation (1), summarized from data in Appendix C, Table C-1.

in Chapters 3 and 4 combined with the specific form of statistical analysis chosen here. While the full form of the process is not amenable to simple identification, the incidence configuration is approximated by the data indicated. A precise specification of the interrelationships and impact of various types of taxes and weightings would require a more rigorous mathematical-statistical formulation beyond the scope of this study.

Tables 6-3 and 6-4 present the same data as in 6-1 and 6-2, except the analysis is applied to the total effective rate—net of that attributable to property taxation. This permits an approximation to the impact of the local sector. Table

Table 6-2
Regression Analysis Taxonomy of State-Local Tax Structure, Total Taxes–Exported[a]

Progressive		$H_1: b_j > 0.0$			
No States					
Proportional (n = 11)		$H_0: b_j = 0.0$			
Colorado		North Carolina			
Delaware		Oregon			
Idaho		South Carolina			
Kentucky		Vermont			
Minnesota		Wisconsin			
New York					
Regressive (n = 39)		$H_2: b_j < 0.0$			
Alabama	5	Louisiana	13	North Dakota	12
Alaska	10	Maine	21	Ohio	33
Arizona	29[b]	Maryland	7	Oklahoma	4
Arkansas	2	Massachusetts	11[b]	Pennsylvania	11[b]
California	25	Michigan	34	Rhode Island	22
Connecticut	18	Mississippi	6	South Dakota	28
Florida	20	Missouri	9	Tennessee	8
Georgia	3	Montana	15	Texas	15
Hawaii	19	Nebraska	26	Utah	27[b]
Illinois	30	Nevada	24	Virginia	1
Indiana	32	New Hampshire	17	Washington	36
Iowa	23	New Jersey	27[b]	West Virginia	14
Kansas	29[b]	New Mexico	31	Wyoming	35

[a]The number beside the state name is its rank within hypothesis H_1 or H_2; Low = 1, High = n.

[b]Tied ranking.

Source: Taxonomy based on estimated values for b_j in equation (1), summarized from data in Appendix C, Table C-2.

6-3 summarizes the results of the regression analysis before adjusting for exporting-importing. The taxonomy shows quite clearly the influence of local sector taxation policy. In this instance, there are ten states that have values for b_j that satisfy H_1. Contrasted with comparable analysis for total burden, it is obvious that local sector influence is highly regressive; the number of states in the proportional category has increased from sixteen to twenty-one. When the influence of local sector taxation policy is eliminated, the total incidence configuration is found to be proportional or progressive in thirty-one states.

Refinement of the analysis to adjust for the impact of spatial incidence

Table 6-3
Regression Analysis Taxonomy of State-Local Tax Structure, Total Taxes Net of Property Tax-Unexported[a]

Progressive (n = 10)		$H_1: b_j > 0.0$		
Delaware	8	Minnesota	7[b]	
Idaho	1	New York	2	
Kentucky	6	North Carolina	4	
Massachusetts	3	Oregon	7[b]	
		Wisconsin	9	
		Vermont	5	
Proportional (n = 21)		$H_0: b_j = 0.0$		
Alaska		Maine		Pennsylvania
Arkansas		Mississippi		Rhode Island
California		Missouri		South Carolina
Colorado		Montana		Tennessee
Connecticut		New Hampshire		Utah
Georgia		North Dakota		Virginia
Iowa		Oklahoma		
Kansas				
Regressive (n = 19)		$H_2: b_j < 0.0$		
Alabama	2	Nevada	16	
Arizona	8	New Jersey	3	
Florida	10[b]	New Mexico	17	
Hawaii	12	Ohio	14	
Illinois	11	South Dakota	5	
Indiana	9	Texas	10[b]	
Louisiana	6	Washington	18	
Maryland	1	West Virginia	7	
Michigan	13	Wyoming	15	
Nebraska	4			

[a]The number beside the state name is its rank within hypothesis H_1 or H_2; Low = 1, High = n.

[b]Tied ranking.

Source: Taxonomy based on estimated values for b_j in equation (1), summarized from data in Appendix C, Table C-3.

substantiates the regressive influence. The number of progressive states changes from ten to two, proportional from twenty-one to twenty and regressive from nineteen to twenty-eight. It is interesting to note that the effect has been to decrease by 80 percent the number of progressive systems and to increase by almost 50 percent the number of regressive systems. Even so, over 40 percent remain classified as progressive-proportional.

Table 6-4
Regression Analysis Taxonomy of State-Local Tax Structure, Total Taxes Net of Property Tax–Exported[a]

Progressive (n = 2)		$H_1: b_j > 0.0$			
Delaware	1				
Wisconsin	2				
Proportional (n = 20)		$H_0: b_j = 0.0$			
Arkansas		Montana			
California		New Hampshire			
Colorado		New York			
Idaho		North Carolina			
Iowa		North Dakota			
Kentucky		Oklahoma			
Massachusetts		Oregon			
Minnesota		Pennsylvania			
Mississippi		South Carolina			
Missouri		Vermont			
Regressive (n = 28)		$H_2: b_j < 0.0$			
Alabama	8[b]	Kansas	7	Ohio	20
Alaska	8[b]	Louisiana	13	Rhode Island	10
Arizona	5	Maine	4	South Dakota	12
Connecticut	15	Maryland	3	Tennessee	6
Florida	16	Michigan	21	Texas	14[b]
Georgia	2	Nebraska	9[b]	Utah	11
Hawaii	18[b]	Nevada	19	Virginia	1
Illinois	18[b]	New Jersey	9[b]	Washington	24
Indiana	17	New Mexico	23	West Virginia	14[b]
				Wyoming	22

[a]The number beside the state name is its rank within hypothesis H_1 or H_2; Low = 1, High = n.

[b]Tied ranking.

Source: Taxonomy based on estimated values for b_j in equation (1), summarized from data in Appendix C, Table C-4.

Isolation of the local sector impact demonstrates quite effectively that in at least twenty-two of the states the regressivity of the total system has resulted from local sector reliance on the property tax. The extreme dependence of the local sector on this form of revenue suggests that the greater the degree of local tax assignment, the more likely a given state will have a regressive tax system.[d]

[d]The case for Alabama and Hawaii is somewhat less tenable on the grounds argued above. Examination of their revenue structures, however, indicates that the nonproperty tax sources of tax revenue are also regressive. Only in Ohio and Kentucky where the local income tax accounts for a relatively large percentage of local tax revenue is the regressivity of the local sector actually overstated.

The regression analysis in this section has served two purposes: (1) the categorical notion that all state-local tax systems are regressive has been undermined empirically, (2) the regressive influence of geographical incidence and local sector activity has been made explicit.

There remain additional dimensions of state-local taxation to be investigated. The following sections will turn attention to: (1) the burden of taxation on a state-by-state basis presenting indices that explicitly incorporate distributional considerations, and (2) the degree of inequality in the distribution of taxes paid by income class.

The Burden of State-Local Taxation

Measurement of the burden of state-local taxation is an elusive endeavor. As indicated in Chapters 3 and 4, it must begin with certain partial equilibrium assumptions concerning shifting and incidence, spatial incidence, secondary effects, and so forth, and then proceed to an empirical implementation based upon statistical series to allocate various taxes by income class. Burden can then be defined, for an income class, as the ratio of taxes paid to income. The problem at this stage, however, is that interpretation must now cope with as many series of data as there are income classes—in this study nine.

Contained in the data on effective rates is rather detailed information on the burden and distributional impact of specific taxes or systems of taxes. The solution to the dilemma is to construct an index that synthesizes the informational content of the (50 x 9) effective rate matrix into a single (50 x 1) vector. With a vector of "burden indices," comparative analysis across states can more easily be effectuated. In addition, due to the unique nature of the data contained in the original matrix, the index will be more representative of the actual position of a particular state-local system vis-à-vis level and incidence of burden. The major considerations are: (1) the loss of information inherent in synthesizing a (50 x 9) effective rate matrix into a (50 x 1) vector and (2) the technique to perform the synthesis; the two are, of course, related.

Before developing the method used in this study it will be useful to reflect briefly on the methodology currently employed to indicate the burden of public sector activity. Basically, it involves relating taxes paid in an economy to some measure of economic well-being. At the national level, the calculation has traditionally involved comparison of taxes with gross national product, taking into consideration the level of per capita income. Such analysis does provide a crude measure of the aggregate impact of the public sector and has often been used to make international comparisons.[6] However, distributional considerations are totally ignored.

A similar type of analysis has been applied to states as distinct fiscal units. Once again, the discussion revolves around aggregate taxes relative to tax-paying ability (some variant of income). Donnahoe, for example, defines tax burden as "some function" that varies directly with tax load (taxes paid) and inversely with tax-paying ability (some function of income). He goes on to state that "the problem of measuring tax burden can . . . be reduced to the selection of a specific locus for the line of equal burden as a standard from which to measure relative deviation."[7] While his analysis is certainly more refined than examination of a simple tax to income ratio, information on the pattern of effective rates is still not reflected in the index.

Examination of current tax burden indices delineates quite clearly the absence of distributional considerations influencing their construction. It is postulated in this study that burden has two distinct components–level and incidence–*both* of which must be reflected in any index purporting to measure the burden of a tax or system of taxes (ordinally or cardinally). Empirical implementation of the model developed in Chapters 3 and 4 offers unique data to construct such an index. Given the effective rate matrices on total tax burden, a technique must be selected to construct an index of burden, that is, synthesize a (50 x 9) matrix into a (50 x 1) vector.

A mathematical-statistical technique designed specifically to accomplish the summarization or comprehension of large numbers of variables has been given the generic name factor analysis. The technique was originally designed for the purpose of isolating a general intelligence factor from masses of data relating to the measurement of intelligence.[8] Factor analysis is equally suited to application on various dimensions of economic activity. It is suggested here that it be applied to an effective rate matrix to summarize data by income class into an index of burden. This permits analysis to reflect both the level of burden and distributional characteristics.

The construction of an index of burden is given more credence in this case, since all the data being synthesized relate specifically to the measurement of tax burden. In other applications of factor analysis, the interpretation is made somewhat less obvious since data often do not measure directly the phenomenon to be indexed; various proxy variables that indirectly measure the phenomena are used.

The mechanics of factor analysis are complex and many nuances on the basic factor model have been developed to deal with specific analytical problems. No attempt will be made to present detail on the mathematics of factor analysis since this would unnecessarily consume a great deal of space. Rather, justification for its application in this instance will be given priority.[9]

Application of factor analysis to data reduction relies upon its capacity to synthesize a given matrix of variables into one or a few factors, with a minimal loss in information content. The factor(s) are identified as representing various dimensions of the information contained in the original matrix. In effect, factor analysis is a technique to construct a new variable called a factor based upon a linear transformation of the original variables in such a way that each factor extracted accounts for a maximum of the variance present in the original variables or not already accounted for by factors previously extracted.[e]

Factor analysis was applied to data on total effective rates. Table 6-5 presents factor scores for the first factor extracted from each matrix. The scores are standardized to zero mean and unit variance and accordingly can be interpreted as Z-scores or the relative deviation of items in a distribution from the mean of the distribution. Rankings based on these scores provide an indication of the relative positioning of each state vis-à-vis the burden of public sector taxation policy.

Comparison of factor scores in Table 6-5 with effective rate data shows the accuracy of using these scores as indices of burden. For example, for the total burden, exported case (col. 1) the lowest level of burden is found in Delaware with a score of –3.57, the highest in Washington with a score of +1.94. State-by-state data substantiate this; Washington has a very high level of burden and Delaware has a level of burden well below other states. It must be remembered, however, that the score or index is a standardized linear combination of effective rates across nine income classes. The weights assigned to each class are calculated so as to maximize the variance accounted for by each factor extracted.[10] Interpretation of the scores as indices of burden must recognize that incidence patterns as well as relative levels of burden are incorporated. Delaware and Washington are useful examples to illustrate the extreme cases.

Delaware has a low level of burden but at the same time incidence is proportional (see Table 6-2). The interaction of these two dimensions results in a low index of burden, –3.57. Washington, at the other extreme, shows an extremely high level of burden combined with a very regressive tax structure; Washington is classified as most regressive.

The extremes defined by Delaware and Washington result from the rather unique tax systems in these states. Delaware relies heavily upon income taxes (37.3 percent) and much less on property (20.5 percent) and sales taxes (no general sales tax, 19.3 percent selective); Washington, at the other extreme, has no income tax and relies heavily on sales taxes (37.8 percent general sales and 22.4 percent selective) with the balance derived mainly from property taxes (30.9 percent).

To complete the example, examination of two states in between serves to make the point. Maine and New York show effective rates that do not differ by much; the burden index, however, is quite different. New York has a score of +0.34 while Maine is +0.95. The reason for the difference is not the level of burden but incidence. New York is classified as proportional while Maine is

[e]Technically speaking the technique used here is components analysis. The major difference is that, while components analysis is variance-oriented, factor analysis is covariance-oriented. In bending to the somewhat confused convention, the text will refer to factor analysis where components analysis is technically correct; the reader is appropriately forewarned.

Table 6-5
Factor Analytic Indices of State-Local Tax Burdens

State	Total Burden				Total Burden Net of Property Tax			
	Exported Score (1)	Rank	Unexported Score (2)	Rank	Exported Score (3)	Rank	Unexported Score (4)	Rank
Alabama	−1.16	07	−1.21	06	+0.88	43	+0.72	41
Alaska	−0.79	11	−0.94	08	+0.60	39	+0.59	39
Arizona	+0.63	37	+1.17	43	+0.27	22	+0.42	35
Arkansas	−0.94	09	−0.94	09	+0.46	38	+0.42	34
California	+1.13	45	+1.21	44	−0.28	21	−0.12	26
Colorado	+0.36	28	+0.39	29	−0.54	18	−0.46	17
Connecticut	−0.09	19	−0.23	15	−0.71	13	−0.67	12
Delaware	−3.57	01	−3.20	01	−1.75	01	−1.35	03
Florida	+0.62	36	+0.44	31	+0.87	42	+0.79	42
Georgia	−0.99	08	−1.03	07	+0.13	32	+0.14	30
Hawaii	+0.82	41	+1.24	47	+2.37	49	+2.67	49
Idaho	−0.07	20	−0.10	19	−0.56	15	−0.78	11
Illinois	+0.41	32	+0.42	30	−0.08	26	−0.06	27
Indiana	+0.41	31	+0.14	25	−0.12	24	−0.36	19
Iowa	+0.69	39	+0.75	39	−0.73	12	−0.64	13[a]
Kansas	+1.03	44	+1.08	42	−0.34	20	−0.37	18
Kentucky	−1.78	02	−1.67	03	−0.54	17	−0.52	16
Louisiana	+0.48	34	+1.23	45	+1.81	47	+2.31	48
Maine	+0.95	43	+0.60	34	−0.06	27	−0.17	25
Maryland	−0.69	12	−0.67	12	−0.06	28	−0.17	24

Massachusetts	+0.39	29	+0.13	24	−1.55	03	−1.52	02
Michigan	+1.33	47	+1.24	46	+0.74	41	+0.55	38
Minnesota	+0.49	35	+0.66	35	−1.33	05	−1.20	06
Mississippi	+0.17	23	+0.32	28	+1.11	44	+1.12	43
Missouri	−1.29	06	−1.45	04[a]	−0.83	10	−0.80	10
Montana	+0.28	25	+0.53	33	−0.87	09	−0.91	09
Nebraska	−0.19	18	−0.38	14	−1.38	04	−1.31	04
Nevada	+0.42	33	+0.71	37	+1.39	45	+1.56	45
New Hampshire	+0.39	30	−0.17	17	−1.07	07	−1.26	05
New Jersey	+0.29	26[a]	−0.02	20	−0.93	08	−1.05	08
New Mexico	+0.71	40	+0.83	40	+1.95	48	+1.95	46
New York	+0.34	20	+0.25	27	−0.57	14	−0.54	15
North Carolina	−1.61	04	−1.45	04[a]	−0.35	19	−0.23	21
North Dakota	−0.20	17	−0.01	21	−0.71	11	−0.57	14
Ohio	+0.29	26[a]	+0.52	32	+0.08	31	+0.00	28
Oklahoma	−0.45	15	−0.18	16	+0.45	37	+0.66	40
Oregon	−0.56	13	−0.58	13	−1.21	06	−1.18	07
Pennsylvania	−0.47	14	−0.72	11	+0.24	33	+0.10	29
Rhode Island	+0.20	24	−0.11	18	−0.01	29	−0.20	22
South Carolina	−1.30	05	−1.29	05	+0.41	36	+0.26	31
South Dakota	+1.14	46	+0.96	41	−0.25	23	−0.19	23
Tennessee	−0.86	10	−0.90	10	+0.28	34	+0.30	33
Texas	−0.37	16	+0.21	26	+0.07	30	+0.44	37
Utah	+0.67	38	+0.74	38	+0.35	35	+0.27	32
Vermont	+0.90	42	+0.67	36	−0.10	25	−0.25	20
Virginia	−1.67	03	−1.92	02	−0.54	16	−0.64	13[a]
Washington	+1.94	49	+1.62	49	+2.53	50	+2.18	47
West Virginia	+0.06	21	−0.01	22	+1.48	46	+1.25	44

Table 6-5 (cont.)

State	Total Burden				Total Burden Net of Property Tax			
	Exported Score (1)	Rank	Unexported Score (2)	Rank	Exported Score (3)	Rank	Unexported Score (4)	Rank
Wisconsin	+0.08	22	+0.08	23	−1.60	02	−1.59	01
Wyoming	+1.38	48	+1.51	48	+0.66	40	+0.43	36
Percentage of Total Variance Accounted for by First Factor	80.2		78.3		83.2		84.1	

[a]Tied Ranking.

regressive (see Table 6-2). The interaction of these forces produces indices that differ substantially; the rank for Maine is 43 while that for New York is 20.

It becomes evident that indices derived from the application of factor analysis to effective rate matrices do provide an accurate indication of the burden of taxation. This permits differentiation among states with similar levels of burden but quite different incidence patterns. Comparison of the exported total burden scores (col. 1, Table 6-5) with the taxonomy of states in Table 6-2 tends to substantiate this. The more regressive states tend to have higher factor scores (e.g., Washington +1.94, Wyoming +1.38, Michigan +1.33) the proportional states lower scores (e.g., Delaware −3.57, Kentucky −1.78, N. Carolina −1.61, S. Carolina −1.30). Perusal of indices for the other three cases (cols. 2-4) reveals the same results. Factor scores serve as indices of both the level and incidence of burden.

A positive feature of the indices constructed by this method is that they reflect virtually all the information (variance) contained in the original effective rate matrix. As indicated in Table 6-5, the percentage of total variance accounted for by the first factor in each case ranges between 78.3 and 84.1 percent. The cost of the data reduction–from the original (50 x 9) matrix to a (50 x 1) vector–has not been a severe loss of information content since between 78.3 and 84.1 percent of the variance in the original data matrices is reflected in the vector of burden indices.

The influence of the property tax on burden is seen by comparing the scores in col. 3 with col. 1. States with high reliance on property taxation (e.g., Nebraska 71 percent, Massachusetts 61 percent) exhibit relatively lower indices when property taxes are netted out (−0.19 to −1.38 and +0.39 to −1.55 respectively); states with low reliance on property taxation show a relative increase in burden (e.g., Hawaii +0.82 to +2.37, Delaware −3.57 to −1.75, S. Carolina −1.30 to +0.41); the rankings indicate the same phenomenon. Thus the indices show quite effectively the impact of property taxation on both level and incidence.

An interesting comparison can be made between Washington and Delaware, both states with low reliance on property taxation (31 percent and 21 percent respectively). After the burden attributable to property taxation is netted out, Washington and Delaware continue to define the extremes. The highly regressive tax structure in Washington and the progressive structure in Delaware, combined with the level of burden, interact to produce such results. In general, reliance on property taxation increases burden through both level and incidence. This is evident from a comparison of the scores for total burden (col. 1) with those net of the property tax (col. 3). Such a comparison makes explicit the influence of the local sector on the burden of the total system. The relationship between local sector activity and burden is generally direct.

These findings concerning the local sector tend to confirm those of the regression analysis in the previous section. It was found that local sector activity was the major contributor to the regressivity of the total tax system. Investigation of the burden of taxation using factor analysis tends to substantiate the impact of the local sector. The indices in Table 6-5, cols. 1 and 3 lend empirical credence to the case.

Inequality in the Distribution of Tax Payments

A third technique for examining the structure of a tax system focuses on inequality in the distribution of taxes paid vis-à-vis the distribution of income or family units. The greater the degree of inequality, the more the burden is imposed upon certain income or family groups; comparative analysis is simplified by using the same definition of income classes as earlier. The estimates of tax payments by income class are those derived from the model in Chapters 3 and 4: tax payments, by income class, represent the numerator of the effective rate.

The Gini Ratio of Concentration (R) is a technique widely used to approximate inequality in the distribution of one variable relative to some criterion distribution, for example, income or family units. The measure defines inequality in a Lorenz curve sense and makes no attempt to indicate social or economic equality (see Appendix B for an explanation of the Gini Ratio). Calculation of R for each state permits them to be ranked and compared vis-à-vis the degree of inequality. Table 6-6 shows R values, by state, for some selected distributions relevant to analysis of state-local tax systems.

The first distribution (taxes paid by income) indicates the degree of inequality in tax payments relative to income. It can be seen that, while the degree of inequality is not extremely high (the maximum value for R is 12.62 for Nebraska), the variation across states is considerable. In addition, closer scrutiny of those states that exhibit high values for R reveals that they are the more regressive: the rankings of regressive states from Tables 6-1 to 6-4 substantite these findings. For example, states such as Wyoming, S. Dakota, and Illinois have high values for R and are among the most regressive; states such as Delaware, Kentucky, N. Carolina, and Wisconsin, with low values for R, are classified as proportional using the regression model. While the R value by itself does not inherently measure the direction of inequality (i.e., toward high or low income classes), comparison with the results of the regression analysis does imply that such inferences can be drawn.

Examination of the distribution of taxes paid by family units reveals greater inequality than by income; the latter exhibits much greater variation. Provisions of state-local taxation seem to be more equitable (in a Lorenz curve sense) vis-à-vis the treatment of income than family units. This is consistent with earlier findings indicating considerable variation across states in the effective rates of certain types of taxation.

Table 6-6
Gini Coefficients of Inequality for Selected Distributions

State	Y = Taxes X = Income		Y = Taxes X = Income (net of property tax)		Y = Taxes X = Families		Y = Taxes X = Families (net of property tax)	
	Index	Rank	Index	Rank	Index	Rank	Index	Rank
Alabama	6.11 R[a]	18	5.09 R[a]	25[b]	36.34	42	41.92	44
Alaska	5.81 R	15	3.56 R	16	30.86	27[b]	36.47	25
Arizona	10.55 R	40	7.86 R	34	27.02	14	37.00	27
Arkansas	6.88 R	25	5.27 P	26	35.79	39	42.21	46
California	7.11 R	26	1.48 P	5	27.36	15	34.43	15
Colorado	5.47 P	14	0.59 P	2	29.27	23	34.76	18
Connecticut	6.71 R	23[b]	3.85 R	18[b]	26.18	11	32.93	3
Delaware	2.59 P	5	6.35 PR	28	40.48	47	38.65	34
Florida	11.76 R	44	11.65 R	46	30.95	28	41.05	39
Georgia	6.06 R	17	3.85 R	18[b]	36.19	41	41.87	43
Hawaii	6.45 R	20	5.01 R	22	29.36	24	35.59	22
Idaho	4.48 P	11	1.29 P	4	29.60	25	34.30	13
Illinois	11.16 R	41	9.63 R	40	24.62	6	35.04	19
Indiana	10.32 R	38[b]	8.50 R	36	24.73	8[b]	34.40	14
Iowa	8.01 R	29	2.54 P	12	29.21	22	36.98	26
Kansas	9.17 R	36	5.08 R	24	27.71	16	36.42	24
Kentucky	1.23 P	1	2.34 P	8	40.05	46	42.13	45
Louisiana	8.04 R	31	6.96 R	32	35.16	38	42.60	47
Maine	7.90 R	30	5.09 R	25[b]	26.21	12	33.87	10
Maryland	6.76 R	24	4.66 R	20	31.11	29	37.74	30
Massachusetts	4.24 R	10	2.98 P	14	28.85	20	33.29	4[b]
Michigan	10.31 R	38[b]	9.03 R	38	24.18	5	33.78	7
Minnesota	3.96 P	8	5.04 P	23	31.54	32	35.96	23
Mississippi	7.98 R	28	6.46 P	29	35.91	40	43.33	48
Missouri	6.69 R	22	2.39 P	10	31.71	33	38.42	33
Montana	6.29 R	19	0.09 P	1	28.22	18	34.70	17
Nebraska	12.62 R	48	11.04 R	44	25.66	7[b]	37.20	29
Nevada	12.07 R	46	11.56 R	45	22.62	1	33.76	6
New Hampshire	6.71 R	23[b]	2.38 P	9[b]	25.73	8[b]	32.56	2
New Jersey	8.18 R	32	5.99 R	20	25.66	7[b]	33.67	5
New Mexico	10.13 R	37	8.87 R	37	28.18	17	37.64	31
New York	2.78 P	6	2.96 P	13	31.99	34	35.35	20
North Carolina	1.98 P	3	1.17 P	3	38.38	45	40.73	37
North Dakota	8.53 R	35	4.32 P	19	28.66	19	37.08	28
Ohio	11.31 R	42	10.50 R	43	23.22	2	35.82	8[b]

Table 6-6 (cont.)

State	Y = Taxes X = Income Index	Rank	Y = Taxes X = Income (net of property tax) Index	Rank	Y = Taxes X = Families Index	Rank	Y = Taxes X = Families (net of property tax) Index	Rank
Oklahoma	5.89 R	16	3.70 P	17	34.89	37	40.54	36
Oregon	2.58 P	4	4.91 P	21	30.86	27[b]	33.86	9
Pennsylvania	5.27 R	13	2.38 P	9[b]	29.10	21	34.65	16
Rhode Island	8.24 R	33	6.49 R	30	25.88	10	33.82	8[b]
South Carolina	4.18 P	9	2.45 P	11	37.02	44	41.22	41
South Dakota	12.29 R	47	10.38 R	42	26.81	13	38.19	32
Tennessee	8.45 R	34	7.11 R	33	34.16	36	41.84	42
Texas	11.82 R	45	11.89 R	47	30.85	26	41.09	40
Utah	6.59 R	21	3.06 R	15	25.85	9	32.36	1
Vermont	3.68 P	7	1.78 P	6	31.43	31	35.39	21
Virginia	5.02 R	12	2.22 R	7	36.38	43	41.04	38
Washington	10.33 R	39	9.37 R	39	23.46	4	33.29	4[b]
West Virginia	7.71 R	27	6.84 R	31	32.83	35	39.74	35
Wisconsin	1.95 P	2	8.21 PR	35	31.38	30	34.28	12
Wyoming	11.53 R	43	10.21 R	41	23.32	3	34.10	11
Mean	7.24		5.53		30.06		36.97	
Standard Deviation	3.05		3.29		4.63		3.33	
Coefficient of Variation	.421		.593		.154		.090	

[a]R = Regressive; P = Proportional; PR = Progressive. Derived from data in Tables 6-2 and 6-4.
[b]Tied Ranking.

In addition, it is interesting to note the change in rankings of the states based on the R values for these two distributions. For example, Kentucky is the most egalitarian based on income and nearly the least based on family units—Nevada is just the reverse. The pattern is fairly consistent, that is, equality based on income implies inequality based on family units, and vice versa. It appears that the structure of the state-local tax system does not result in equity in the distribution of tax payments in relation to both income and family units. This implies that policy to achieve equity must be clearly defined as equity vis-à-vis some particular criterion.

The R values for the second distribution—taxes net of property taxes—show slightly less inequality than for total taxes (the average is 5.53); the variation is substantially greater, however (the coefficient of variation is 0.593). Comparison of the R values before and after the influence of property taxation is eliminated proves interesting. Several states show considerable shifts in inequality when property taxes are netted out. This would perhaps be expected a priori due to the incidence of this tax. However, examination of the change in rankings of states reveals that it is not simply a function of the relative importance of property taxes in a particular state. Rather, states whose rankings change the most (not necessarily in a given direction) are those with high reliance on property taxation. In other words, the influence of the property tax is considerable but not simple enough to suggest that the direction of influence will always be the same such as toward greater inequality. The phenomenon is more complex than this. For example, the ranking for Wisconsin changes from 2 to 35 with the elimination of property taxes (greater inequality), while the ranking for California changes from 26 to 5; both of these states derive about one-half their tax revenue from the property tax. Obviously, the change depends upon the distribution of income and each type of tax in a state. The point is that the property tax is too complex an institution to express its influence in categorical terms. Forces acting in each state must serve to temper any empirical findings.

The property tax influences the incidence of tax payments toward greater inequality; with a netting out of property tax payments, the average value for R declines from 7.24 to 5.53. Simultaneously, the variation across states increases considerably, the coefficient of variation changes from 0.421 to 0.593. This implies that, on the average, the distribution of property tax payments acts in favor of greater inequality in the distribution of total tax payments.

This makes sense a priori since property taxation has been found to be regressive. Interestingly, however, the property tax also lessens the variation across states in the degree of inequality, although variation is still considerable.

Summary

The features of one particular tax can be properly understood only when it is related to the system of taxes of which it is a part. Chapter 5 provided data on effective rates for each state-local tax. The task of this chapter has been to examine the features of the total tax structure for each of the fifty states and then make comparative analysis across governmental systems.

Three techniques were used to examine total tax burden for each state. First, a regression model was specified relating effective rate of taxation to average income. This permits states to be classified as to overall incidence–regressive, proportional, or progressive. The results clearly demonstrate that all states are not regressive. The pattern that emerges is rather a function of many forces including types of taxes used, their incidence and relative importance in the system. It was found that eleven states were proportional with respect to total tax burden. Among the thirty-nine classified as regressive, there is a considerable range in the degree of regressivity. When the influence of property taxation, as a proxy for the local sector, was netted out, it was found that two states were progressive and twenty proportional. This served to emphasize the strong regressive influence local sector taxation policy exerts on the total system of state-local taxes. Once again, within the regressive group of states, there was much variance in the extent of regressivity.

The second technique employed was factor analysis. Given the effective rate matrix on total tax burden, factor analysis was used to construct an index of burden. The indices developed using this technique reflect not only the level of tax burden within a state but also the incidence of this burden. The advantage to such an index is that it summarizes information on effective rates by income class, changing a (50 x 9) matrix into a (50 x 1) vector of numbers reflecting both level and distribution of the tax burden. This greatly facilitates analysis of the comparative burden of taxation among states and refines the classification given by the regression model.

Finally, inequality in the distribution of taxes in relation to income and family units was examined. The technique used was the Gini Ratio. It was found that there is a fair amount of variation across states in inequality but that it is much more extreme in the case of family units. In addition, equality of tax payments relative to income consistently meant inequality relative to family units.

Each of the techniques selected for examining state-local taxation has its own informational content. All three taken together, however, provide a great deal of data on the characteristics of each system and their comparative positions. The task of the remaining chapters will be to examine what shifts have occurred since the study year that might alter the results indicated here and synthesize the findings of the study as they relate to public policy.

7 Recent Developments in State-Local Tax Policy

There have been numerous changes in the provisions of state and local tax policy since the study year reported on here. The politics of state-local finance is, in fact, characterized by a constant process of incremental alterations to an existing tax structure. Rates are increased, deductions modified, tax bases redefined and special provisions developed to meet with politically or socially sensitive concerns. To document all such nuances would serve little purpose as one would soon become lost in a mire of seemingly uncomprehensible, unrelated information. To discuss trends and relate major changes in state-local finance, however, seems a fitting manner in which to close this study. Accordingly, in the pages that follow attention will be given to some of the major revisions that have occurred in the state-local sector's taxation policy. To facilitate discussion, each major tax will be dealt with separately. Since property, income and general sales and gross receipts taxes comprise most state-local tax revenue, they will be discussed in some detail.[1]

Property Taxation

The property tax has been a fiscal mainstay of government in the United States since its founding. Its evolution has been from a tax used to support the federal and state governments to a tax that is presently uniquely local both in terms of providing tax revenue for the local sector and being almost entirely locally collected. When one discusses the property tax today one is discussing the backbone of local government finance in the United States and all the problems accruing thereto.

As has been empirically documented in Chapters 5 and 6, the property tax exerts a regressive influence in every state. Changes in this tax therefore have important ramifications for the equity of a set of taxes within any state-local system. The only way to define exactly what has occurred since the study year would be to redo the analysis, not a feasible alternative at this point in time. An acceptable form of speculation about changes in the impact of the property tax is to examine the relative reliance of state-local systems on this source of revenue and special provisions that have been designed to deal with its inequities.

Examination of data for 1962 and 1970 uncovers a marked decline in relative reliance on this tax. Table 7-1 gives a distribution of states according to relative changes in property taxes as a source of tax revenue. Out of fifty states, two

Table 7-1
State-Local Taxes as a Percentage of Total State-Local Tax Revenue: Changes, 1962-1970

	Change	Property	(Number of States) Income	General Sales and Gross Receipts
Minus	1-5	22	3	8
Minus	6-10	15	–	–
Minus over	10	7	–	–
Zero		2	2	1
Plus	1-5	4	27	14
Plus	6-10	–	9	15
Plus over	10	–	3	8
Total		50	44	46

Source: Advisory Commission on Intergovernmental Relations, STATE-LOCAL FINANCES: SIGNIFICANT FEATURES AND SUGGESTED LEGISLATION: 1972 (Washington, D.C.: ACIR, 1972), various tables.

show no change, four an increased reliance (with a maximum of 4 percent for Washington) and forty-four a decrease. The maximum decline was in Nebraska, where property taxes fell from 71 to 53 percent of tax revenue. Seven states showed a decline of over 10 percent and fifteen a decline of between 6 and 10 percent. All-in-all, the trend is clearly defined. While property taxation remains the major tax for local governments, it is assuming a less important role in the broader context of state-local fiscal activity.

The U.S. average of property taxes as a proportion of state-local tax revenue has declined from 46 to 39 percent between 1962 and 1970, not an insignificant decline. To the extent that revenue has been maintained or increased by a state income tax, the effect on equity is beneficial. Many of the states that showed the largest fall in the role of the property tax are states that have adopted a state personal income tax (Illinois, Indiana, Michigan, Nebraska, Maine). Most of the remaining states simply altered the provisions of their existing income tax to increase its role in financing state-local public goods. The net effect of shifting from reliance on property taxation to increased use of personal income taxation is less regressivity for the total tax structure.

A second important development in property taxation policy has resulted from the financial burden this tax exerts on low income households. Prior to 1963, there were virtually no instances of state-financed, residential property tax relief schemes for low income households, often called the "circuit-breaker." At this writing, there are eleven states that finance property tax relief for low income households. While each state has varying features, there is some agreement in limiting the benefits to homeowners sixty-five and older. A few states also permit renters and persons less than sixty-five to receive relief. Of these eleven states, nine have explicitly stated income limits while in Vermont the limit is not explicit and Oregon has no limit.[2]

The net effect of a circuit-breaker allowance is to lessen the burden of the property tax on those with the least capacity to bear such a burden. It seems unfortunate that the limitations are couched in terms of age, since age has no sole claim on poverty. The obvious reason is the potential loss in tax yield if just an income limit were stipulated. The framework is provided, however, for extending such low income exemptions to other classes of poor, if and when states decide to assume the fiscal consequences.

In discussing its "high quality state-local fiscal system," the Advisory Commission on Intergovernmental Relations has emphasized that the regressive sting of the local property tax should be lessened by provisions such as the circuit-breaker. While this has become fact in eleven states, there remain thirty-nine that have no such provisions. Also, no states have seen fit to define poverty more broadly than an elderly homeowner or renter. It can only be hoped that this trend will be maintained to include additional states and a broader spectrum of the poor. If this becomes fact, then the sting of the local property tax can be ameliorated if not eliminated.

Personal Income Tax

For the study year, there were thirty-seven states that levied a personal income tax, Pennsylvania being the only one in which the tax was entirely local. By 1972, this number had risen to forty-four, all of which included a state levy. There remain six states that have not as yet adopted a state personal income tax: Florida, Nevada, South Dakota, Texas, Washington, and Wyoming.[3] Use of the personal income tax is now almost unanimous. During the period 1962-72, reliance on this tax increased in thirty-nine states and decreased in three, with two states showing no change. Table 7-1 gives the distribution of these changes. While most of the states (twenty-seven) fall in a 1-5 percent increase range, there are twelve states with increases of 6 percent or more. The maximum is 13 percent in Michigan which adopted a personal income tax in 1967. Of three states showing a decline, the maximum was 2 percent. Broader use of this tax is evident as indicated by the U.S. average rising from 7 to 11 percent between 1962 and 1970. Such a shift implies less regressive overall tax incidence for those state-local systems that have either recently adopted the tax or changed its rate, deduction, or exemption provisions toward greater progressivity.

Detailed examination of changes in rates, deductions, and exemptions tells more about the gross shifts indicated above. Table 7-2 gives revisions in the percentage, single, and joint standard deduction provisions since 1962. Seven states have increased the percentage deduction and twelve the single and

Table 7-2
Personal Income Tax Provisions: Changes, 1962-71

	Personal Exemption			Standard Deduction		
Change	Single	Married	Dependent	Percentage	Single	Married-Joint
Increase	7	8	13	7	12	12
No Change	22	21	18	24	20	20
Decrease	3	3	1	1	0	0
New Tax	8	8	8	8	8	8
Total[a]	40	40	40	40	40	40

[a]The total is 40 rather than 44 since 4 states tax only interest, capital gains, dividends, or commuter income and have no such provisions.

Source: Advisory Commission on Intergovernmental Relations, STATE-LOCAL FINANCES: SIGNIFICANT FEATURES AND SUGGESTED LEGISLATION: 1972 (Washington, D.C.: ACIR, 1972), pp. 208 and 210.

married-joint amounts. Only one state decreased any of its deduction provisions; California removed its percentage deduction while increasing its single and married-joint amounts. The balance of the states did not alter any deduction provisions. The tendency toward increasing the size of the allowances for standard deductions helps to increase the progressive influence of the personal income tax in the total state-local tax structure. Even though the impact might be slight, it exists.

A second feature of the personal income tax is an allowance for personal exemptions. Between 1962 and 1971, seven states increased the single exemption, eight the married, and thirteen the exemption for dependents (see Table 7-2). On the other side, three states decreased both the single and married exemption and one the allowance for dependents. Thus there is a slight trend toward increasing the exemption allowance of the personal income tax. The net effect of these higher exemptions is also to increase the progressive impact of the personal income tax in the total tax structure, however slight it may be.

A final important feature of the personal income tax is its rate structure. Most states have an explicit system of marginal rates applied to ranges of income. The nominal rates are designed to vary from near proportionality in Mississippi to considerable progressivity in New York and Delaware.[a] Five states, however, have a flat percentage rate applied to the income base, and four tax only interest, dividends, capital gains, or the income of commuters. Of the states that have a system of marginal rates, four rely on the federal tax base in determining state tax liability. This is *de facto* a system of implicit marginal rates.

[a]It must be emphasized that progressivity in nominal rate structure is not the same as progressivity in effective rates of taxation. The latter can be, and usually is, drastically different from the former.

During the period 1962-71, twenty-one states revised their personal income tax rates nominally in the direction of greater progression. This implies either an increase in rates falling more heavily on upper income classes or a finer disaggregation of income into more classes with an adjustment of rates to produce a nominal increase in progression. Two states, Idaho and Mississippi, altered the nominal rates toward less progressivity. Of the remaining states, thirteen showed no change and eight were new taxes.[4]

All-in-all, it becomes obvious that the personal income tax is assuming a more important role in state-local finance. It has increased from 7 to 11 percent of total state-local tax revenue between 1962-71 and there is a clearly defined tendency for those states that do not have a personal income tax to adopt one. Of those that had one in effect, the trend has been in the direction of altering the rates, exemptions, and deductions toward producing a greater share of tax revenue for the system while at the same time increasing the progressivity of the total tax structure.

The Advisory Commission on Intergovernmental Relations has defined what it feels to be a "high quality state-local fiscal system." About the personal income tax, it states:

> The personal income tax should stand out as the single most important revenue instrument in the State capable of producing close to 25 percent of total State-local tax revenue.[5]

While this is far from a reality, there are four states that approximate such a position: Alaska, Delaware, Hawaii, and Oregon. If one also includes the local income tax, then Maryland and New York must be added to this list. Continued movement toward greater reliance on the personal income tax would "tone up the equity features of the system and insure an overall State-local system elasticity of between 1 and 1.2." Both are highly desirable goals for state-local tax policy to strive for.

General Sales and Gross Receipts Taxes

The third major tax for the state-local sector is that levied on general sales and gross receipts. For the study year, there were forty-one states that had such a tax; in four states—New York, Virginia, Alsaka, and Oregon—the levy was entirely local. By 1971, forty-six states had adopted such a tax (Alaska remains all local). Only Delaware, Montana, New Hampshire, and Oregon do not currently have a general sales tax either at the state or local level. Use of this type of taxation is now almost as widespread as the property tax.

Examination of changes since 1962, helps to emphasize increased reliance on this tax. Table 7-1 shows these changes. Eight states had a relative decrease, although not by much; in most states the decline has been 1 percent with a maximum of 3 percent in Michigan. One state shows no change and the remaining thirty-seven have increased usage of the general sales tax. Fourteen states have increased from 1-5 percent, fifteen between 6 and 10 percent and eight over 10 percent. The maximum increase was 18 percent in Virginia, which adopted the tax in 1966, followed closely by a 17 percent rise in Idaho. Between 1962 and 1970, the U.S. average rose from 15 to 19 percent.

The general sales tax is increasingly one of the most important revenue sources for the state-local sector and has been subject to numerous rate increases since the study year. During the period 1962-72, rates were increased in every state that had such a tax. In eight states the increases were 3 percent or more, with a maximum of 5 percent in New Jersey. This constant revision of rates accounts for much of the increased relative reliance on the tax. Virginia, for example, went from 0.1 percent in 1962 (a local levy in Bristol) to 18 percent in 1970, most of which is accountable for by the adoption of a state general sales tax in 1966. Currently, the highest state rate is levied in Pennsylvania at 6 percent. The trend is clearly in favor of more states using the tax combined with increases in the rates of the state levy. The modal rate is currently 4 percent (seventeen states) an increase from a mode in 1962 of 3 percent (seventeen states).

At the local level, change has been almost as prevalent. In 1962 local sales taxation was permitted in twelve states; the number is now up to twenty-five with authorization for use in Oregon and Wisconsin that has not yet been put into effect. One system, Mississippi, stopped using a local tax but the rest have, generally speaking, increased use of the tax. Since the study year, the local maximum rates have gone up in twenty states, decreased in two, and remained constant in three. The trend here is also clearly defined. Within the constitutional limitations set by respective state governments, local governments have made wider use of local general sales taxation. While the modal rate has remained at 1 percent, the number of states permitting a local levy has more than doubled. The number of local governments relying on the tax has increased from about 1,900 in 1962 to nearly 5,000 in 1972.

As was documented empirically in Chapter 5, the general sales tax tends to be regressive in incidence. Since it is a main source of state-local tax revenue, many states have designed tax policy to eliminate or lessen its regressive sting. In 1962 nine states exempted food, twelve medicine, and two clothing from the base of general sales taxation. It was found that the exemption of food did serve to lessen, but not eliminate, the regressive impact of this tax (see Chapter 5). As of 1972, sixteen states exempt food and twenty-nine medicine from general sales taxation. It is expected that wider exemption of food does serve to ameliorate its regressive incidence. The wider exemption for medicine probably has little impact on the incidence of the tax since it generally accounts for such a small proportion of total consumption. This treatment seems based more on the psychological impact of not taxing medicine than any expected economic consequences.

In addition to these exemption provisions, seven states have adopted—all since the study year—a personal income tax rebate to minimize or offset the regressivity of the general sales tax. While its form and extent varies, Colorado, Hawaii, Idaho, Indiana, Massachusetts, Nebraska, and Vermont all give rebates tied to the state personal income tax. Thus, aside from those states having specific exemptions, several states have chosen to adopt personal income tax rebates to lessen the regressivity of the general sales tax. A tally shows exemptions or rebates affecting medicine in thirty states, food in twenty-one states, and an additional two states (Idaho and Vermont) rebating on sales taxes paid.

All-in-all, there is a clear trend toward more states using a general sales tax, more states permitting local governments to use this tax, an increased reliance on the tax and concurrent rate increases. Simultaneously, there is a movement in the design of tax policy to do something about the regressivity of the tax. Currently, two-thirds of the states exempt medicine and almost one-half food, either as a specific exemption or in the form of a rebate on the personal income tax. Greater reliance on this tax as a revenue source has at least been tempered by policy designed to lessen its regressive burden.

The "Big Three" State-Local Taxes

Property, income, and general sales and gross receipts taxes are the main fiscal resources for the state-local sector. Taken together, they accounted for 69 percent of tax revenue in 1970, up from 68 percent in 1962. It is interesting to note that there has been little shift in this U.S. average over an eight-year period. Like any average, however, it is extremely deceptive in terms of underlying variation. Between 1962-70, thirty-eight states increased relative reliance on these three taxes while seven remained constant and five declined. Of the thirty-eight that increased, thirty-one rose from 1-5 percent, six from 6-10 percent and one by 13 percent (Virginia). There has, in fact, been considerable change across the fifty states in their use of these taxes.

Even more interesting is the trend indicating relative utilization of these three taxes. As was mentioned earlier (see Table 7-1), forty-four states have decreased their reliance on property taxation in the total tax structure. Most of the drastic shifts away from property taxation have been in favor of one or both of the other major taxes. For example, Illinois showed a 12 percent decrease in the property tax and an 11 percent increase in the personal income tax, Maryland changed by −10 percent and +10 percent and Michigan −9 percent and +13 percent, respectively. Of the twenty-two states that had declines in use of property taxation by 6 percent or more, fifteen of them picked up most of the relative loss by wider use of personal income taxation. The remaining states either split the increase between the other two taxes or shifted to a wider use of the general sales tax. For example, New Jersey decreased the property tax by 11 percent and increased general sales taxation by 11 percent, Wisconsin was −13 percent and +11 percent, Nebraska −18 percent and +13 percent and Idaho −13 percent and +17 percent.

The tendency, however, is clearly in favor of wider use of the personal income tax to offset any decreased reliance on property taxation rather than a total shift to the general sales tax. That is, the number of states doing the former was greater than those doing the latter during the period 1962-70. On the whole, this seems a most desirable tendency for state-local finance to be manifesting. Reliance on the property tax, with all its many inequities, not the least of which is its regressive incidence, is being offset by wider use of a state personal income tax, generally with a marginal rate structure and deduction and exemption features enhancing its progressive impact, or wider use of a general sales tax, which while regressive, is not nearly as severe as the property tax. In addition, there are many states that have adopted special provisions to lessen the regressive sting of both the general sales and property tax. When all this is combined with a general increase in progressive features for the state personal income tax, the tendency of state-local taxation seems clearly in the direction of lessened regressivity for the overall tax system.

Reflecting back on the Advisory Commission's high quality state-local fiscal system, there does seem to be substantial movement toward meeting their recommendations. The property tax is being relied on less for tax revenue and its inequities are at least partially offset by circuit-breaker type provisions in several states. The general sales tax is approaching the 20-25 percent productivity figure postulated and its regressivity is being ameliorated either by exemptions or an income tax rebate. Six states currently meet the commission's specifications on productivity and antiregressivity: Florida, Hawaii, Indiana, Maine, Pennsylvania, and Rhode Island.[6] Most importantly, the personal income tax is becoming a more important tax instrument. Using the Commission's 25 percent guideline for productivity, four states currently approximate this figure (Alaska, 25.8; Delaware, 27.8; Hawaii, 23.8; and Oregon, 25.5).[7] The features of the tax are also being redefined to increase its progressive influence. The combination of all these factors leads to one conclusion—the state-local tax system is becoming less regressive overall. The ultimate test is, of course, empirical, and must await future research.

Conclusions, Implications, and Future Research

The purpose of this research has been to uncover differences among states in the incidence of their taxes. The focus has not been specifically on rates, types of taxation, and relative reliance per se but rather on the differential impact that state-local taxation exerts on various income levels. It soon becomes obvious that this variation is considerable both across states and income groups; variation by type of tax is also found to exist.

In light of the increasing plight of the state-local sector, knowledge of all aspects of its fiscal activity must be uncovered. The previous chapters represent an attempt to investigate the question of tax incidence. Several major issues relevant to state-local taxation and the continued viability of this sector have been brought to focus and need to be emphasized in conclusion.

Summary of Empirical Findings

Previous studies of the incidence of taxation all possess one deficiency: the analysis is either highly aggregate or focused on one specific state. While such a focus does offer knowledge of a governmental sector or a particular state, there is a potential danger in interpretation. There is absolutely no reason to assume that any aggregate or disaggregate series on tax burdens, for any given tax or system of taxes, will be representative of *each* state-local system. In effect, the process of aggregation or disaggregation provides an empirical hiding place to disguise extreme variation across states, types of taxes, and income classes. In addition, past studies are nearly void of comparative analysis.

As a result of the degree of aggregation employed, most of these studies have either ignored or assumed away the phenomenon of spatial redistribution of taxes. As discussed earlier (Chapter 4), the volume of these flows cannot be dismissed. Given the nature of the estimates discussed in Chapter 4, it was found that 21 percent of total state-local tax revenue for the study year was spatially "rearranged" among states or between levels of government. Of the $8.3 billion represented, $3.0 billion was absorbed by the federal government as reduced federal tax yield. The balance, some $5.3 billion, remained as a burden in the form of state-local taxes. This spatial tax rearrangement has important implications for both the level of tax burden and its incidence. It is therefore imperative that it be accounted for in any empirical study concerned with making comparative inferences.

The model developed here has been designed to cope with these weaknesses in earlier studies. Building on the historical perspective in Chapter 2, Chapter 3 presents a model to estimate the incidence of each type of tax and the total tax structure for each state. The focus is placed explicitly on interstate comparisons. Chapter 4 completes the model by incorporating the spatial flow of taxes into estimates of incidence. Only when they are explicitly accounted for do the empirical results more closely approximate actual tax incidence. The empirical results derived from the model are given in full in Appendix D. These data provide the base for a detailed comparative analysis of the structure of state-local tax systems.

It was found that the incidence of specific taxes varies considerably among states. Also, variation across income class is clearly defined; the most extreme instance being the personal income tax where exemption, deduction, and rate features result in a constant increase in variation as income decreases. Differences in the extent of variation for specific taxes were also found to be considerable. Thus, no matter how tax burden is examined, variation emerges as a major feature of state-local taxation. The purpose of this study has been to uncover this variation, making explicit its magnitude and impact.

Analysis of each state's tax system reveals several points of interest. The classification of states by incidence—based upon the regression model—shows quite clearly that all are not regressive. This is a major point! Just because specific taxes are regressive, it should not be assumed categorically that the same is true for systems of taxes. Overall incidence depends upon the weighting of each tax in its system, both level and incidence. The regression analysis reveals eleven states with average incidence patterns that are proportional rather than regressive. Closer examination shows these to be states with individual income taxes of sufficient relative importance to exert a significant progressive-proportional impact.

The influence of spatial tax flows is also found to be regressive. Comparison of the regression analysis results before and after adjusting for tax-exporting and importing shows the number of regressive states increasing when the estimates are revised to adjust for spatial incidence. This shifting of taxes has an important effect in each state. Perusal of data on tax-exporting shows that those taxes more amenable to exporting tend to be more progressive. This, combined with the incidence of imported taxes, leads to greater overall regressivity.

The most pronounced regressive influence on state-local tax systems is a result of local sector policy. When this influence is "netted out," the regression analysis uncovers more states to be progressive or proportional. Tables 6-3 and 6-4 give the unexported and exported classification of states, net of local sector influence. The number of progressive-proportional states before and after adjusting for spatial incidence is thirty-one and twenty-two respectively. When the regressivity of the local sector is made explicit, it is found that many systems are actually progressive or proportional, except for the effect of the local property tax. Comparison of Tables 6-1 and 6-2 with 6-3 and 6-4 delineates the influence of both spatial incidence and local sector tax policy.

As has been discussed, the incidence of a system of taxes is a complex phenomenon to quantify. Appendix D contains detailed data on level and incidence, by type of tax and state. However, some method of summarization is necessary to facilitate their comprehension. A new method for quantifying the burden of a specific tax or system of taxes has been suggested in this study. It relies on properties of factor analysis, a mathematical technique designed to summarize large numbers of variables and uncover interrelationships and patterns of variation that exist among them. Given the total effective tax rates in Appendix D, an opportunity is presented to apply factor analysis to the construction of tax burden indices that reflect *both* level and incidence. The results of this analysis are given in Table 6-5. The indices contained therein reflect the relative positions of each state. Lower scores indicate the interaction of a lower level of burden and less regressive incidence, higher scores a greater burden and more regressive incidence. While factor analysis is applied here only to total tax burden, it is equally applicable to each specific tax. Using the data in Appendix D, a comparative analysis for each type of tax could be undertaken.

It is felt that the application of factor analysis to the comprehension of state-local tax incidence offers considerable promise. This technique is uniquely suited to the task of uncovering common patterns of variation and relationships among large numbers of variables. It has been used here to summarize data on effective tax rates by income class. Use of these indices greatly facilitates any comparative analysis.

Tax Burden and the Distribution of Aid

The measurement of tax burden has implications for the allocation of federal aid among states. Most aid formulae use an index of tax effort to account for above or below average effort. The amount of aid is then adjusted upward or downward according to relative effort. It was suggested in Chapter 6 that such a measure may not reflect actual effort in a state since it ignores specific features of each tax, the interaction of taxes as a system and the distributional impact of taxes relative to income. For example, so many dollars in taxes per $1,000 of personal income tells nothing of how this tax burden affects various levels of income. A more accurate measure would indicate both the level of taxation and the incidence of the entire tax system. Just such a measure was developed earlier by applying factor analysis to effective tax rate data.

A simplified aid formula to allocate aid according to population, per capita personal income, and tax effort might look as follows:

$$F_i = \frac{(P_i \cdot Y)}{Y_i} \; (E_i)$$

F_i = state i's share of total aid

E_i = tax effort of ith state

P_i = population of ith state

P = population of United States

Y = per capita personal income for United States

Y_i = per capita personal income for ith state

Traditionally, tax effort (E_i) has been defined as:[1]

$$\frac{T_i}{(Y_i \cdot P_i)} \Bigg/ \frac{T}{(Y \cdot P)}$$

This measure relates taxes paid as a percentage of personal income in the ith state to that for the total United States. It is suggested here that tax effort be measured to reflect both the level and incidence of taxes relative to income. Table 6-5 contains indices that do just that. Use of such an index would adjust the distribution of aid to be more reflective of variations in tax effort among states.[2] This would provide a more equitable allocation of funds earmarked for revenue-sharing type programs.

Tax Burden and Local Sector Fiscal Activity

One important policy implication of this research relates to the fiscal impact of the local sector. The extreme dependence of this sector on property taxation as a source of revenue produces a strong regressive force. The impact of this tax is extreme from two points of view: first, the level of burden is by far the highest of any state-local tax; second, its incidence is highly regressive. The combined effect places the local sector in an increasingly less viable position. Local reliance on property taxation in a particular system depends upon the nature of assignment for taxation. A state with high local responsibility for raising taxes will exhibit a level of property tax burden considerably above those that raise revenue through state-wide taxation. High local assignment in effect forces local units to utilize the property tax more intensively.

Empirical examination of the local sector serves to emphasize its regressive tax policy. In many instances, the state component of a system's burden is proportional or progressive while the local component is regressive. Thus the

impact of local fiscal activity on
interaction of level and incidence, as i
good approximation to the total influ
positions are influenced to the extent
reinforce each other.

Local sector tax burden has substantial i
to expand its current quantity and quality of
the state assumes greater responsibility for raisin
and their bases are considerably more responsive
the local level, however, the base is more narrow
forms of taxation are generally not available. In fa
the capacity of this sector to keep pace with dema
becomes increasingly less certain. Despite rather rema ,
increasing fiscal pressure raises serious doubt about the c on past
trends. Perusal of the features of state-local taxation reve ost constant
alteration of the tax structure in an attempt to "squeeze ut" an additional
dollar. Rates are increased, tax bases defined more inclusively, assessments redone, exemptions and deductions revised and where politically feasible, new taxes are introduced. (This has been discussed in Chapter 7.)

Fiscal problems of local governments are increasing in intensity. One need only examine local newspapers, Senate hearings or academic journals to get a feel for their fiscal plight. At the state level, the situation is perhaps somewhat less intense but no less politically sensitive. Attempts to impose new taxes are generally met with unpopular citizen reaction. However, the broad base of state-wide taxation and the increasing use of a progressive income tax, grant the state a certain fiscal responsiveness that is not available to local government.

In essence, it seems that the state-local sector is becoming a second-rate partner in the American federal system. The burden of its structure has been increasing steadily, to a large extent in response to the process of urbanization. At the same time, the distributional impact of most state-local taxes raise questions of purpose in light of recent proposals for income maintenance and the alleviation of poverty. To a considerable extent states, and more especially local governments, have borne the heaviest part of the costs associated with urbanization. These costs have been placed on a tax system that is inferior when viewed relative to the federal revenue structure.

Interlocal fiscal tensions are now emerging in the form of disparities among local governments. Once again, much of the tension relates directly to the tax instruments available, the often extreme differentials in taxable capacity, and the level and incidence of the existing burden. More recently these disparities have raised constitutional questions concerning continued use of the property tax to finance local education. In cases such as *Serrano* v. *Priest* in California, the courts have declared that a fragmented local property tax base gives rise to disparities that deny students equal protection under the fourteenth Amend-

ears to settle the legal issues, the fiscal consequences ly obvious. The pressure for a basic revision of fiscal ntensifying from all sides.

sed in Chapter 7, in certain few instances policy has been designed with situations entailing excessive burden, extreme regressivity, or other ms of "hardship." For example, some states exempt certain classes of goods from the base of general sales taxation (e.g., food, clothing, medicine). There has been an increasing tendency for states to lessen regressivity and burden by adopting such provisions. A novel method to cope with inequities in property taxation was initially implemented in Wisconsin and has since been adopted by eleven other states. Called the "circuit breaker," it serves to lessen any extreme burden imposed on low income families. At the same time, however, it does not exempt an entire group of people (e.g., the aged) since it defines relief in terms of need for relief.[3] Other attempts to cope with the level and incidence of state-local tax burdens are conspicuously absent. The loss in yield resulting from such provisions accounts for the scarcity of notable examples.

Regressivity and Spatial Incidence

The spatial facets of tax incidence represent one of the least understood topics in state-local finance. The physical dimension of a taxing jurisdiction is one of the determinants of the flow of tax burdens. Boundaries for tax purposes, while legally defined, bear no necessary relationship to economically defined areas; taxes flow accordingly. The openness of states as economic units dictates the need for more exact knowledge concerning the influence of these flows on state-local taxation. Some attempt has been made here to do just this.

A major component of tax flows is the implicit subsidy provided state-local governments through the deductibility provisions of federal tax law. It has been estimated that some $3 billion in state-local taxes are effectively shifted to the federal tax structure. The extent of the subsidy depends upon the features of each state's tax structure. However, implications for the use of various taxes by state and local governments is evident. For example, local property taxes are fully deductible against federal tax liability. This provides a lessening in the burden of this tax and therefore an implicit grant to local governments. The effect of the subsidy becomes greater as the federal marginal tax rate increases and is a function of the distribution of income and property in each state. At the state level, the income tax is also fully deductible and its burden is increasingly lessened as the tax-paying unit falls into higher and higher marginal rates. The situation remains, however, that it is the tax-paying units with the highest income that benefit the most. While federal tax deductions do lessen the burden of state-local taxes, relief is not necessarily a function of "need for relief."

Given the regressiveness of state-local taxation, there is an offsetting role for the federal government, if one makes the assumption that taxation in this sector should be less regressive. One could propose for example, elimination of the property and general sales tax, and their replacement with an equal yield state income tax with progressive marginal rates. This is likely to occur, at best, only slowly over time. The federal government does have the machinery, however, to simultaneously lessen regressivity and decrease the burden of state-local taxation. By setting up a system of weighted deductibility provisions for various state-local taxes, it could accomplish several tasks. First, total burden could be lessened by decreasing federal tax liability. Second, the incidence of a tax system can be altered by weighting the deduction of state-local taxes differently at various levels of income. For example, by permitting a weight greater than 1.0 for deductions in lower income classes, the incidence of the system could be made less regressive overall. Questions of loss of federal tax yield and the selection of weights are, of course, more complicated issues. Finally, the federal government could encourage increased reliance on certain types of taxation such as the income tax. By assigning a set of weights greater than 1.0 (by level of income) to deduction of the state income tax, it would be made a much more attractive alternative. These provisions could be designed to encourage greater state assumption of fiscal responsibility to replace a piecemeal local approach.

In a recent report by the Committee for Economic Development it was suggested that:

> Both state and Federal aid systems should be restructured in order to put resources where they are most needed. Equally important, state and Federal aid should be used to stimulate government reorganization. The use of aid for this purpose has a precedent in its use in promoting school consolidation by the states. Therefore, we recommend that state and Federal aid should be used as an incentive to promote the kind of restructured government outlined in this statement.[4]

An implicit form of state and federal aid is represented by deductibility provisions incorporated in their tax laws. There seems no reason why these provisions could not be refined to encourage whatever governmental reorganization is deemed most desirable.

Summary and Conclusion

The nuances of state-local taxation are complex and many. Attempts at comprehending all aspects of this sector's fiscal activity have resulted in much empirical and analytical research. This study has contributed to this literature by estimating the incidence of state-local taxes for each state and type of tax. A contribution has been made by providing comparative empirical content to the question "who pays the taxes?"

It seems appropriate, however, to close with a caveat. The research reported on here has focused entirely upon the tax side of the budget. The purpose was to achieve better understanding of the structure of state-local taxation. Complete understanding, however, must involve data on the incidence of expenditures. Thus far research on expenditure incidence is limited to total governmental sectors. With further refinements in data on consumption and income patterns and some hard conceptual rethinking concerning the incidence of expenditures, it may well be possible to replicate this study for state-local expenditures. Such analysis would then permit inferences about the total distributional impact of state-local fiscal activity. Its implementation, however, must await these advancements.

Appendixes

Appendix A: The Allocation of Personal Income by Income Class

Data on the distribution of income for states are not available in published form. Therefore, a method must be devised to allocate personal income (as defined by the Department of Commerce) for each state by income class. The resulting distribution can then be used as a base for effective rate calculations.

The most comprehensive data on the distribution of income and consumption patterns are available from the Bureau of Labor Statistics (BLS) for the period 1960-61.[1] However, the income definition used by BLS differs from that of personal income in the national income accounts. (See Table A-1 for a detailed breakdown of the items that make up the difference between personal income as defined by the Department of Commerce and BLS money income.)

The method that was used to allocate state personal income from the Department of Commerce by income class employs the percentage distribution of income derived from BLS data. These percentages were applied to the total state personal income figures for each state to arrive at a distribution of income for each state.

The distortion that results from using BLS data to distribute personal income ultimately depends upon the distribution of items that comprise the difference. Table A-1 enumerates these components, and there seems to be no reason to assume that the net distribution of these items favors either end of the income distribution. Therefore, the assumption is made that the difference is neutral in its impact and the BLS percentages are close approximations to those for the actual distribution of personal income. While it is a somewhat biased assumption for some states, it does not appear to seriously impair the significance of the resulting data.[a]

[a]It is also assumed that there was no significant redistribution of income between the BLS 1960-61 income data and the Department of Commerce personal income data for 1962, a reasonable assumption.

Table A-1
Relation of BLS Money Income to Net National Product (Millions)

BLS money income before taxes		$348,041
Plus:	"Other labor income"	12,746
	Net rent, owner-occupied dwellings	6,992
	Services furnished by financial institutions[a]	5,296
	Food grown and consumed on farms	1,105
	Food furnished employees	2,113
	Difference between personal taxes in BLS survey and in national income accounts	13,731
	Imputed items in personal saving	15,500
	Other and unaccounted	11,290
	Capital gains	13,837
Equals:	Personal income and capital gains	430,651
	Personal income excluding capital gains*	416,814
Less:	Transfers to persons	
	Social insurance benefits	18,034
	Civilian government pensions	2,499
	Veterans benefits and pensions	5,544
	Relief and other	4,344
	Net interest paid by government	7,390
	Net interest paid by consumers and subsidies less current surplus of government enterprises	9,067
Plus:	Non-personal taxes	
	Corporate profits tax liabilities	
	Half on consumption	11,552
	Half on dividends	11,552
	Contributions for social insurance	
	Personal contributions	9,598
	Employer contributions	11,843
	Indirect business tax & non-tax liability	47,699
	Undistributed corporate profits[b]	12,687
Equals:	Net national product	474,865

[a]Excludes insurance companies.

[b]Includes inventory valuation adjustment.

*Department of Commerce definition.

Source: Tax Foundation, TAX BURDENS AND BENEFITS OF GOVERNMENT EXPENDITURES BY INCOME CLASS, 1961 and 1965 (N.Y.: Tax Foundation, 1967), p. 42. The data are for 1961.

Appendix B: The Gini Ratio of Concentration

The Gini coefficient provides an index of the degree of inequality in a distribution.[2] It is generally applicable to a frequency distribution and is constructed relative to a line of perfect equality, in a Lorenz curve sense. Figure B-1 indicates what the Gini Ratio measures.

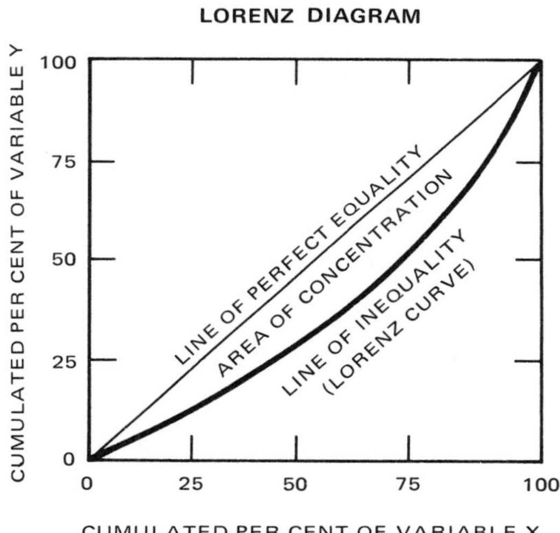

The ratio is defined as the area under a Lorenz curve ("area of concentration") relative to the total area under the main diagonal. Inequality is expressed as actual deviation from perfect equality (i.e., an equal percentage distribution) relative to total possible deviation. Calculation of the Ratio involves the use of the following approximation formula:

$$R = \frac{\frac{1}{2} \Sigma [(Y \cdot X_{+1}) - (X \cdot Y_{+1})]}{5{,}000}$$

The method approximates the area under a Lorenz curve by summation over triangles, "any one of which is determined by the origin and two successive observational points."[3]

A specific case for the distribution of taxes paid by family units provides a good illustration. The results for New York state can be compared with the data in Table 6-5; the data are computed by applying this technique to each state.

Table B-1
Gini Ratio for Inequality of Taxes by Family Units, New York State

Income Class	Cumulative % Taxes Paid (Y) (1)	Cumulative % Families (X) (2)	(X_{+1}) (3)	(Y_{+1}) (4)	$(Y)\cdot(X_{+1})$ (5)	$(X)\cdot(Y_{+1})$ (6)	(5)-(6)
$0-1,999	2.1	7.7	—	—	0	0	0
2,000-2,999	4.5	13.8	7.7	2.1	34.7	29.0	5.67
3,000-3,999	8.8	22.1	13.8	4.5	121.4	99.5	21.99
4,000-4,999	15.6	32.8	22.1	8.8	344.8	288.7	56.12
5,000-5,999	25.2	45.7	32.8	15.6	826.6	712.9	113.64
6,000-7,499	39.4	61.9	45.7	25.2	1800.6	1559.9	240.70
7,500-9,999	58.9	79.9	61.9	39.4	3645.9	3148.1	497.85
10,000-14,999	78.5	93.1	79.9	58.9	6272.1	5483.6	788.56
Over 15,000	99.9	99.8	93.1	78.5	9300.6	7834.3	1488.39
	—	—	99.9	99.9	0	0	0
							3135.

$$R = \frac{\frac{1}{2}\,(3135.)}{5000.}$$

$$R = 0.31$$

Gini's R is a percentage figure bounded above by 1.0 and below by 0.0. As such, it enables comparisons to be made across states vis-à-vis the degree of deviation from perfect equality, that is, a line of equal percentage distribution.[a]

[a]There is, of course, a weakness in attributing to such a line anything resembling political, social, or economic equality. Such a line is purely statistical in nature and must be interpreted accordingly.

Appendix C: Statistical Results from the Regression Model of State-Local Tax Incidence

The following four tables present the complete empirical results of the regression analyses based on equation (1). Statistics are reported by state for each of the alternative sets of data discussed in Chapter 6: (1) total tax burden-exported, (2) total tax burden net of the property tax-exported, (3) total tax burden--unexported and (4) total tax burden net of the property tax-unexported. Tables C-1 through C-4 are the source of the information summarized in Tables 6-1 through 6-4 in Chapter 6. They permit a somewhat more detailed examination of a specific state or comparison across sets of states than was possible in earlier discussion.

Table C-1
Regression Analysis of State-Local Tax Structure, Total Taxes–Unexported

State	Regression Coefficient*	Standard Error*	F-Value**	Level of Significance
Alabama	–.074	.021	12.61	.01
Alaska	–.102	.035	8.45	.05
Arizona	–.233	.071	10.76	.05
Arkansas	–.054	.028	3.69	–
California	–.186	.075	6.18	.05
Colorado	–.125	.064	3.82	–
Connecticut	–.140	.051	7.39	.05
Delaware	+.078	.010	62.11	.01
Florida	–.167	.027	36.88	.01
Georgia	–.066	.024	7.25	.05
Hawaii	–.163	.058	7.66	.05
Idaho	–.114	.059	3.74	–
Illinois	–.242	.059	16.67	.01
Indiana	–.237	.053	19.64	.01
Iowa	–.182	.056	10.29	.05
Kansas	–.209	.063	10.85	.05
Kentucky	+.027	.025	1.15	–
Louisiana	–.113	.043	9.55	.05
Maine	–.161	.051	9.79	.05
Maryland	–.095	.095	25.71	.01
Massachusetts	–.088	.042	4.27	–
Michigan	–.270	.060	20.11	.01
Minnesota	–.092	.064	2.06	–

Table C-1 (cont.)

State	Regression Coefficient*	Standard Error*	F-Value**	Level of Significance
Mississippi	–.076	.041	3.36	–
Missouri	–.092	.039	5.35	–
Montana	–.150	.067	4.90	–
Nebraska	–.204	.040	25.19	.01
Nevada	–.205	.048	17.90	.01
New Hampshire	–.139	.056	6.13	.05
New Jersey	–.190	.054	12.35	.01
New Mexico	–.243	.064	14.08	.01
New York	–.053	.050	1.12	–
North Carolina	+.023	.019	1.49	–
North Dakota	–.129	.046	7.63	.05
Ohio	–.254	.060	17.90	.01
Oklahoma	–.080	.031	6.41	.05
Oregon	–.062	.051	1.47	–
Pennsylvania	–.087	.047	3.41	–
Rhode Island	–.140	.048	8.32	.05
South Carolina	–.016	.023	0.49	–
South Dakota	–.210	.048	18.73	.01
Tennessee	–.093	.031	9.08	.05
Texas	–.173	.031	30.15	.01
Utah	–.199	.069	8.12	.05
Vermont	–.055	.040	1.89	–
Virginia	–.048	.015	9.67	.05
Washington	–.291	.081	12.68	.01
West Virginia	–.135	.028	23.05	.01
Wisconsin	–.045	.068	0.45	–
Wyoming	–.303	.078	15.15	.01

*Multiplied by 100,000 for convenience of presentation.

**F distributed as F (1,7): .01 level = 12.25; .05 level = 5.59.

–Regression coefficient not statistically different from zero at .05 level of significance.

Table C-2
Regression Analysis of State-Local Tax Structure, Total Taxes–Exported

State	Regression Coefficient*	Standard Error*	F-Value**	Level of Significance
Alabama	–.094	.020	20.68	.01
Alaska	–.118	.036	10.57	.05
Arizona	–.209	.061	11.69	.05

Table C-2 (cor

State	Regression Coefficient*	Standard Error*	F-Value**	Level of Significance
Arkansas	–.077	.026	8.84	.05
California	–.192	.068	7.97	.05
Colorado	–.140	.060	5.46	–
Connecticut	–.159	.046	11.95	.05
Delaware	+.009	.008	1.47	–
Florida	–.168	.026	40.89	.01
Georgia	–.086	.023	13.60	.01
Hawaii	–.162	.054	8.98	.05
Idaho	–.135	.057	5.57	–
Illinois	–.228	.054	17.65	.01
Indiana	–.231	.051	19.95	.01
Iowa	–.177	.053	10.91	.05
Kansas	–.209	.057	13.05	.01
Kentucky	–.008	.024	0.11	–
Louisiana	–.132	.036	13.53	.01
Maine	–.170	.051	12.67	.01
Maryland	–.104	.018	30.91	.01
Massachusetts	–.120	.041	8.64	.05
Michigan	–.265	.055	22.75	.01
Minnesota	–.117	.058	4.11	–
Mississippi	–.097	.036	7.09	.05
Missouri	–.111	.039	8.14	.05
Montana	–.147	.061	5.73	.05
Nebraska	–.195	.040	23.86	.01
Nevada	–.184	.044	17.27	.01
New Hampshire	–.157	.055	8.00	.05
New Jersey	–.197	.051	14.88	.01
New Mexico	–.230	.060	14.59	.01
New York	–.098	.046	4.56	–
North Carolina	–.015	.017	0.81	–
North Dakota	–.125	.042	8.65	.05
Ohio	–.247	.056	19.15	.01
Oklahoma	–.092	.029	10.04	.05
Oregon	–.094	.051	3.33	–
Pennsylvania	–.120	.043	7.69	.05
Rhode Island	–.173	.043	16.15	.01
South Carolina	–.047	.021	4.76	–
South Dakota	–.200	.046	18.79	.01
Tennessee	–.107	.028	13.83	.01

Table C-2 (cont.)

State	Regression Coefficient*	Standard Error*	F-Value**	Level of Significance
Texas	−.156	.026	35.00	.01
Utah	−.197	.065	9.27	.05
Vermont	−.091	.040	5.14	–
Virginia	−.073	.016	18.88	.01
Washington	−.280	.078	12.93	.01
West Virginia	−.137	.028	23.89	.01
Wisconsin	−.079	.063	1.58	–
Wyoming	−.277	.070	15.66	.01

*Multiplied by 100,000 for convenience of presentation.

**F distributed as F (1,7): .01 level = 12.25; .05 level = 5.59.

–Regression coefficient not statistically different from zero at .05 level of significance.

Table C-3
Regression Analysis of State-Local Tax Structure, Total Taxes Net of Property Tax–Unexported

State	Regression Coefficient*	Standard Error*	F-Value**	Level of Significance
Alabama	−.040	.014	7.70	.05
Alaska	−.046	.020	5.01	–
Arizona	−.087	.031	7.45	.05
Arkansas	−.009	.019	0.21	–
California	−.023	.031	0.54	–
Colorado	+.019	.025	0.55	–
Connecticut	−.021	.020	1.06	–
Delaware	+.106	.006	303.06	.01
Florida	−.093	.013	46.48	.01
Georgia	−.013	.014	0.88	–
Hawaii	−.108	.044	5.95	.05
Idaho	+.046	.018	6.59	.05
Illinois	−.101	.026	15.22	.01
Indiana	−.089	.018	22.70	.01
Iowa	−.014	.017	0.70	–
Kansas	−.033	.022	2.24	–
Kentucky	+.078	.015	24.50	.01
Louisiana	−.081	.033	6.03	.05
Maine	−.029	.019	2.43	–

Table C-3 (cont.)

State	Regression Coefficient*	Standard Error*	F-Value**	Level of Significance
Maryland	–.026	.008	9.95	.05
Massachusetts	+.065	.007	78.14	.01
Michigan	–.119	.024	23.44	.01
Minnesota	+.088	.021	17.27	.01
Mississippi	–.018	.031	0.35	–
Missouri	–.001	.018	0.00	–
Montana	+.024	.021	1.21	–
Nebraska	–.056	.006	75.98	.01
Nevada	–.134	.029	20.68	.01
New Hampshire	+.010	.019	0.28	–
New Jersey	–.041	.015	7.26	.05
New Mexico	–.159	.042	13.88	.01
New York	+.064	.019	10.67	.05
North Carolina	+.067	.011	33.69	.01
North Dakota	–.014	.019	0.49	–
Ohio	–.122	.029	17.93	.01
Oklahoma	–.020	.020	0.98	–
Oregon	+.088	.013	45.98	.01
Pennsylvania	–.007	.027	0.06	–
Rhode Island	–.032	.021	2.36	–
South Carolina	+.022	.016	1.86	–
South Dakota	–.073	.016	19.95	.01
Tennessee	–.039	.021	3.51	–
Texas	–.093	.016	32.66	.01
Utah	–.052	.031	2.86	–
Vermont	+.071	.008	78.93	.01
Virginia	+.003	.006	0.23	–
Washington	–.188	.054	12.11	.05
West Virginia	–.082	.018	20.28	.01
Wisconsin	+.133	.027	23.81	.01
Wyoming	–.128	.031	17.14	.01

*Multiplied by 100,000 for convenience of presentation.
**F distributed as F (1,7): .01 level = 12.25; .05 level = 5.59.
–Regression coefficient not statistically different from zero at .05 level of significance.

Table C-4
Regression Analysis of State-Local Tax Structure, Total Taxes Net of Property Tax-Exported

State	Regression Coefficient*	Standard Error*	F-Value**	Level of Significance
Alabama	−.068	.015	18.80	.01
Alaska	−.068	.023	8.70	.05
Arizona	−.100	.032	9.87	.05
Arkansas	−.040	.019	4.57	–
California	−.053	.031	2.99	–
Colorado	−.018	.027	0.44	–
Connecticut	−.057	.019	9.21	.05
Delaware	+.032	.004	46.08	.01
Florida	−.105	.014	53.85	.01
Georgia	−.042	.015	7.88	.05
Hawaii	−.115	.041	7.66	.05
Idaho	−.008	.024	0.13	–
Illinois	−.115	.027	17.50	.01
Indiana	−.113	.023	22.45	.01
Iowa	−.038	.021	3.42	–
Kansas	−.066	.024	7.50	.05
Kentucky	+.032	.016	4.07	–
Louisiana	−.090	.027	10.48	.05
Maine	−.054	.021	6.58	.05
Maryland	−.051	.009	28.95	.01
Massachusetts	+.014	.006	4.80	–
Michigan	−.143	.026	28.82	.01
Minnesota	+.033	.022	2.19	–
Mississippi	−.049	.027	3.19	–
Missouri	−.035	.021	2.76	–
Montana	−.014	.026	0.28	–
Nebraska	−.072	.011	42.18	.01
Nevada	−.129	.029	19.10	.01
New Hampshire	−.026	.021	1.42	–
New Jersey	−.072	.017	16.76	.01
New Mexico	−.163	.042	14.70	.01
New York	+.005	.018	0.10	–
North Carolina	+.020	.010	3.58	–
North Dakota	−.033	.021	3.55	–
Ohio	−.138	.030	20.28	.01
Oklahoma	−.042	.019	4.64	–
Oregon	+.032	.018	3.11	–

Table C-4 (cont.)

State	Regression Coefficient*	Standard Error*	F-Value**	Level of Significance
Pennsylvania	−.051	.025	4.06	–
Rhode Island	−.080	.018	18.99	.01
South Carolina	−.018	.016	1.25	–
South Dakota	−.083	.018	20.00	.01
Tennessee	−.062	.020	9.35	.05
Texas	−.096	.015	41.60	.01
Utah	−.081	.033	5.74	.05
Vermont	+.020	.010	3.46	–
Virginia	−.030	.008	11.55	.05
Washington	−.194	.054	12.56	.01
West Virginia	−.096	.020	22.48	.01
Wisconsin	+.070	.028	6.08	.05
Wyoming	−.146	.034	17.62	.01

*Multiplied by 100,000 for convenience of presentation.

**F distributed as F (1,7): .01 level = 12.25; .05 level = 5.59.

–Regression coefficient not statistically different from zero at .05 level of significance.

Appendix D: State-by-State Data on Effective Rates of Taxation by Type of Tax

The data in the following Tables D-1 through D-22 represent the basic effective tax rates estimated from the model developed in Chapters 3 and 4 and discussed in Chapters 5 and 6. Effective rates of taxation—defined as taxes paid relative to income—are given for each of nine income classes, ranging from $0-$1,999 to over $15,000, for each of the fifty states. Separate tables are provided for each state-local tax. In addition, for several of the taxes, tables are given that provide effective rate estimates based upon alternative shifting-incidence assumptions. For example, in the case of the property tax the following allocators are used to estimate effective tax rates and are shown in the table indicated:

Allocator	*Table*
Housing Expenditures	D-11
1/2 housing, 1/2 consumption	D-12
Consumption	D-13
1/2 property taxes, 1/2 consumption	D-14

The data in Tables D-1 through D-22 permit comparisons across individual states to be made and some analyses to be done that were not done explicitly in the previous text. In short, it permits the reader to tailor the analysis to his own needs by using this detailed information.

Table D-1
Effective Rates of Taxation: Corporation Income Tax (Allocator-Consumption)

	$ 0- 1,999	2,000- 2,999	3,000- 3,999	4,000- 4,999	5,000- 5,999	6,000- 7,499	7,500- 9,999	10,000- 14,999	OVER 15,000
ALABAMA	.00298	.00267	.00263	.00232	.00225	.00209	.00196	.00180	.00127
ALASKA	.00376	.00279	.00267	.00237	.00217	.00217	.00196	.00174	.00125
ARIZONA	.00211	.00156	.00150	.00134	.00123	.00123	.00111	.00099	.00070
ARKANSAS	.00324	.00290	.00285	.00252	.00244	.00227	.00213	.00196	.00138
CALIFORNIA	.00680	.00504	.00484	.00432	.00395	.00395	.00357	.00318	.00227
COLORADO	.00481	.00356	.00343	.00306	.00280	.00279	.00252	.00225	.00161
CONNECTICUT	.00442	.00391	.00356	.00328	.00302	.00290	.00269	.00250	.00191
DELAWARE	.00437	.00391	.00385	.00340	.00329	.00305	.00287	.00264	.00186
FLORIDA	.00000	.00000	.00000	.00000	.00000	.00000	.00000	.00000	.00000
GEORGIA	.00303	.00271	.00267	.00236	.00228	.00212	.00199	.00183	.00129
HAWAII	.00495	.00367	.00353	.00315	.00288	.00288	.00260	.00231	.00165
IDAHO	.00417	.00309	.00297	.00265	.00242	.00242	.00219	.00195	.00139
ILLINOIS	.00000	.00000	.00000	.00000	.00000	.00000	.00000	.00000	.00000
INDIANA	.00000	.00000	.00000	.00000	.00000	.00000	.00000	.00000	.00000
IOWA	.00071	.00058	.00052	.00049	.00045	.00042	.00040	.00036	.00026
KANSAS	.00197	.00163	.00144	.00137	.00126	.00118	.00111	.00102	.00073
KENTUCKY	.00364	.00326	.00321	.00284	.00275	.00255	.00240	.00220	.00155
LOUISIANA	.00568	.00508	.00501	.00443	.00428	.00398	.00374	.00344	.00242
MAINE	.00000	.00000	.00000	.00000	.00000	.00000	.00000	.00000	.00000
MARYLAND	.00222	.00199	.00196	.00173	.00168	.00156	.00146	.00134	.00094

MASSACHUSETTS	.00715	.00632	.00576	.00530	.00489	.00470	.00436	.00404	.00309
MICHIGAN	.00000	.00000	.00000	.00000	.00000	.00000	.00000	.00000	.00000
MINNESOTA	.00430	.00357	.00316	.00299	.00275	.00257	.00243	.00223	.00159
MISSISSIPPI	.00458	.00409	.00403	.00357	.00345	.00320	.00301	.00277	.00195
MISSOURI	.00173	.00143	.00127	.00120	.00110	.00103	.00098	.00089	.00064
MONTANA	.00302	.00224	.00215	.00192	.00175	.00175	.00158	.00141	.00101
NEBRASKA	.00000	.00000	.00000	.00000	.00000	.00000	.00000	.00000	.00000
NEVADA	.00000	.00000	.00000	.00000	.00000	.00000	.00000	.00000	.00000
NEW HAMPSHIRE	.00000	.00000	.00000	.00000	.00000	.00000	.00000	.00000	.00000
NEW JERSEY	.00293	.00259	.00236	.00217	.00200	.00192	.00179	.00165	.00127
NEW MEXICO	.00000	.00000	.00000	.00000	.00000	.00000	.00000	.00000	.00000
NEW YORK	.00512	.00452	.00412	.00379	.00350	.00336	.00312	.00289	.00221
NORTH CAROLINA	.00609	.00545	.00537	.00475	.00459	.00426	.00401	.00368	.00259
NORTH DAKOTA	.00095	.00079	.00070	.00066	.00060	.00057	.00053	.00049	.00035
OHIO	.00000	.00000	.00000	.00000	.00000	.00000	.00000	.00000	.00000
OKLAHOMA	.00341	.00305	.00301	.00266	.00258	.00239	.00225	.00206	.00145
OREGON	.00522	.00387	.00372	.00332	.00304	.00303	.00274	.00244	.00175
PENNSYLVANIA	.00784	.00694	.00632	.00582	.00537	.00515	.00478	.00443	.00339
RHODE ISLAND	.00370	.00327	.00298	.00274	.00253	.00243	.00226	.00209	.00160
SOUTH CAROLINA	.00407	.00364	.00358	.00317	.00307	.00285	.00268	.00246	.00172
SOUTH DAKOTA	.00034	.00028	.00025	.00023	.00022	.00020	.00019	.00017	.00012
TENNESSEE	.00411	.00368	.00362	.00320	.00310	.00288	.00271	.00249	.00175
TEXAS	.00000	.00000	.00000	.00000	.00000	.00000	.00000	.00000	.00000
UTAH	.00400	.00296	.00285	.00254	.00232	.00232	.00210	.00187	.00133
VERMONT	.00286	.00252	.00230	.00212	.00195	.00187	.00174	.00161	.00123
VIRGINIA	.00320	.00287	.00282	.00250	.00242	.00224	.00213	.00194	.00136
WASHINGTON	.00000	.00000	.00000	.00000	.00000	.00000	.00000	.00000	.00000
WEST VIRGINIA	.00000	.00000	.00000	.00000	.00000	.00000	.00000	.00000	.00000
WISCONSIN	.00588	.00487	.00431	.00409	.00376	.00351	.00332	.00304	.00217
WYOMING	.00000	.00000	.00000	.00000	.00000	.00000	.00000	.00000	.00000

Table D-2
Effective Rates of Taxation: Corporation Income Tax (Allocator-1/2 Consumption, 1/2 Dividends)

	$ 0- 1,999	2,000- 2,999	3,000- 3,999	4,000- 4,999	5,000- 5,999	6,000- 7,499	7,500- 9,999	10,000- 14,999	OVER 15,000
ALABAMA	.00162	.00143	.00156	.00123	.00160	.00125	.00130	.00228	.00616
ALASKA	.00241	.00174	.00242	.00153	.00121	.00145	.00146	.00155	.00261
ARIZONA	.00146	.00105	.00159	.00093	.00071	.00089	.00093	.00101	.00188
ARKANSAS	.00178	.00158	.00174	.00135	.00182	.00140	.00146	.00272	.00767
CALIFORNIA	.00455	.00327	.00477	.00290	.00225	.00277	.00284	.00305	.00544
COLORADO	.00337	.00242	.00368	.00215	.00163	.00206	.00214	.00235	.00442
CONNECTICUT	.00253	.00239	.00215	.00199	.00184	.00155	.00167	.00213	.00541
DELAWARE	.00228	.00203	.00211	.00175	.00201	.00169	.00168	.00239	.00520
FLORIDA	.00000	.00000	.00000	.00000	.00000	.00000	.00000	.00000	.00000
GEORGIA	.00163	.00144	.00155	.00124	.00156	.00125	.00128	.00214	.00554
HAWAII	.00328	.00236	.00341	.00209	.00163	.00199	.00204	.00218	.00385
IDAHO	.00305	.00218	.00345	.00194	.00144	.00187	.00197	.00220	.00430
ILLINOIS	.00000	.00000	.00000	.00000	.00000	.00000	.00000	.00000	.00000
INDIANA	.00000	.00000	.00000	.00000	.00000	.00000	.00000	.00000	.00000
IOWA	.00045	.00038	.00030	.00029	.00030	.00031	.00032	.00034	.00105
KANSAS	.00124	.00106	.00085	.00080	.00082	.00084	.00087	.00093	.00275
KENTUCKY	.00196	.00174	.00189	.00149	.00191	.00151	.00156	.00267	.00708
LOUISIANA	.00304	.00270	.00289	.00232	.00288	.00232	.00236	.00387	.00983
MAINE	.00000	.00000	.00000	.00000	.00000	.00000	.00000	.00000	.00000
MARYLAND	.00116	.00104	.00108	.00089	.00104	.00087	.00087	.00127	.00286

MASSACHUSETTS	.00420	.00403	.00361	.00335	.00310	.00254	.00281	.00377	.01032
MICHIGAN	.00000	.00000	.00000	.00000	.00000	.00000	.00000	.00000	.00000
MINNESOTA	.00270	.00231	.00185	.00175	.00179	.00184	.00190	.00201	.00594
MISSISSIPPI	.00252	.00223	.00247	.00191	.00258	.00199	.00208	.00390	.01106
MISSOURI	.00108	.00093	.00074	.00070	.00072	.00074	.00076	.00081	.00239
MONTANA	.00218	.00156	.00244	.00139	.00104	.00134	.00140	.00155	.00300
NEBRASKA	.00000	.00000	.00000	.00000	.00000	.00000	.00000	.00000	.00000
NEVADA	.00000	.00000	.00000	.00000	.00000	.00000	.00000	.00000	.00000
NEW HAMPSHIRE	.00000	.00000	.00000	.00000	.00000	.00000	.00000	.00000	.00000
NEW JERSEY	.00168	.00160	.00143	.00133	.00123	.00103	.00111	.00143	.00366
NEW MEXICO	.00000	.00000	.00000	.00000	.00000	.00000	.00000	.00000	.00000
NEW YORK	.00294	.00279	.00250	.00232	.00214	.00179	.00194	.00250	.00641
NORTH CAROLINA	.00331	.00294	.00321	.00251	.00329	.00258	.00267	.00474	.01289
NORTH DAKOTA	.00062	.00054	.00042	.00040	.00042	.00044	.00046	.00049	.00161
OHIO	.00000	.00000	.00000	.00000	.00000	.00000	.00000	.00000	.00000
OKLAHOMA	.00183	.00162	.00175	.00139	.00174	.00140	.00143	.00237	.00610
OREGON	.00369	.00265	.00407	.00236	.00178	.00226	.00236	.00260	.00494
PENNSYLVANIA	.00469	.00454	.00406	.00377	.00349	.00281	.00317	.00438	.01254
RHODE ISLAND	.00225	.00220	.00196	.00182	.00169	.00134	.00153	.00217	.00647
SOUTH CAROLINA	.00222	.00197	.00216	.00168	.00223	.00173	.00180	.00326	.00898
SOUTH DAKOTA	.00022	.00019	.00015	.00014	.00015	.00016	.00016	.00018	.00059
TENNESSEE	.00222	.00197	.00214	.00169	.00217	.00172	.00177	.00307	.00819
TEXAS	.00000	.00000	.00000	.00000	.00000	.00000	.00000	.00000	.00000
UTAH	.00287	.00205	.00320	.00183	.00137	.00176	.00184	.00204	.00393
VERMONT	.00178	.00175	.00156	.00145	.00134	.00104	.00122	.00178	.00554
VIRGINIA	.00170	.00151	.00161	.00130	.00158	.00129	.00131	.00205	.00501
WASHINGTON	.00000	.00000	.00000	.00000	.00000	.00000	.00000	.00000	.00000
WEST VIRGINIA	.00000	.00000	.00000	.00000	.00000	.00000	.00000	.00000	.00000
WISCONSIN	.00366	.00313	.00251	.00238	.00243	.00249	.00257	.00271	.00790
WYOMING	.00000	.00000	.00000	.00000	.00000	.00000	.00000	.00000	.00000

Table D-3
Effective Rates of Taxation: Total Sales and Gross Receipts Taxes (Allocator-Consumption)

	\$ 0- 1,999	2,000- 2,999	3,000- 3,999	4,000- 4,999	5,000- 5,999	6,000- 7,499	7,500- 9,999	10,000- 14,999	OVER 15,000
ALABAMA	.05116	.04815	.04999	.04523	.04259	.04084	.03652	.03366	.02176
ALASKA	.03431	.02553	.02797	.02580	.02362	.02173	.02080	.01826	.01129
ARIZONA	.05805	.04252	.04346	.03917	.03560	.03358	.03153	.02777	.01862
ARKANSAS	.04664	.04398	.04536	.04104	.03892	.03700	.03321	.03030	.01942
CALIFORNIA	.04641	.03383	.03634	.03298	.02995	.02861	.02711	.02408	.01668
COLORADO	.03926	.02888	.03038	.02751	.02508	.02325	.02232	.01992	.01290
CONNECTICUT	.03303	.03175	.03029	.02887	.02666	.02499	.02279	.02064	.01471
DELAWARE	.01797	.01708	.01770	.01609	.01511	.01442	.01260	.01132	.00671
FLORIDA	.04480	.04198	.04392	.03971	.03736	.03630	.03269	.03073	.02077
GEORGIA	.04654	.04367	.04542	.04102	.03847	.03708	.03341	.03123	.02080
HAWAII	.09531	.06946	.06838	.06139	.05609	.05327	.04919	.04336	.02942
IDAHO	.02386	.01755	.02068	.01889	.01697	.01474	.01477	.01250	.00725
ILLINOIS	.04606	.03841	.03450	.03239	.02953	.02737	.02561	.02252	.01508
INDIANA	.04404	.03813	.03560	.03423	.03117	.02862	.02743	.02412	.01591
IOWA	.03356	.02976	.02795	.02691	.02439	.02217	.02124	.01839	.01183
KANSAS	.03821	.03313	.03089	.02956	.02689	.02466	.02355	.02054	.01340
KENTUCKY	.04003	.03802	.03993	.03625	.03415	.03294	.02969	.02776	.01849
LOUISIANA	.05240	.04799	.04886	.04370	.04077	.03910	.03506	.03247	.02133
MAINE	.03521	.03576	.03613	.03505	.03289	.03115	.02840	.02565	.01767
MARYLAND	.03553	.03251	.03275	.02926	.02775	.02631	.02374	.02160	.01407

MASSACHUSETTS	.01276	.01407	.01425	.01408	.01318	.01241	.01110	.00961	.00612
MICHIGAN	.04597	.04147	.03913	.03664	.03350	.03109	.02926	.02700	.01807
MINNESOTA	.02516	.02177	.02077	.01942	.01754	.01604	.01513	.01244	.00731
MISSISSIPPI	.05594	.05257	.05378	.04858	.04635	.04371	.03944	.03570	.02286
MISSOURI	.03462	.02986	.02728	.02581	.02341	.02143	.02018	.01743	.01133
MONTANA	.02829	.02081	.02425	.02236	.02018	.01774	.01746	.01471	.00855
NEBRASKA	.01714	.01662	.01692	.01653	.01481	.01310	.01285	.01051	.00591
NEVADA	.05671	.04185	.04342	.03920	.03537	.03357	.03134	.02701	.01820
NEW HAMPSHIRE	.01954	.02075	.02149	.02116	.01995	.01882	.01685	.01463	.00914
NEW JERSEY	.02434	.02368	.02250	.02153	.01976	.01817	.01597	.01351	.00843
NEW MEXICO	.06460	.04732	.05093	.04610	.04142	.03826	.03652	.03133	.02045
NEW YORK	.03295	.03073	.02859	.02685	.02461	.02305	.02076	.01833	.01285
NORTH CAROLINA	.03769	.03556	.03723	.03374	.03175	.03070	.02750	.02558	.01698
NORTH DAKOTA	.03167	.02762	.02646	.02539	.02310	.02124	.02043	.01762	.01120
OHIO	.03474	.03100	.02906	.02807	.02539	.02340	.02239	.01959	.01276
OKLAHOMA	.04079	.03830	.03932	.03553	.03359	.03191	.02839	.02571	.01606
OREGON	.01506	.01107	.01333	.01205	.01085	.00912	.00956	.00835	.00467
PENNSYLVANIA	.03138	.03149	.03132	.03010	.02826	.02655	.02441	.02219	.01590
RHODE ISLAND	.03750	.03678	.03589	.03436	.03194	.03020	.02752	.02485	.01750
SOUTH CAROLINA	.05041	.04712	.04920	.04441	.04143	.04018	.03604	.03389	.02256
SOUTH DAKOTA	.03735	.03277	.03119	.03004	.02732	.02500	.02411	.02090	.01341
TENNESSEE	.04166	.03913	.04041	.03652	.03447	.03291	.02948	.02703	.01742
TEXAS	.03343	.03104	.03151	.02834	.02676	.02538	.02253	.02027	.01252
UTAH	.05090	.03730	.03974	.03582	.03227	.02995	.02871	.02507	.01652
VERMONT	.02628	.02845	.02826	.02814	.02646	.02489	.02248	.01984	.01276
VIRGINIA	.02622	.02412	.02498	.02252	.02086	.02027	.01762	.01587	.00962
WASHINGTON	.09789	.07142	.07098	.06388	.05825	.05538	.05113	.04482	.03040
WEST VIRGINIA	.05911	.05419	.05428	.04848	.04638	.04335	.03964	.03584	.02353
WISCONSIN	.02233	.01992	.01929	.01832	.01652	.01499	.01432	.01181	.00696
WYOMING	.04376	.03210	.03486	.03144	.02823	.02593	.02498	.02153	.01395

Table D-4
Effective Rates of Taxation: General Sales and Gross Receipts Taxes (Allocator-Consumption Net of Excluded Items)

	$ 0- 1,999	2,000- 2,999	3,000- 3,999	4,000- 4,999	5,000- 5,999	6,000- 7,499	7,500- 9,999	10,000- 14,999	OVER 15,000
ALABAMA	.02451	.02183	.02137	.01878	.01807	.01676	.01590	.01466	.01053
ALASKA	.00875	.00642	.00615	.00549	.00499	.00496	.00448	.00400	.00291
ARIZONA	.03697	.02708	.02602	.02330	.02117	.02103	.01904	.01700	.01237
ARKANSAS	.02387	.02127	.02081	.01829	.01759	.01632	.01548	.01428	.01025
CALIFORNIA	.02751	.01991	.02036	.01841	.01678	.01704	.01559	.01418	.01083
COLORADO	.02136	.01563	.01503	.01346	.01223	.01215	.01100	.00982	.00715
CONNECTICUT	.01351	.01242	.01191	.01108	.01024	.00986	.00940	.00918	.00755
DELAWARE	.00000	.00000	.00000	.00000	.00000	.00000	.00000	.00000	.00000
FLORIDA	.01536	.01445	.01487	.01337	.01303	.01242	.01196	.01143	.00860
GEORGIA	.02532	.02256	.02207	.01940	.01866	.01731	.01642	.01515	.01087
HAWAII	.06389	.04682	.04498	.04031	.03661	.03637	.03291	.02938	.02139
IDAHO	.00000	.00000	.00000	.00000	.00000	.00000	.00000	.00000	.00000
ILLINOIS	.02499	.02049	.01790	.01701	.01564	.01465	.01377	.01269	.00914
INDIANA	.02899	.02376	.02077	.01974	.01814	.01700	.01597	.01472	.01060
IOWA	.01864	.01528	.01335	.01269	.01167	.01093	.01027	.00947	.00681
KANSAS	.02229	.01829	.01598	.01519	.01396	.01308	.01229	.01133	.00816
KENTUCKY	.02081	.01855	.01815	.01595	.01534	.01423	.01350	.01245	.00894
LOUISIANA	.02192	.01953	.01911	.01680	.01615	.01499	.01421	.01311	.00941
MAINE	.01615	.01501	.01447	.01349	.01253	.01214	.01152	.01119	.00911
MARYLAND	.01100	.01035	.01065	.00957	.00933	.00890	.00857	.00818	.00616

MASSACHUSETTS	.00000	.00000	.00000	.00000	.00000	.00000	.00000	.00000	.00000
MICHIGAN	.03006	.02641	.02431	.02237	.02073	.01970	.01829	.01783	.01298
MINNESOTA	.00000	.00000	.00000	.00000	.00000	.00000	.00000	.00000	.00000
MISSISSIPPI	.03212	.02861	.02800	.02462	.02367	.02197	.02083	.01922	.01380
MISSOURI	.01709	.01402	.01225	.01165	.01071	.01003	.00943	.00869	.00625
MONTANA	.00000	.00000	.00000	.00000	.00000	.00000	.00000	.00000	.00000
NEBRASKA	.00000	.00000	.00000	.00000	.00000	.00000	.00000	.00000	.00000
NEVADA	.01858	.01365	.01307	.01170	.01062	.01055	.00956	.00853	.00621
NEW HAMPSHIRE	.00000	.00000	.00000	.00000	.00000	.00000	.00000	.00000	.00000
NEW JERSEY	.00000	.00000	.00000	.00000	.00000	.00000	.00000	.00000	.00000
NEW MEXICO	.03442	.02522	.02421	.02170	.01971	.01958	.01773	.01582	.01152
NEW YORK	.01404	.01228	.01113	.01022	.00937	.00895	.00830	.00770	.00596
NORTH CAROLINA	.01776	.01603	.01574	.01388	.01332	.01240	.01178	.01086	.00783
NORTH DAKOTA	.01420	.01166	.01023	.00974	.00896	.00840	.00789	.00729	.00525
OHIO	.01327	.01154	.01021	.01013	.00926	.00889	.00854	.00822	.00615
OKLAHOMA	.01497	.01334	.01305	.01147	.01104	.01024	.00971	.00896	.00643
OREGON	.00002	.00001	.00001	.00001	.00001	.00001	.00001	.00000	.00000
PENNSYLVANIA	.01743	.01590	.01508	.01385	.01293	.01218	.01161	.01120	.00929
RHODE ISLAND	.01353	.01259	.01214	.01132	.01050	.01018	.00967	.00939	.00764
SOUTH CAROLINA	.02251	.02006	.01963	.01725	.01659	.01540	.01460	.01347	.00963
SOUTH DAKOTA	.01577	.01293	.01129	.01074	.00987	.00925	.00869	.00801	.00577
TENNESSEE	.02047	.01824	.01785	.01569	.01510	.01401	.01328	.01225	.00880
TEXAS	.00722	.00679	.00699	.00628	.00612	.00584	.00562	.00537	.00404
UTAH	.03153	.02307	.02218	.01986	.01804	.01792	.01623	.01449	.01054
VERMONT	.00000	.00000	.00000	.00000	.00000	.00000	.00000	.00000	.00000
VIRGINIA	.00011	.00010	.00009	.00008	.00008	.00007	.00007	.00006	.00004
WASHINGTON	.06069	.04446	.04273	.03829	.03478	.03456	.03128	.02793	.02033
WEST VIRGINIA	.03493	.03105	.03040	.02672	.02569	.02384	.02261	.02085	.01497
WISCONSIN	.00209	.00172	.00150	.00142	.00131	.00123	.00115	.00106	.00076
WYOMING	.02357	.01728	.01657	.01481	.01346	.01338	.01210	.01080	.00787

Table D-5
Effective Rates of Taxation: Total Selective Sales and Gross Receipts Taxes (Allocator-Consumption)

	$ 0- 1,999	2,000- 2,999	3,000- 3,999	4,000- 4,999	5,000- 5,999	6,000- 7,499	7,500- 9,999	10,000- 14,999	OVER 15,000
ALABAMA	.02664	.02632	.02862	.02645	.02452	.02407	.02062	.01899	.01122
ALASKA	.02556	.01911	.02181	.02031	.01862	.01677	.01631	.01425	.00838
ARIZONA	.02107	.01543	.01744	.01586	.01442	.01255	.01249	.01077	.00624
ARKANSAS	.02277	.02271	.02454	.02275	.02132	.02067	.01772	.01601	.00917
CALIFORNIA	.01890	.01391	.01598	.01457	.01316	.01157	.01151	.00989	.00584
COLORADO	.01789	.01324	.01535	.01404	.01285	.01110	.01132	.01010	.00575
CONNECTICUT	.01952	.01933	.01838	.01778	.01642	.01512	.01338	.01146	.00715
DELAWARE	.01797	.01708	.01770	.01609	.01511	.01442	.01260	.01132	.00671
FLORIDA	.02944	.02752	.02904	.02634	.02432	.02387	.02072	.01930	.01217
GEORGIA	.02121	.02111	.02335	.02162	.01980	.01976	.01698	.01608	.00992
HAWAII	.03141	.02263	.02339	.02108	.01948	.01689	.01628	.01397	.00802
IDAHO	.02386	.01755	.02068	.01889	.01697	.01474	.01477	.01250	.00725
ILLINOIS	.02106	.01792	.01659	.01537	.01389	.01272	.01183	.00983	.00594
INDIANA	.01504	.01437	.01483	.01448	.01302	.01162	.01145	.00939	.00530
IOWA	.01491	.01448	.01460	.01422	.01272	.01124	.01097	.00892	.00501
KANSAS	.01592	.01484	.01490	.01437	.01292	.01158	.01125	.00920	.00523
KENTUCKY	.01921	.01947	.02177	.02030	.01881	.01870	.01619	.01530	.00955
LOUISIANA	.03048	.02845	.02975	.02690	.02461	.02410	.02084	.01936	.01191
MAINE	.01905	.02074	.02165	.02156	.02035	.01901	.01688	.01445	.00856
MARYLAND	.02453	.02216	.02209	.01968	.01841	.01741	.01516	.01341	.00790

MASSACHUSETTS	.01276	.01407	.01425	.01408	.01318	.01241	.01110	.00961	.00612
MICHIGAN	.01591	.01506	.01481	.01427	.01277	.01138	.01097	.00916	.00508
MINNESOTA	.02516	.02177	.02077	.01942	.01754	.01604	.01513	.01244	.00731
MISSISSIPPI	.02381	.02396	.02577	.02396	.02267	.02174	.01861	.01648	.00906
MISSOURI	.01752	.01583	.01502	.01416	.01269	.01140	.01075	.00874	.00507
MONTANA	.02829	.02081	.02425	.02236	.02018	.01774	.01746	.01471	.00855
NEBRASKA	.01714	.01662	.01692	.01653	.01481	.01310	.01285	.01051	.00591
NEVADA	.03813	.02819	.03035	.02750	.02474	.02302	.02178	.01847	.01199
NEW HAMPSHIRE	.01954	.02075	.02149	.02116	.01995	.01882	.01685	.01463	.00914
NEW JERSEY	.02434	.02368	.02250	.02153	.01976	.01817	.01597	.01351	.00843
NEW MEXICO	.03018	.02210	.02671	.02440	.02170	.01867	.01879	.01550	.00892
NEW YORK	.01890	.01845	.01746	.01663	.01523	.01410	.01245	.01062	.00689
NORTH CAROLINA	.01993	.01953	.02149	.01986	.01843	.01830	.01572	.01471	.00914
NORTH DAKOTA	.01747	.01595	.01623	.01565	.01414	.01283	.01254	.01033	.00595
OHIO	.02146	.01945	.01885	.01794	.01612	.01450	.01385	.01137	.00661
OKLAHOMA	.02581	.02495	.02626	.02406	.02255	.02166	.01868	.01674	.00963
OREGON	.01503	.01106	.01331	.01204	.01084	.00910	.00955	.00834	.00466
PENNSYLVANIA	.01394	.01559	.01624	.01624	.01533	.01437	.01279	.01099	.00661
RHODE ISLAND	.02397	.02419	.02374	.02304	.02143	.02001	.01785	.01546	.00986
SOUTH CAROLINA	.02789	.02706	.02956	.02715	.02483	.02478	.02143	.02041	.01292
SOUTH DAKOTA	.02157	.01984	.01989	.01930	.01744	.01575	.01541	.01289	.00764
TENNESSEE	.02119	.02089	.02255	.02082	.01937	.01890	.01619	.01478	.00862
TEXAS	.02621	.02425	.02452	.02205	.02063	.01954	.01690	.01490	.00848
UTAH	.01936	.01422	.01756	.01595	.01422	.01202	.01248	.01058	.00597
VERMONT	.02628	.02845	.02826	.02814	.02646	.02489	.02248	.01984	.01276
VIRGINIA	.02611	.02402	.02488	.02244	.02078	.02020	.01754	.01580	.00957
WASHINGTON	.03719	.02695	.02824	.02558	.02346	.02082	.01985	.01688	.01006
WEST VIRGINIA	.02418	.02313	.02387	.02176	.02069	.01951	.01703	.01498	.00856
WISCONSIN	.02023	.01820	.01779	.01689	.01520	.01376	.01316	.01074	.00619
WYOMING	.02018	.01481	.01829	.01662	.01477	.01255	.01287	.01072	.00608

Table D-6
Effective Rates of Taxation: Alcoholic Beverages Tax (Allocator-Alcohol Expenditures)

	$ 0- 1,999	2,000- 2,999	3,000- 3,999	4,000- 4,999	5,000- 5,999	6,000- 7,499	7,500- 9,999	10,000- 14,999	OVER 15,000
ALABAMA	.00272	.00262	.00377	.00348	.00253	.00341	.00303	.00401	.00362
ALASKA	.00525	.00428	.00346	.00366	.00405	.00416	.00372	.00430	.00252
ARIZONA	.00174	.00142	.00115	.00122	.00135	.00139	.00124	.00144	.00084
ARKANSAS	.00163	.00157	.00227	.00209	.00152	.00205	.00182	.00241	.00218
CALIFORNIA	.00137	.00111	.00090	.00096	.00106	.00109	.00098	.00113	.00066
COLORADO	.00205	.00166	.00135	.00143	.00158	.00162	.00145	.00168	.00098
CONNECTICUT	.00166	.00207	.00168	.00179	.00169	.00163	.00158	.00156	.00122
DELAWARE	.00092	.00089	.00128	.00118	.00086	.00116	.00103	.00136	.00123
FLORIDA	.00279	.00269	.00388	.00358	.00260	.00350	.00311	.00412	.00372
GEORGIA	.00306	.00295	.00425	.00392	.00285	.00384	.00341	.00452	.00408
HAWAII	.00274	.00222	.00180	.00192	.00212	.00217	.00195	.00225	.00132
IDAHO	.00173	.00140	.00114	.00121	.00134	.00137	.00123	.00142	.00083
ILLINOIS	.00162	.00099	.00132	.00126	.00123	.00130	.00136	.00121	.00073
INDIANA	.00164	.00100	.00134	.00128	.00125	.00132	.00138	.00123	.00074
IOWA	.00064	.00039	.00052	.00050	.00049	.00052	.00054	.00048	.00029
KANSAS	.00156	.00095	.00127	.00121	.00119	.00125	.00131	.00117	.00070
KENTUCKY	.00248	.00238	.00344	.00317	.00230	.00310	.00276	.00365	.00330
LOUISIANA	.00325	.00313	.00451	.00416	.00303	.00407	.00362	.00480	.00433
MAINE	.00111	.00138	.00111	.00119	.00112	.00108	.00105	.00104	.00081
MARYLAND	.00088	.00085	.00122	.00113	.00082	.00110	.00098	.00130	.00117

MASSACHUSETTS	.00154	.00192	.00155	.00166	.00156	.00151	.00147	.00145	.00113
MICHIGAN	.00077	.00047	.00063	.00060	.00059	.00062	.00065	.00060	.00035
MINNESOTA	.00287	.00176	.00235	.00223	.00219	.00231	.00242	.00215	.00129
MISSISSIPPI	.00105	.00101	.00146	.00135	.00098	.00132	.00117	.00156	.00141
MISSOURI	.00074	.00045	.00061	.00058	.00056	.00060	.00062	.00056	.00033
MONTANA	.00337	.00274	.00222	.00236	.00261	.00268	.00240	.00277	.00162
NEBRASKA	.00100	.00061	.00082	.00078	.00076	.00080	.00084	.00075	.00045
NEVADA	.00135	.00110	.00089	.00095	.00104	.00107	.00096	.00111	.00065
NEW HAMPSHIRE	.00052	.00065	.00052	.00056	.00052	.00051	.00049	.00049	.00038
NEW JERSEY	.00099	.00124	.00100	.00107	.00101	.00097	.00095	.00094	.00073
NEW MEXICO	.00148	.00120	.00097	.00104	.00115	.00118	.00105	.00122	.00071
NEW YORK	.00087	.00109	.00088	.00094	.00088	.00085	.00083	.00082	.00064
NORTH CAROLINA	.00214	.00206	.00297	.00274	.00199	.00268	.00239	.00316	.00286
NORTH DAKOTA	.00272	.00166	.00222	.00211	.00207	.00219	.00229	.00204	.00123
OHIO	.00148	.00090	.00120	.00114	.00112	.00118	.00124	.00111	.00066
OKLAHOMA	.00151	.00145	.00210	.00193	.00140	.00189	.00168	.00223	.00201
OREGON	.00048	.00039	.00031	.00033	.00037	.00038	.00034	.00039	.00023
PENNSYLVANIA	.00140	.00175	.00141	.00151	.00142	.00137	.00134	.00132	.00103
RHODE ISLAND	.00133	.00166	.00134	.00143	.00135	.00131	.00127	.00125	.00098
SOUTH CAROLINA	.00391	.00376	.00542	.00500	.00364	.00489	.00435	.00577	.00519
SOUTH DAKOTA	.00223	.00136	.00182	.00173	.00170	.00179	.00188	.00167	.00100
TENNESSEE	.00187	.00180	.00260	.00240	.00174	.00235	.00209	.00277	.00250
TEXAS	.00107	.00103	.00148	.00137	.00099	.00134	.00119	.00157	.00142
UTAH	.00061	.00050	.00040	.00043	.00047	.00049	.00043	.00050	.00029
VERMONT	.00472	.00587	.00476	.00507	.00478	.00462	.00450	.00444	.00347
VIRGINIA	.00189	.00182	.00263	.00242	.00176	.00237	.00213	.00279	.00252
WASHINGTON	.00318	.00258	.00210	.00223	.00246	.00253	.00226	.00262	.00153
WEST VIRGINIA	.00050	.00048	.00070	.00065	.00047	.00063	.00056	.00074	.00067
WISCONSIN	.00212	.00129	.00173	.00164	.00161	.00170	.00178	.00159	.00095
WYOMING	.00070	.00057	.00046	.00049	.00054	.00056	.00050	.00058	.00034

Table D-7
Effective Rates of Taxation: Tobacco Products Tax (Allocator-Tobacco Expenditures)

	$ 0– 1,999	2,000– 2,999	3,000– 3,999	4,000– 4,999	5,000– 5,999	6,000– 7,499	7,500– 9,999	10,000– 14,999	OVER 15,000
ALABAMA	.00733	.00601	.00515	.00428	.00390	.00338	.00287	.00215	.00081
ALASKA	.00662	.00469	.00543	.00500	.00420	.00400	.00334	.00194	.00141
ARIZONA	.00236	.00167	.00193	.00179	.00150	.00143	.00119	.00069	.00050
ARKANSAS	.00618	.00507	.00434	.00361	.00328	.00285	.00242	.00182	.00068
CALIFORNIA	.00247	.00175	.00203	.00188	.00157	.00150	.00125	.00073	.00053
COLORADO	.00068	.00048	.00055	.00051	.00043	.00041	.00034	.00020	.00014
CONNECTICUT	.00392	.00416	.00385	.00351	.00298	.00267	.00213	.00147	.00088
DELAWARE	.00566	.00465	.00398	.00330	.00301	.00261	.00221	.00166	.00063
FLORIDA	.00408	.00335	.00287	.00239	.00217	.00188	.00160	.00120	.00045
GEORGIA	.00616	.00506	.00433	.00360	.00328	.00284	.00241	.00181	.00068
HAWAII	.00276	.00195	.00226	.00209	.00176	.00167	.00140	.00081	.00059
IDAHO	.00430	.00304	.00353	.00326	.00274	.00261	.00218	.00126	.00092
ILLINOIS	.00383	.00339	.00285	.00252	.00221	.00202	.00173	.00123	.00069
INDIANA	.00330	.00292	.00246	.00217	.00191	.00174	.00149	.00106	.00060
IOWA	.00383	.00339	.00285	.00252	.00222	.00202	.00173	.00124	.00069
KANSAS	.00386	.00341	.00287	.00254	.00223	.00203	.00174	.00124	.00070
KENTUCKY	.00303	.00249	.00213	.00177	.00161	.00140	.00118	.00089	.00033
LOUISIANA	.01055	.00866	.00742	.00616	.00561	.00486	.00413	.00310	.00117
MAINE	.00540	.00571	.00528	.00481	.00409	.00367	.00292	.00202	.00121
MARYLAND	.00693	.00569	.00487	.00405	.00368	.00319	.00271	.00204	.00077

MASSACHUSETTS	.00444	.00471	.00436	.00397	.00337	.00302	.00241	.00166	.00100
MICHIGAN	.00558	.00493	.00415	.00367	.00322	.00294	.00252	.00185	.00101
MINNESOTA	.00599	.00530	.00446	.00395	.00347	.00316	.00271	.00193	.00108
MISSISSIPPI	.00674	.00553	.00474	.00394	.00358	.00311	.00264	.00198	.00075
MISSOURI	.00477	.00421	.00355	.00314	.00276	.00252	.00216	.00154	.00086
MONTANA	.00730	.00517	.00598	.00553	.00465	.00443	.00370	.00215	.00157
NEBRASKA	.00344	.00304	.00256	.00226	.00199	.00181	.00155	.00111	.00062
NEVADA	.00616	.00438	.00505	.00467	.00392	.00373	.00312	.00181	.00132
NEW HAMPSHIRE	.00494	.00522	.00483	.00440	.00373	.00335	.00267	.00184	.00110
NEW JERSEY	.00560	.00593	.00549	.00500	.00425	.00381	.00303	.00209	.00126
NEW MEXICO	.00711	.00503	.00583	.00539	.00453	.00431	.00361	.00209	.00153
NEW YORK	.00478	.00506	.00468	.00427	.00363	.00325	.00259	.00179	.00107
NORTH CAROLINA	.00000	.00000	.00000	.00000	.00000	.00000	.00000	.00000	.00000
NORTH DAKOTA	.00482	.00426	.00358	.00317	.00278	.00254	.00218	.00155	.00087
OHIO	.00473	.00418	.00351	.00311	.00273	.00249	.00214	.00152	.00085
OKLAHOMA	.00797	.00654	.00560	.00465	.00424	.00367	.00312	.00234	.00088
OREGON	.00000	.00000	.00000	.00000	.00000	.00000	.00000	.00000	.00000
PENNSYLVANIA	.00444	.00470	.00435	.00397	.00337	.00302	.00241	.00166	.00099
RHODE ISLAND	.00515	.00545	.00505	.00460	.00391	.00350	.00279	.00193	.00115
SOUTH CAROLINA	.00634	.00520	.00445	.00370	.00337	.00292	.00248	.00186	.00070
SOUTH DAKOTA	.00401	.00355	.00298	.00264	.00232	.00212	.00181	.00129	.00072
TENNESSEE	.00598	.00491	.00421	.00350	.00318	.00276	.00234	.00176	.00066
TEXAS	.00952	.00782	.00669	.00556	.00506	.00439	.00372	.00280	.00106
UTAH	.00227	.00161	.00186	.00172	.00145	.00138	.00115	.00067	.00048
VERMONT	.00576	.00609	.00565	.00514	.00437	.00391	.00312	.00215	.00129
VIRGINIA	.00377	.00309	.00265	.00220	.00200	.00174	.00149	.00111	.00042
WASHINGTON	.00524	.00371	.00430	.00398	.00334	.00318	.00266	.00154	.00113
WEST VIRGINIA	.00690	.00565	.00484	.00402	.00366	.00317	.00269	.00203	.00076
WISCONSIN	.00573	.00506	.00426	.00377	.00331	.00302	.00259	.00185	.00104
WYOMING	.00375	.00265	.00307	.00283	.00238	.00227	.00189	.00110	.00080

Table D-8
Effective Rates of Taxation: Public Utilities Tax (Allocator-Telephone and Telegraph Expenditures)

	$ 0- 1,999	2,000- 2,999	3,000- 3,999	4,000- 4,999	5,000- 5,999	6,000- 7,499	7,500- 9,999	10,000- 14,999	OVER 15,000
ALABAMA	.00117	.00101	.00100	.00092	.00088	.00091	.00082	.00067	.00044
ALASKA	.00000	.00000	.00000	.00000	.00000	.00000	.00000	.00000	.00000
ARIZONA	.00266	.00179	.00177	.00141	.00129	.00130	.00113	.00100	.00059
ARKANSAS	.00054	.00046	.00046	.00042	.00040	.00042	.00038	.00031	.00020
CALIFORNIA	.00113	.00076	.00075	.00060	.00055	.00055	.00048	.00042	.00025
COLORADO	.00137	.00092	.00091	.00073	.00066	.00067	.00058	.00051	.00030
CONNECTICUT	.00648	.00535	.00436	.00399	.00381	.00346	.00302	.00273	.00209
DELAWARE	.00013	.00011	.00011	.00010	.00010	.00010	.00009	.00007	.00005
FLORIDA	.00477	.00413	.00409	.00379	.00360	.00374	.00337	.00277	.00181
GEORGIA	.00011	.00010	.00009	.00009	.00008	.00009	.00008	.00006	.00004
HAWAII	.00922	.00621	.00613	.00491	.00449	.00451	.00393	.00346	.00206
IDAHO	.00138	.00093	.00092	.00073	.00067	.00067	.00059	.00052	.00031
ILLINOIS	.00571	.00466	.00400	.00365	.00340	.00301	.00270	.00240	.00166
INDIANA	.00000	.00000	.00000	.00000	.00000	.00000	.00000	.00000	.00000
IOWA	.00024	.00019	.00017	.00015	.00014	.00012	.00011	.00010	.00007
KANSAS	.00110	.00089	.00077	.00070	.00065	.00058	.00052	.00046	.00032
KENTUCKY	.00004	.00003	.00003	.00003	.00003	.00003	.00003	.00002	.00001
LOUISIANA	.00222	.00192	.00190	.00176	.00167	.00174	.00156	.00129	.00084
MAINE	.00349	.00288	.00234	.00214	.00205	.00186	.00162	.00147	.00112
MARYLAND	.00319	.00276	.00274	.00253	.00241	.00250	.00225	.00185	.00121

MASSACHUSETTS	.00000	.00000	.00000	.00000	.00000	.00000	.00000	.00000	.00000
MICHIGAN	.00000	.00000	.00000	.00000	.00000	.00000	.00000	.00000	.00000
MINNESOTA	.00547	.00447	.00383	.00350	.00326	.00289	.00259	.00230	.00159
MISSISSIPPI	.00011	.00009	.00009	.00008	.00008	.00008	.00007	.00006	.00004
MISSOURI	.00315	.00257	.00220	.00201	.00188	.00166	.00149	.00132	.00091
MONTANA	.00155	.00104	.00103	.00082	.00075	.00075	.00066	.00058	.00034
NEBRASKA	.00058	.00047	.00040	.00037	.00034	.00030	.00027	.00024	.00017
NEVADA	.00049	.00033	.00033	.00026	.00024	.00024	.00021	.00018	.00011
NEW HAMPSHIRE	.00085	.00070	.00057	.00052	.00050	.00045	.00039	.00035	.00027
NEW JERSEY	.00769	.00635	.00518	.00473	.00452	.00410	.00358	.00324	.00249
NEW MEXICO	.00147	.00099	.00097	.00078	.00071	.00071	.00062	.00055	.00032
NEW YORK	.00419	.00346	.00282	.00258	.00246	.00223	.00195	.00176	.00135
NORTH CAROLINA	.00403	.00349	.00346	.00320	.00304	.00316	.00285	.00234	.00153
NORTH DAKOTA	.00011	.00009	.00007	.00007	.00006	.00005	.00005	.00004	.00003
OHIO	.00326	.00266	.00228	.00209	.00194	.00172	.00154	.00137	.00095
OKLAHOMA	.00092	.00079	.00078	.00072	.00069	.00072	.00064	.00053	.00034
OREGON	.00129	.00087	.00086	.00069	.00063	.00063	.00055	.00048	.00029
PENNSYLVANIA	.00162	.00134	.00109	.00100	.00095	.00087	.00075	.00068	.00052
RHODE ISLAND	.00451	.00373	.00304	.00278	.00265	.00241	.00210	.00190	.00146
SOUTH CAROLINA	.00165	.00143	.00141	.00131	.00124	.00129	.00116	.00096	.00062
SOUTH DAKOTA	.00004	.00003	.00002	.00002	.00002	.00002	.00002	.00001	.00001
TENNESSEE	.00093	.00081	.00080	.00074	.00070	.00073	.00066	.00054	.00035
TEXAS	.00202	.00175	.00173	.00160	.00152	.00158	.00142	.00117	.00076
UTAH	.00073	.00049	.00048	.00038	.00035	.00035	.00031	.00027	.00016
VERMONT	.00316	.00260	.00213	.00194	.00186	.00168	.00147	.00133	.00102
VIRGINIA	.00594	.00514	.00509	.00471	.00448	.00466	.00424	.00345	.00225
WASHINGTON	.00811	.00546	.00540	.00432	.00395	.00397	.00346	.00305	.00182
WEST VIRGINIA	.00026	.00023	.00022	.00021	.00020	.00020	.00018	.00015	.00010
WISCONSIN	.00244	.00199	.00171	.00156	.00145	.00129	.00115	.00102	.00071
WYOMING	.00069	.00047	.00046	.00037	.00033	.00034	.00029	.00026	.00015

Table D-9
Effective Rates of Taxation: Public Utilities Tax (Allocator-Gas and Electric Expenditures)

	$ 0- 1,999	2,000- 2,999	3,000- 3,999	4,000- 4,999	5,000- 5,999	6,000- 7,499	7,500- 9,999	10,000- 14,999	OVER 15,000
ALABAMA	.00179	.00134	.00114	.00092	.00084	.00077	.00067	.00056	.00036
ALASKA	.00000	.00000	.00000	.00000	.00000	.00000	.00000	.00000	.00000
ARIZONA	.00352	.00240	.00181	.00151	.00147	.00128	.00104	.00082	.00049
ARKANSAS	.00079	.00059	.00050	.00040	.00037	.00034	.00029	.00024	.00016
CALIFORNIA	.00156	.00106	.00080	.00067	.00065	.00056	.00046	.00036	.00022
COLORADO	.00182	.00124	.00093	.00078	.00076	.00066	.00054	.00042	.00025
CONNECTICUT	.00860	.00680	.00542	.00479	.00417	.00357	.00305	.00250	.00158
DELAWARE	.00023	.00017	.00015	.00012	.00011	.00010	.00008	.00007	.00004
FLORIDA	.00765	.00573	.00489	.00393	.00360	.00329	.00286	.00239	.00154
GEORGIA	.00018	.00013	.00011	.00009	.00008	.00007	.00006	.00005	.00003
HAWAII	.01264	.00863	.00650	.00545	.00528	.00460	.00374	.00296	.00178
IDAHO	.00180	.00123	.00092	.00077	.00075	.00065	.00053	.00042	.00025
ILLINOIS	.00762	.00576	.00454	.00380	.00343	.00321	.00262	.00219	.00143
INDIANA	.00000	.00000	.00000	.00000	.00000	.00000	.00000	.00000	.00000
IOWA	.00031	.00023	.00018	.00015	.00014	.00013	.00010	.00009	.00005
KANSAS	.00142	.00107	.00084	.00071	.00064	.00060	.00049	.00041	.00026
KENTUCKY	.00006	.00005	.00004	.00003	.00003	.00002	.00002	.00002	.00001
LOUISIANA	.00348	.00261	.00223	.00179	.00164	.00150	.00130	.00109	.00070
MAINE	.00425	.00335	.00267	.00236	.00206	.00176	.00150	.00123	.00078
MARYLAND	.00546	.00409	.00349	.00280	.00257	.00235	.00204	.00170	.00110

MASSACHUSETTS	.00000	.00000	.00000	.00000	.00000	.00000	.00000	.00000	.00000
MICHIGAN	.00000	.00000	.00000	.00000	.00000	.00000	.00000	.00000	.00000
MINNESOTA	.00710	.00537	.00424	.00355	.00320	.00300	.00244	.00205	.00134
MISSISSIPPI	.00015	.00011	.00010	.00008	.00007	.00006	.00005	.00004	.00003
MISSOURI	.00404	.00306	.00241	.00202	.00182	.00170	.00139	.00116	.00076
MONTANA	.00203	.00138	.00104	.00087	.00084	.00073	.00060	.00047	.00028
NEBRASKA	.00074	.00056	.00044	.00037	.00033	.00031	.00025	.00021	.00014
NEVADA	.00068	.00046	.00035	.00029	.00028	.00024	.00020	.00016	.00009
NEW HAMPSHIRE	.00107	.00084	.00067	.00059	.00051	.00044	.00037	.00031	.00019
NEW JERSEY	.01017	.00804	.00640	.00567	.00493	.00423	.00360	.00295	.00187
NEW MEXICO	.00193	.00132	.00099	.00083	.00080	.00070	.00057	.00045	.00027
NEW YORK	.00548	.00433	.00345	.00305	.00266	.00228	.00194	.00159	.00101
NORTH CAROLINA	.00619	.00464	.00396	.00318	.00291	.00266	.00231	.00193	.00125
NORTH DAKOTA	.00014	.00010	.00008	.00007	.00006	.00005	.00004	.00004	.00002
OHIO	.00430	.00325	.00256	.00215	.00194	.00181	.00148	.00124	.00081
OKLAHOMA	.00146	.00109	.00093	.00075	.00068	.00062	.00054	.00045	.00029
OREGON	.00172	.00117	.00088	.00074	.00072	.00062	.00051	.00040	.00024
PENNSYLVANIA	.00206	.00163	.00130	.00115	.00100	.00086	.00073	.00060	.00038
RHODE ISLAND	.00568	.00449	.00357	.00316	.00275	.00236	.00201	.00165	.00104
SOUTH CAROLINA	.00252	.00188	.00161	.00129	.00118	.00108	.00094	.00078	.00050
SOUTH DAKOTA	.00005	.00004	.00003	.00002	.00002	.00002	.00001	.00001	.00001
TENNESSEE	.00144	.00108	.00092	.00074	.00067	.00062	.00054	.00045	.00029
TEXAS	.00326	.00244	.00208	.00167	.00153	.00140	.00122	.00102	.00065
UTAH	.00097	.00066	.00050	.00042	.00040	.00035	.00028	.00022	.00013
VERMONT	.00388	.00306	.00244	.00216	.00188	.00161	.00137	.00112	.00071
VIRGINIA	.00964	.00721	.00616	.00495	.00453	.00415	.00364	.00301	.00194
WASHINGTON	.01094	.00746	.00562	.00472	.00457	.00398	.00324	.00256	.00154
WEST VIRGINIA	.00042	.00031	.00026	.00021	.00019	.00018	.00015	.00013	.00008
WISCONSIN	.00320	.00242	.00191	.00160	.00144	.00135	.00110	.00092	.00060
WYOMING	.00093	.00063	.00047	.00040	.00038	.00033	.00027	.00021	.00013

Table D-10
Effeetive Rates of Taxation: Motor Fuel Tax (Allocator-Auto Operation Expenditures)

	$ 0- 1,999	2,000- 2,999	3,000- 3,999	4,000- 4,999	5,000- 5,999	6,000- 7,499	7,500- 9,999	10,000- 14,999	OVER 15,000
ALABAMA	.01304	.01478	.01700	.01640	.01592	.01528	.01289	.01119	.00567
ALASKA	.01127	.00835	.01121	.01012	.00897	.00721	.00798	.00689	.00364
ARIZONA	.01045	.00772	.01040	.00943	.00835	.00671	.00743	.00641	.00339
ARKANSAS	.01168	.01325	.01524	.01470	.01427	.01369	.01155	.01003	.00508
CALIFCRNIA	.00926	.00684	.00922	.00836	.00740	.00594	.00659	.00569	.00300
COLORADO	.01061	.00783	.01056	.00957	.00848	.00681	.00754	.00651	.00344
CONNECTICUI	.00326	.00446	.00576	.00616	.00616	.00588	.00536	.00475	.00256
DELAWARE	.00584	.00662	.00761	.00734	.00713	.00684	.00577	.00501	.00254
FLORIDA	.01006	.01142	.01313	.01267	.01229	.01180	.00996	.00864	.00438
GEORGIA	.01003	.01138	.01309	.01262	.01225	.01176	.00992	.00862	.00436
HAWAII	.01185	.00877	.01181	.01071	.00948	.00761	.00844	.00728	.00385
IDAHO	.01293	.00957	.01288	.01167	.01034	.00830	.00920	.00794	.00420
ILLINOIS	.00510	.00538	.00575	.00577	.00515	.00445	.00448	.00368	.00201
INDIANA	.00914	.00966	.01033	.01037	.00925	.00798	.00803	.00660	.00361
IOWA	.00913	.00964	.01031	.01035	.00923	.00797	.00802	.00659	.00360
KANSAS	.00818	.00865	.00925	.00928	.00828	.00715	.00720	.00591	.00323
KENTUCKY	.00980	.01112	.01279	.01233	.01197	.01149	.00969	.00842	.00426
LOUISIANA	.00938	.01064	.01224	.01181	.01146	.01100	.00928	.00806	.00408
MAINE	.00615	.00841	.01085	.01160	.01161	.01109	.01009	.00895	.00483
MARYLAND	.00610	.00691	.00796	.00767	.00745	.00715	.00603	.00524	.00265

MASSACHUSETTS	.00298	.00408	.00527	.00563	.00564	.00538	.00490	.00435	.00234
MICHIGAN	.00765	.00808	.00864	.00867	.00773	.00668	.00672	.00569	.00302
MINNESOTA	.00750	.00793	.00848	.00851	.00759	.00655	.00660	.00542	.00296
MISSISSIPPI	.01299	.01472	.01694	.01634	.01586	.01522	.01284	.01115	.00565
MISSOURI	.00657	.00695	.00743	.00746	.00665	.00574	.00578	.00475	.00259
MONTANA	.01383	.01022	.01375	.01247	.01105	.00887	.00983	.00848	.00448
NEBRASKA	.01095	.01157	.01236	.01242	.01108	.00956	.00962	.00791	.00432
NEVADA	.00961	.00713	.00957	.00867	.00767	.00616	.00683	.00589	.00311
NEW HAMPSHIRE	.00525	.00718	.00924	.00987	.00988	.00944	.00859	.00761	.00411
NEW JERSEY	.00364	.00498	.00643	.00687	.00688	.00657	.00598	.00530	.00286
NEW MEXICO	.01734	.01282	.01726	.01565	.01386	.01113	.01234	.01064	.00563
NEW YORK	.00228	.00311	.00402	.00430	.00430	.00411	.00374	.00331	.00179
NORTH CAROLINA	.01021	.01158	.01333	.01285	.01247	.01197	.01010	.00877	.00444
NORTH DAKOTA	.00795	.00840	.00898	.00901	.00804	.00694	.00698	.00574	.00314
OHIO	.00892	.00943	.01007	.01011	.00902	.00779	.00784	.00644	.00352
OKLAHOMA	.01070	.01214	.01396	.01347	.01307	.01255	.01058	.00919	.00465
OREGON	.01048	.00774	.01043	.00946	.00838	.00673	.00746	.00643	.00340
PENNSYLVANIA	.00448	.00613	.00792	.00846	.00847	.00809	.00736	.00653	.00352
RHODE ISLAND	.00443	.00606	.00783	.00836	.00837	.00799	.00727	.00645	.00348
SOUTH CAROLINA	.01118	.01268	.01459	.01407	.01366	.01311	.01106	.00960	.00485
SOUTH DAKOTA	.00976	.01032	.01102	.01107	.00987	.00852	.00858	.00705	.00385
TENNESSEE	.01024	.01161	.01336	.01289	.01251	.01201	.01013	.00880	.00446
TEXAS	.00795	.00902	.01038	.01001	.00971	.00932	.00787	.00683	.00346
UTAH	.01325	.00978	.01318	.01195	.01058	.00850	.00942	.00813	.00429
VERMONT	.00607	.00828	.01071	.01144	.01144	.01092	.00994	.00882	.00476
VIRGINIA	.00926	.01050	.01208	.01165	.01131	.01086	.00925	.00795	.00403
WASHINGTON	.01235	.00913	.01230	.01115	.00988	.00793	.00879	.00759	.00401
WEST VIRGINIA	.00868	.00983	.01131	.01091	.01059	.01016	.00857	.00744	.00377
WISCONSIN	.00796	.00840	.00899	.00902	.00805	.00694	.00699	.00574	.00314
WYOMING	.01321	.00977	.01314	.01188	.01053	.00846	.00937	.00808	.00427

Table D-11
Effective Rates of Taxation: Property Tax (Allocator-Housing Expenditures)

	$ 0- 1,999	2,000- 2,999	3,000- 3,999	4,000- 4,999	5,000- 5,999	6,000- 7,499	7,500- 9,999	10,000- 14,999	OVER 15,000
ALABAMA	.01838	.01640	.01611	.01365	.01324	.01246	.01195	.01100	.00844
ALASKA	.03811	.02855	.02312	.02199	.02051	.01951	.01704	.01434	.01074
ARIZONA	.07778	.05818	.04725	.04511	.04205	.03998	.03495	.02942	.02204
ARKANSAS	.02914	.02601	.02554	.02165	.02100	.01977	.01896	.01744	.01339
CALIFORNIA	.10111	.07563	.06143	.05867	.05469	.05201	.04546	.03827	.02866
COLORADO	.08821	.06593	.05357	.05115	.04768	.04534	.03963	.03336	.02499
CONNECTICUT	.07790	.06749	.05539	.04845	.04597	.04154	.03721	.03481	.03132
DELAWARE	.02062	.01840	.01806	.01531	.01485	.01397	.01340	.01233	.00946
FLORIDA	.04985	.04452	.04372	.03706	.03594	.03383	.03244	.02986	.02291
GEORGIA	.03407	.03041	.02986	.02531	.02454	.02310	.02216	.02039	.01564
HAWAII	.03475	.02601	.02112	.02017	.01880	.01788	.01562	.01315	.00985
IDAHO	.07846	.05874	.04767	.04550	.04241	.04033	.03525	.02968	.02223
ILLINOIS	.07490	.06060	.05164	.04815	.04406	.04200	.03676	.03255	.02327
INDIANA	.07479	.06050	.05158	.04809	.04400	.04195	.03672	.03251	.02325
IOWA	.09108	.07368	.06279	.05856	.05359	.05108	.04471	.03959	.02831
KANSAS	.09040	.07320	.06239	.05816	.05323	.05073	.04442	.03933	.02812
KENTUCKY	.03080	.02749	.02700	.02288	.02219	.02089	.02003	.01844	.01415
LOUISIANA	.03093	.02761	.02712	.02298	.02229	.02098	.02012	.01852	.01421
MAINE	.08479	.07333	.06017	.05266	.04997	.04514	.04043	.03783	.03404
MARYLAND	.04232	.03778	.03711	.03145	.03050	.02871	.02753	.02534	.01944

MASSACHUSETTS	.10322	.08941	.07340	.06421	.06092	.05505	.04931	.04613	.04152
MICHIGAN	.07685	.06218	.05299	.04942	.04522	.04311	.03773	.03444	.02389
MINNESOTA	.09825	.07956	.06780	.06322	.05786	.05514	.04828	.04275	.03057
MISSISSIPPI	.03688	.03290	.03233	.02740	.02657	.02502	.02398	.02208	.01694
MISSOURI	.05316	.04303	.03667	.03420	.03130	.02983	.02611	.02312	.01653
MONTANA	.09337	.06981	.05665	.05412	.05045	.04797	.04193	.03530	.02644
NEBRASKA	.08734	.07071	.06025	.05620	.05143	.04901	.04291	.03800	.02716
NEVADA	.04939	.03707	.03000	.02863	.02668	.02536	.02217	.01867	.01398
NEW HAMPSHIRE	.09461	.08186	.06701	.05863	.05562	.05026	.04503	.04211	.03791
NEW JERSEY	.09092	.07878	.06463	.05653	.05364	.04847	.04342	.04062	.03655
NEW MEXICO	.04166	.03117	.02530	.02417	.02253	.02141	.01872	.01576	.01180
NEW YORK	.08239	.07136	.05856	.05123	.04861	.04393	.03935	.03681	.03313
NORTH CAROLINA	.02994	.02674	.02627	.02226	.02159	.02032	.01949	.01794	.01376
NORTH DAKOTA	.07253	.05870	.05005	.04665	.04269	.04069	.03561	.03154	.02256
OHIO	.06892	.05579	.04753	.04433	.04056	.03866	.03385	.02997	.02143
OKLAHOMA	.03735	.03334	.03274	.02775	.02692	.02534	.02430	.02236	.01716
OREGON	.08127	.06080	.04937	.04716	.04395	.04180	.03654	.03076	.02304
PENNSYLVANIA	.04911	.04256	.03492	.03056	.02899	.02620	.02347	.02195	.01975
RHODE ISLAND	.06926	.05998	.04924	.04308	.04086	.03693	.03308	.03095	.02785
SOUTH CAROLINA	.02291	.02044	.02009	.01702	.01650	.01554	.01490	.01371	.01048
SOUTH DAKOTA	.09100	.07364	.06271	.05851	.05355	.05103	.04468	.03956	.02828
TENNESSEE	.03377	.03015	.02962	.02510	.02435	.02292	.02198	.02023	.01552
TEXAS	.04639	.04141	.04067	.03447	.03343	.03147	.03018	.02777	.02131
UTAH	.07628	.05700	.04631	.04421	.04121	.03917	.03425	.02883	.02159
VERMONT	.08342	.07204	.05922	.05178	.04910	.04436	.03974	.03719	.03348
VIRGINIA	.03366	.03004	.02950	.02500	.02425	.02283	.02212	.02015	.01546
WASHINGTON	.05735	.04290	.03486	.03330	.03104	.02951	.02579	.02172	.01626
WEST VIRGINIA	.02905	.02587	.02542	.02154	.02089	.01966	.01886	.01735	.01332
WISCONSIN	.09478	.07668	.06538	.06096	.05578	.05316	.04654	.04120	.02946
WYOMING	.08651	.06476	.05250	.05003	.04665	.04436	.03876	.03263	.02445

Table D-12
Effective Rates of Taxation: Property Tax (Allocator-1/2 Housing, 1/2 Consumption)

	$ 0- 1,999	2,000- 2,999	3,000- 3,999	4,000- 4,999	5,000- 5,999	6,000- 7,499	7,500- 9,999	10,000- 14,999	OVER 15,000
ALABAMA	.01826	.01631	.01605	.01389	.01346	.01258	.01195	.01099	.00808
ALASKA	.03546	.02646	.02324	.02137	.01976	.01925	.01709	.01480	.01083
ARIZONA	.07311	.05444	.04801	.04431	.04093	.03987	.03543	.03071	.02247
ARKANSAS	.02895	.02588	.02545	.02204	.02135	.01996	.01895	.01743	.01282
CALIFORNIA	.09441	.07032	.06197	.05724	.05287	.05151	.04576	.03966	.02903
COLORADO	.08282	.06164	.05437	.05019	.04636	.04517	.04014	.03479	.02546
CONNECTICUT	.07148	.06250	.05389	.04834	.04523	.04212	.03843	.03578	.02973
DELAWARE	.02056	.01837	.01807	.01564	.01516	.01416	.01345	.01237	.00909
FLORIDA	.04961	.04435	.04363	.03778	.03660	.03421	.03249	.02987	.02197
GEORGIA	.03387	.03027	.02977	.02578	.02497	.02334	.02217	.02039	.01499
HAWAII	.03245	.02418	.02130	.01968	.01817	.01770	.01572	.01362	.00997
IDAHO	.07396	.05512	.04858	.04483	.04140	.04034	.03584	.03107	.02274
ILLINOIS	.07073	.05787	.05022	.04719	.04329	.04088	.03719	.03351	.02394
INDIANA	.07099	.05809	.05043	.04740	.04346	.04105	.03735	.03366	.02405
IOWA	.08683	.07104	.06166	.05797	.05317	.05021	.04569	.04118	.02942
KANSAS	.08604	.07046	.06116	.05748	.05273	.04978	.04532	.04084	.02918
KENTUCKY	.03060	.02735	.02690	.02330	.02257	.02109	.02003	.01842	.01355
LOUISIANA	.03077	.02750	.02705	.02342	.02269	.02121	.02014	.01852	.01362
MAINE	.07838	.06842	.05901	.05296	.04957	.04615	.04212	.03922	.03256
MARYLAND	.04218	.03770	.03708	.03211	.03111	.02907	.02761	.02539	.01867

MASSACHUSETTS	.09478	.08287	.07147	.06410	.05999	.05586	.05098	.04746	.03943
MICHIGAN	.07274	.05953	.05165	.04856	.04453	.04206	.03827	.03554	.02464
MINNESOTA	.09339	.07648	.06637	.06240	.05723	.05404	.04918	.04433	.03167
MISSISSIPPI	.03665	.03274	.03222	.02791	.02702	.02527	.02399	.02206	.01623
MISSOURI	.05062	.04145	.03598	.03382	.03102	.02929	.02666	.02403	.01716
MONTANA	.08792	.06545	.05767	.05327	.04919	.04793	.04259	.03692	.02702
NEBRASKA	.08334	.06824	.05921	.05568	.05107	.04822	.04389	.03956	.02826
NEVADA	.04610	.03446	.03025	.02792	.02578	.02510	.02231	.01933	.01415
NEW HAMPSHIRE	.08701	.07599	.06536	.05864	.05487	.05110	.04663	.04341	.03607
NEW JERSEY	.08344	.07297	.06289	.05641	.05279	.04916	.04486	.04176	.03470
NEW MEXICO	.03917	.02918	.02572	.02375	.02194	.02136	.01899	.01646	.01204
NEW YORK	.07579	.06626	.05713	.05125	.04796	.04467	.04076	.03795	.03153
NORTH CAROLINA	.02974	.02659	.02616	.02265	.02194	.02051	.01948	.01791	.01317
NORTH DAKOTA	.06937	.05678	.04932	.04634	.04250	.04013	.03652	.03292	.02353
OHIO	.06529	.05345	.04637	.04359	.03998	.03776	.03436	.03096	.02212
OKLAHOMA	.03712	.03317	.03263	.02826	.02738	.02559	.02430	.02234	.01644
OREGON	.07633	.05687	.05012	.04629	.04275	.04166	.03702	.03208	.02348
PENNSYLVANIA	.04520	.03954	.03409	.03059	.02862	.02666	.02433	.02265	.01881
RHODE ISLAND	.06376	.05574	.04808	.04314	.04035	.03758	.03430	.03193	.02653
SOUTH CAROLINA	.02275	.02033	.02000	.01732	.01677	.01568	.01489	.01369	.01003
SOUTH DAKOTA	.08720	.07137	.06191	.05823	.05341	.05043	.04592	.04138	.02956
TENNESSEE	.03355	.02999	.02951	.02556	.02476	.02314	.02198	.02021	.01487
TEXAS	.04616	.04125	.04058	.03515	.03404	.03182	.03022	.02779	.02044
UTAH	.07163	.05329	.04701	.04339	.04007	.03903	.03469	.03007	.02200
VERMONT	.07716	.06726	.05812	.05212	.04874	.04538	.04142	.03859	.03205
VIRGINIA	.03349	.02993	.02944	.02549	.02469	.02308	.02215	.02016	.01483
WASHINGTON	.05374	.04002	.03529	.03260	.03011	.02933	.02606	.02259	.01653
WEST VIRGINIA	.02883	.02571	.02531	.02191	.02122	.01983	.01884	.01732	.01274
WISCONSIN	.08995	.07360	.06390	.06006	.05508	.05201	.04733	.04265	.03047
WYOMING	.08119	.06051	.05326	.04907	.04533	.04417	.03923	.03400	.02490

Table D-13
Effective Rates of Taxation: Property Tax (Allocator-Consumption)

	$ 0- 1,999	2,000- 2,999	3,000- 3,999	4,000- 4,999	5,000- 5,999	6,000- 7,499	7,500- 9,999	10,000- 14,999	OVER 15,000
ALABAMA	.01814	.01622	.01599	.01414	.01368	.01270	.01195	.01098	.00773
ALASKA	.03282	.02436	.02335	.02076	.01900	.01899	.01714	.01527	.01093
ARIZONA	.06843	.05071	.04876	.04352	.03980	.03976	.03592	.03200	.02291
ARKANSAS	.02876	.02574	.02536	.02243	.02170	.02015	.01895	.01741	.01225
CALIFORNIA	.08772	.06502	.06251	.05581	.05105	.05100	.04607	.04104	.02939
COLORADO	.07744	.05735	.05516	.04923	.04504	.04499	.04064	.03621	.02592
CONNECTICUT	.06505	.05751	.05238	.04822	.04450	.04270	.03965	.03675	.02814
DELAWARE	.02051	.01835	.01807	.01598	.01547	.01435	.01350	.01240	.00873
FLORIDA	.04936	.04418	.04353	.03851	.03726	.03459	.03253	.02989	.02104
GEORGIA	.03367	.03013	.02968	.02625	.02540	.02358	.02218	.02038	.01434
HAWAII	.03015	.02235	.02149	.01919	.01755	.01753	.01583	.01410	.01009
IDAHO	.06945	.05151	.04949	.04416	.04039	.04036	.03644	.03247	.02326
ILLINOIS	.06656	.05515	.04879	.04624	.04251	.03976	.03762	.03448	.02461
INDIANA	.06720	.05567	.04928	.04671	.04292	.04015	.03799	.03481	.02485
IOWA	.08258	.06841	.06053	.05738	.05275	.04934	.04668	.04278	.03054
KANSAS	.08169	.06773	.05994	.05680	.05222	.04884	.04622	.04235	.03023
KENTUCKY	.03041	.02721	.02681	.02372	.02294	.02130	.02003	.01841	.01295
LOUISIANA	.03060	.02738	.02697	.02386	.02309	.02143	.02016	.01852	.01303
MAINE	.07197	.06352	.05785	.05327	.04917	.04717	.04380	.04061	.03109
MARYLAND	.04203	.03761	.03706	.03277	.03171	.02944	.02769	.02544	.01790

MASSACHUSETTS	.08633	.07632	.06954	.06400	.05907	.05668	.05264	.04879	.03735
MICHIGAN	.06863	.05687	.05032	.04770	.04384	.04101	.03881	.03665	.02538
MINNESOTA	.08853	.07341	.06495	.06157	.05660	.05293	.05009	.04590	.03277
MISSISSIPPI	.03643	.03258	.03211	.02841	.02748	.02552	.02399	.02205	.01552
MISSOURI	.04809	.03987	.03528	.03344	.03074	.02875	.02721	.02493	.01780
MONTANA	.08246	.06109	.05868	.05241	.04794	.04789	.04325	.03854	.02759
NEBRASKA	.07933	.06577	.05818	.05517	.05072	.04742	.04487	.04113	.02935
NEVADA	.04282	.03184	.03050	.02721	.02488	.02485	.02245	.02000	.01432
NEW HAMPSHIRE	.07941	.07012	.06371	.05865	.05412	.05193	.04823	.04470	.03423
NEW JERSEY	.07596	.06716	.06116	.05629	.05195	.04985	.04630	.04291	.03285
NEW MEXICO	.03669	.02720	.02613	.02334	.02135	.02132	.01926	.01716	.01229
NEW YORK	.06918	.06115	.05570	.05127	.04732	.04541	.04217	.03909	.02993
NORTH CAROLINA	.02953	.02644	.02605	.02304	.02230	.02070	.01947	.01789	.01259
NORTH DAKOTA	.06621	.05487	.04858	.04603	.04231	.03957	.03743	.03431	.02450
OHIO	.06166	.05111	.04521	.04286	.03940	.03685	.03487	.03195	.02281
OKLAHOMA	.03689	.03301	.03252	.02877	.02784	.02584	.02430	.02233	.01572
OREGON	.07140	.05293	.05088	.04543	.04154	.04151	.03749	.03341	.02392
PENNSYLVANIA	.04129	.03652	.03326	.03062	.02826	.02712	.02519	.02334	.01787
RHODE ISLAND	.05825	.05149	.04691	.04319	.03985	.03824	.03551	.03292	.02520
SOUTH CAROLINA	.02259	.02021	.01992	.01762	.01704	.01583	.01488	.01367	.00959
SOUTH DAKOTA	.08339	.06911	.06111	.05795	.05328	.04982	.04715	.04321	.03084
TENNESSEE	.03334	.02984	.02941	.02601	.02517	.02337	.02198	.02019	.01421
TEXAS	.04592	.04109	.04049	.03582	.03465	.03217	.03025	.02780	.01956
UTAH	.06699	.04959	.04770	.04257	.03894	.03889	.03513	.03130	.02241
VERMONT	.07090	.06249	.05701	.05246	.04838	.04641	.04311	.03998	.03062
VIRGINIA	.03332	.02981	.02937	.02598	.02514	.02334	.02218	.02017	.01419
WASHINGTON	.05012	.03715	.03573	.03191	.02918	.02915	.02633	.02346	.01679
WEST VIRGINIA	.02862	.02556	.02519	.02228	.02155	.02001	.01882	.01729	.01217
WISCONSIN	.08511	.07052	.06242	.05916	.05438	.05086	.04813	.04410	.03148
WYOMING	.07587	.05627	.05401	.04811	.04402	.04398	.03970	.03537	.02534

Table D-14
Effective Rates of Taxation: Property Tax (Allocator-1/2 Property Taxes, 1/2 Consumption)

	$ 0- 1,999	2,000- 2,999	3,000- 3,999	4,000- 4,999	5,000- 5,999	6,000- 7,499	7,500- 9,999	10,000- 14,999	OVER 15,000
ALABAMA	.01475	.01347	.01311	.01187	.01261	.01346	.01313	.01258	.01129
ALASKA	.03351	.02264	.01782	.01657	.01705	.01890	.01684	.01574	.01244
ARIZONA	.07237	.04867	.03811	.03564	.03681	.04095	.03651	.03418	.02711
ARKANSAS	.02396	.02193	.02131	.01932	.02059	.02207	.02156	.02068	.01866
CALIFORNIA	.09082	.06120	.04816	.04500	.04634	.05145	.04588	.04291	.03397
COLORADO	.08204	.05512	.04317	.04037	.04171	.04642	.04138	.03874	.03074
CONNECTICUT	.06727	.05523	.04419	.04150	.04107	.04159	.03946	.03859	.03123
DELAWARE	.01566	.01428	.01390	.01256	.01322	.01394	.01356	.01295	.01143
FLORIDA	.03914	.03576	.03478	.03148	.03332	.03539	.03450	.03301	.02943
GEORGIA	.02709	.02476	.02407	.02180	.02312	.02463	.02402	.02300	.02058
HAWAII	.03144	.02118	.01664	.01555	.01603	.01781	.01587	.01485	.01176
IDAHO	.07492	.05033	.03921	.03670	.03800	.04237	.03776	.03538	.02812
ILLINOIS	.05942	.05300	.04391	.03988	.03905	.04028	.03782	.03430	.02896
INDIANA	.06091	.05440	.04503	.04087	.04006	.04140	.03886	.03525	.02984
IOWA	.07546	.06743	.05576	.05060	.04964	.05134	.04819	.04370	.03705
KANSAS	.07438	.06650	.05502	.04991	.04897	.05061	.04752	.04309	.03651
KENTUCKY	.02464	.02252	.02190	.01983	.02105	.02246	.02191	.02099	.01882
LOUISIANA	.02448	.02237	.02175	.01969	.02087	.02221	.02166	.02073	.01853
MAINE	.07781	.06357	.05055	.04754	.04721	.04791	.04550	.04459	.03617
MARYLAND	.03219	.02937	.02860	.02584	.02721	.02871	.02794	.02669	.02357

MASSACHUSETTS	.09043	.07417	.05925	.05566	.05514	.05587	.05304	.05189	.04203
MICHIGAN	.06174	.05511	.04563	.04144	.04060	.04192	.03935	.03679	.03018
MINNESOTA	.08029	.07177	.05939	.05390	.05285	.05461	.05127	.04650	.03937
MISSISSIPPI	.03037	.02778	.02700	.02449	.02609	.02798	.02733	.02621	.02366
MISSOURI	.04375	.03911	.03236	.02937	.02880	.02977	.02795	.02534	.02147
MONTANA	.08847	.05940	.04632	.04338	.04489	.05001	.04458	.04176	.03317
NEBRASKA	.07266	.06500	.05373	.04876	.04784	.04949	.04645	.04213	.03572
NEVADA	.04443	.03004	.02353	.02197	.02263	.02512	.02241	.02096	.01660
NEW HAMPSHIRE	.08465	.06927	.05505	.05174	.05131	.05205	.04942	.04839	.03923
NEW JERSEY	.07860	.06454	.05161	.04847	.04797	.04858	.04610	.04508	.03648
NEW MEXICO	.03886	.02614	.02045	.01914	.01977	.02199	.01961	.01836	.01456
NEW YORK	.07191	.05901	.04718	.04431	.04387	.04444	.04218	.04125	.03339
NORTH CAROLINA	.02413	.02208	.02146	.01944	.02066	.02208	.02155	.02065	.01855
NORTH DAKOTA	.06109	.05466	.04520	.04097	.04022	.04164	.03908	.03544	.03010
OHIO	.05554	.04960	.04105	.03728	.03654	.03772	.03541	.03212	.02716
OKLAHOMA	.02952	.02697	.02623	.02375	.02517	.02678	.02612	.02500	.02234
OREGON	.07559	.05084	.03979	.03723	.03845	.04279	.03815	.03572	.02833
PENNSYLVANIA	.04364	.03578	.02854	.02682	.02659	.02696	.02559	.02505	.02029
RHODE ISLAND	.06194	.05074	.04045	.03802	.03769	.03823	.03630	.03554	.02881
SOUTH CAROLINA	.01850	.01691	.01645	.01490	.01584	.01694	.01653	.01584	.01419
SOUTH DAKOTA	.07713	.06902	.05699	.05169	.05077	.05257	.04935	.04475	.03800
TENNESSEE	.02709	.02477	.02409	.02182	.02317	.02473	.02413	.02312	.02074
TEXAS	.03627	.03312	.03223	.02916	.03084	.03274	.03191	.03053	.02719
UTAH	.07123	.04783	.03742	.03500	.03618	.04026	.03590	.03362	.02667
VERMONT	.07625	.06223	.04960	.04661	.04623	.04690	.04455	.04367	.03542
VIRGINIA	.02625	.02396	.02331	.02109	.02230	.02366	.02330	.02205	.01963
WASHINGTON	.05265	.03543	.02780	.02600	.02683	.02982	.02659	.02489	.01973
WEST VIRGINIA	.02309	.02106	.02049	.01855	.01967	.02097	.02046	.01959	.01754
WISCONSIN	.07692	.06868	.05687	.05162	.05060	.05226	.04906	.04449	.03765
WYOMING	.08041	.05411	.04227	.03946	.04078	.04539	.04044	.03787	.03006

Table D-15
Effective Rates of Taxation: Other Selective Sales Taxes (Allocator-Consumption)

	$ 0- 1,999	2,000- 2,999	3,000- 3,999	4,000- 4,999	5,000- 5,999	6,000- 7,499	7,5.00- 9,999	10,000- 14,999	OVER 15,000
ALABAMA	.00174	.00155	.00153	.00135	.00131	.00122	.00114	.00105	.00074
ALASKA	.00239	.00177	.00170	.00151	.00138	.00138	.00125	.00111	.00079
ARIZONA	.00298	.00221	.00212	.00189	.00173	.00173	.00156	.00139	.00099
ARKANSAS	.00246	.00220	.00217	.00192	.00186	.00172	.00162	.00149	.00105
CALIFORNIA	.00422	.00313	.00301	.00268	.00245	.00245	.00221	.00197	.00141
COLORADO	.00272	.00201	.00194	.00173	.00158	.00158	.00143	.00127	.00091
CONNECTICUT	.00206	.00182	.00165	.00152	.00140	.00135	.00125	.00116	.00089
DELAWARE	.00529	.00473	.00466	.00412	.00399	.00370	.00348	.00320	.00225
FLORIDA	.00482	.00432	.00425	.00376	.00364	.00338	.00318	.00292	.00205
GEORGIA	.00176	.00157	.00155	.00137	.00132	.00123	.00116	.00106	.00075
HAWAII	.00140	.00104	.00099	.00089	.00081	.00081	.00073	.00065	.00046
IDAHO	.00308	.00228	.00219	.00196	.00179	.00179	.00161	.00144	.00103
ILLINOIS	.00288	.00238	.00211	.00200	.00184	.00172	.00162	.00149	.00106
INDIANA	.00094	.00078	.00069	.00065	.00060	.00056	.00053	.00048	.00034
IOWA	.00098	.00081	.00072	.00068	.00062	.00058	.00055	.00050	.00036
KANSAS	.00088	.00073	.00065	.00061	.00056	.00053	.00050	.00045	.00032
KENTUCKY	.00381	.00341	.00336	.00297	.00288	.00267	.00251	.00231	.00162
LOUISIANA	.00379	.00339	.00334	.00295	.00285	.00265	.00249	.00229	.00161
MAINE	.00213	.00188	.00171	.00157	.00145	.00139	.00129	.00120	.00092
MARYLAND	.00514	.00460	.00453	.00401	.00388	.00360	.00339	.00311	.00219

MASSACHUSETTS	.00378	.00334	.00305	.00280	.00259	.00248	.00231	.00214	.00163
MICHIGAN	.00189	.00157	.00139	.00131	.00121	.00113	.00107	.00101	.00070
MINNESOTA	.00168	.00139	.00123	.00116	.00107	.00100	.00095	.00087	.00062
MISSISSIPPI	.00286	.00255	.00252	.00223	.00215	.00200	.00188	.00173	.00121
MISSOURI	.00138	.00114	.00101	.00096	.00088	.00082	.00078	.00071	.00051
MONTANA	.00175	.00129	.00124	.00111	.00101	.00101	.00091	.00081	.00058
NEBRASKA	.00099	.00082	.00072	.00069	.00063	.00059	.00056	.00051	.00036
NEVADA	.02031	.01510	.01447	.01291	.01180	.01179	.01065	.00949	.00679
NEW HAMPSHIRE	.00775	.00684	.00621	.00572	.00528	.00506	.00470	.00436	.00334
NEW JERSEY	.00392	.00346	.00315	.00290	.00268	.00257	.00239	.00221	.00169
NEW MEXICO	.00231	.00171	.00164	.00147	.00134	.00134	.00121	.00108	.00077
NEW YORK	.00547	.00484	.00440	.00405	.00374	.00359	.00333	.00309	.00236
NORTH CAROLINA	.00137	.00123	.00121	.00107	.00104	.00096	.00090	.00083	.00058
NORTH DAKOTA	.00183	.00151	.00134	.00127	.00116	.00109	.00103	.00094	.00067
OHIO	.00201	.00167	.00148	.00140	.00129	.00120	.00114	.00104	.00074
OKLAHOMA	.00415	.00372	.00366	.00324	.00313	.00291	.00273	.00251	.00177
OREGON	.00235	.00174	.00167	.00149	.00136	.00136	.00123	.00110	.00078
PENNSYLVANIA	.00154	.00136	.00124	.00114	.00105	.00101	.00094	.00087	.00066
RHODE ISLAND	.00736	.00651	.00593	.00546	.00503	.00483	.00449	.00416	.00318
SOUTH CAROLINA	.00393	.00352	.00346	.00306	.00296	.00275	.00259	.00238	.00167
SOUTH DAKOTA	.00550	.00455	.00403	.00382	.00351	.00328	.00311	.00284	.00203
TENNESSEE	.00163	.00146	.00144	.00127	.00123	.00114	.00108	.00099	.00069
TEXAS	.00439	.00393	.00387	.00342	.00331	.00307	.00289	.00266	.00187
UTAH	.00223	.00165	.00159	.00142	.00130	.00130	.00117	.00104	.00074
VERMONT	.00583	.00513	.00468	.00431	.00397	.00381	.00354	.00328	.00251
VIRGINIA	.00153	.00137	.00135	.00119	.00115	.00107	.00101	.00092	.00065
WASHINGTON	.00546	.00405	.00389	.00348	.00318	.00318	.00287	.00255	.00183
WEST VIRGINIA	.00765	.00683	.00673	.00596	.00576	.00535	.00503	.00462	.00325
WISCONSIN	.00121	.00100	.00089	.00084	.00077	.00072	.00068	.00062	.00044
WYOMING	.00157	.00117	.00112	.00100	.00091	.00091	.00082	.00073	.00052

Table D-16
Effective Rates of Taxation: All Other Taxes (Allocator-Consumption)

	$ 0- 1,999	2,000- 2,999	3,000- 3,999	4,000- 4,999	5,000- 5,999	6,000- 7,499	7,500- 9,999	10,000- 14,999	OVER 15,000
ALABAMA	.01134	.01014	.00999	.00884	.00855	.00794	.00747	.00686	.00483
ALASKA	.02872	.02132	.02044	.01817	.01663	.01662	.01500	.01336	.00957
ARIZONA	.00891	.00660	.00635	.00566	.00518	.00517	.00467	.00416	.00298
ARKANSAS	.01324	.01185	.01168	.01033	.00999	.00928	.00873	.00802	.00564
CALIFORNIA	.00927	.00687	.00661	.00590	.00540	.00539	.00487	.00434	.00310
COLORADO	.01292	.00956	.00920	.00821	.00751	.00750	.00678	.00604	.00432
CONNECTICUT	.00480	.00424	.00387	.00356	.00328	.00315	.00293	.00271	.00207
DELAWARE	.00832	.00744	.00733	.00648	.00627	.00582	.00547	.00503	.00354
FLORIDA	.01662	.01488	.01466	.01297	.01255	.01165	.01095	.01007	.00708
GEORGIA	.00732	.00655	.00645	.00571	.00552	.00513	.00482	.00443	.00312
HAWAII	.00934	.00693	.00666	.00594	.00544	.00543	.00490	.00437	.00313
IDAHO	.02177	.01614	.01551	.01384	.01266	.01265	.01142	.01017	.00729
ILLINOIS	.01078	.00893	.00790	.00749	.00688	.00643	.00609	.00558	.00398
INDIANA	.00768	.00636	.00563	.00533	.00490	.00458	.00434	.00397	.00284
IOWA	.01242	.01029	.00910	.00863	.00793	.00742	.00702	.00643	.00459
KANSAS	.01120	.00929	.00822	.00779	.00716	.00670	.00634	.00581	.00414
KENTUCKY	.00728	.00651	.00641	.00567	.00549	.00510	.00479	.00440	.00310
LOUISIANA	.02800	.02506	.02468	.02184	.02113	.01961	.01845	.01695	.01193
MAINE	.01213	.01071	.00975	.00898	.00829	.00795	.00738	.00684	.00524
MARYLAND	.00909	.00813	.00801	.00709	.00686	.00636	.00599	.00550	.00387

MASSACHUSETTS	.00652	.00577	.00525	.00483	.00446	.00428	.00398	.00368	.00282
MICHIGAN	.01964	.01628	.01440	.01365	.01255	.01174	.01110	.01049	.00726
MINNESOTA	.01377	.01142	.01010	.00958	.00880	.00823	.00779	.00714	.00510
MISSISSIPPI	.01351	.01208	.01191	.01053	.01019	.00946	.00890	.00818	.00575
MISSOURI	.01187	.00984	.00871	.00825	.00759	.00709	.00671	.00615	.00439
MONTANA	.01654	.01225	.01177	.01051	.00962	.00960	.00867	.00773	.00553
NEBRASKA	.01147	.00950	.00841	.00797	.00733	.00685	.00648	.00594	.00424
NEVADA	.03319	.02468	.02364	.02109	.01928	.01926	.01740	.01550	.01110
NEW HAMPSHIRE	.01303	.01150	.01045	.00962	.00888	.00852	.00791	.00733	.00561
NEW JERSEY	.00839	.00742	.00675	.00622	.00574	.00550	.00511	.00474	.00363
NEW MEXICO	.02754	.02041	.01961	.01752	.01602	.01600	.01445	.01288	.00922
NEW YORK	.00996	.00880	.00802	.00738	.00681	.00653	.00607	.00562	.00430
NORTH CAROLINA	.00901	.00807	.00795	.00703	.00680	.00632	.00594	.00546	.00384
NORTH DAKOTA	.01852	.01535	.01359	.01288	.01183	.01107	.01047	.00960	.00685
OHIO	.01248	.01034	.00915	.00867	.00797	.00745	.00705	.00646	.00461
OKLAHOMA	.01792	.01603	.01579	.01397	.01352	.01255	.01180	.01084	.00763
OREGON	.01738	.01288	.01239	.01106	.01011	.01010	.00913	.00813	.00582
PENNSYLVANIA	.01403	.01240	.01130	.01040	.00960	.00921	.00855	.00793	.00607
RHODE ISLAND	.00925	.00817	.00745	.00686	.00633	.00607	.00564	.00523	.00400
SOUTH CAROLINA	.00858	.00767	.00756	.00669	.00647	.00601	.00565	.00519	.00364
SOUTH DAKOTA	.01567	.01298	.01148	.01088	.01001	.00936	.00886	.00811	.00579
TENNESSEE	.01151	.01030	.01015	.00898	.00869	.00807	.00759	.00697	.00491
TEXAS	.01658	.01483	.01461	.01293	.01251	.01161	.01092	.01003	.00706
UTAH	.01399	.01036	.00996	.00889	.00813	.00812	.00734	.00654	.00468
VERMONT	.01984	.01748	.01595	.01468	.01354	.01298	.01206	.01118	.00856
VIRGINIA	.01423	.01273	.01255	.01110	.01074	.00997	.00947	.00861	.00606
WASHINGTON	.01320	.00978	.00941	.00840	.00768	.00767	.00693	.00618	.00442
WEST VIRGINIA	.01244	.01111	.01095	.00968	.00936	.00869	.00818	.00751	.00529
WISCONSIN	.01025	.00850	.00752	.00713	.00655	.00613	.00580	.00531	.00379
WYOMING	.02547	.01889	.01813	.01615	.01477	.01476	.01333	.01187	.00850

Table D-17
Effective Rates of Taxation: Personal Income Tax (Allocator-Personal Income Tax Payments)

	$ 0- 1,999	2,000- 2,999	3,000- 3,999	4,000- 4,999	5,000- 5,999	6,000- 7,499	7,500- 9,999	10,000- 14,999	OVER 15,000
ALABAMA	.00000	.00000	.00000	.00060	.00175	.00345	.00603	.00951	.01459
ALASKA	.00335	.00609	.00804	.00883	.00983	.01122	.01267	.01515	.02301
ARIZONA	.00000	.00000	.00028	.00066	.00119	.00196	.00325	.00517	.00967
ARKANSAS	.00000	.00000	.00000	.00000	.00000	.00189	.00346	.00695	.01938
CALIFORNIA	.00000	.00000	.00000	.00044	.00082	.00148	.00261	.00571	.01339
COLORADO	.00000	.00034	.00261	.00364	.00502	.00694	.00916	.01287	.02414
CONNECTICUT	.00000	.00000	.00000	.00000	.00000	.00000	.00000	.00000	.00000
DELAWARE	.00019	.00069	.00390	.00619	.00817	.00873	.01612	.02092	.02797
FLORIDA	.00000	.00000	.00000	.00000	.00000	.00000	.00000	.00000	.00000
GEORGIA	.00000	.00000	.00000	.00017	.00064	.00197	.00499	.00947	.01644
HAWAII	.00105	.00364	.00640	.00772	.00959	.01162	.01404	.01724	.02469
IDAHO	.00000	.00196	.00374	.00554	.00766	.01117	.01518	.02070	.03000
ILLINOIS	.00000	.00000	.00000	.00000	.00000	.00000	.00000	.00000	.00000
INDIANA	.00000	.00000	.00000	.00000	.00000	.00000	.00000	.00000	.00000
IOWA	.00000	.00000	.00033	.00125	.00235	.00436	.00744	.00929	.01270
KANSAS	.00000	.00070	.00134	.00177	.00253	.00354	.00486	.00491	.01150
KENTUCKY	.00000	.00000	.00000	.00120	.00293	.00551	.00798	.01660	.03314
LOUISIANA	.00000	.00000	.00000	.00000	.00000	.00077	.00237	.00404	.01002
MAINE	.00000	.00000	.00000	.00000	.00000	.00000	.00000	.00000	.00000
MARYLAND	.00000	.00151	.00739	.00656	.00731	.00843	.00953	.01072	.01248

MASSACHUSETTS	.00000	.00000	.00372	.00626	.00800	.00933	.01074	.01224	.01413
MICHIGAN	.00000	.00000	.00000	.00000	.00000	.00000	.00000	.00000	.00000
MINNESOTA	.00000	.00021	.00152	.00345	.00526	.00793	.01209	.01859	.03470
MISSISSIPPI	.00000	.00000	.00000	.00000	.00000	.00000	.00000	.00222	.01860
MISSOURI	.00000	.00000	.00000	.00162	.00304	.00489	.00740	.01101	.01868
MONTANA	.00000	.00058	.00134	.00216	.00325	.00523	.00745	.01144	.02061
NEBRASKA	.00000	.00000	.00000	.00000	.00000	.00000	.00000	.00000	.00000
NEVADA	.00000	.00000	.00000	.00000	.00000	.00000	.00000	.00000	.00000
NEW HAMPSHIRE	.00000	.00000	.00000	.00000	.00000	.00000	.00000	.00000	.00857
NEW JERSEY	.00003	.00007	.00012	.00015	.00018	.00022	.00028	.00041	.00065
NEW MEXICO	.00000	.00000	.00131	.00287	.00385	.00486	.00578	.00657	.01154
NEW YORK	.00000	.00280	.00490	.00623	.00765	.00909	.01149	.01511	.03062
NORTH CAROLINA	.00000	.00000	.00211	.00471	.00631	.00862	.01131	.01573	.02602
NORTH DAKOTA	.00000	.00000	.00033	.00092	.00123	.00154	.00246	.00622	.01946
OHIO	.01198	.00733	.00521	.00394	.00321	.00258	.00200	.00144	.00071
OKLAHOMA	.00000	.00000	.00049	.00118	.00186	.00305	.00475	.00837	.01427
OREGON	.00073	.00323	.00630	.00839	.01108	.01421	.01823	.02250	.02944
PENNSYLVANIA	.00456	.00446	.00442	.00444	.00446	.00450	.00448	.00450	.00448
RHODE ISLAND	.00000	.00000	.00000	.00000	.00000	.00000	.00000	.00000	.00000
SOUTH CAROLINA	.00000	.00000	.00000	.00209	.00298	.00481	.00685	.01095	.02450
SOUTH DAKOTA	.00000	.00000	.00000	.00000	.00000	.00000	.00000	.00000	.00000
TENNESSEE	.00030	.00036	.00038	.00019	.00031	.00025	.00038	.00107	.00374
TEXAS	.00000	.00000	.00000	.00000	.00000	.00000	.00000	.00000	.00000
UTAH	.00023	.00077	.00159	.00227	.00343	.00524	.00769	.01031	.01434
VERMONT	.00039	.00240	.00437	.00687	.00852	.01087	.01405	.02327	.02844
VIRGINIA	.00000	.00105	.00386	.00392	.00497	.00657	.01090	.01193	.01581
WASHINGTON	.00000	.00000	.00000	.00000	.00000	.00000	.00000	.00000	.00000
WEST VIRGINIA	.00000	.00080	.00281	.00400	.00439	.00513	.00576	.00710	.01166
WISCONSIN	.00000	.00000	.00289	.00439	.00524	.00771	.00842	.01568	.03934
WYOMING	.00000	.00000	.00000	.00000	.00000	.00000	.00000	.00000	.00000

Table D-18
Effective Rates of Taxation: Death and Gift Taxes (Allocator-All to Highest Income Class)

	OVER 15,000
ALABAMA	.00042
ALASKA	.00025
ARIZONA	.00040
ARKANSAS	.00068
CALIFORNIA	.00449
COLORADO	.00643
CONNECTICUT	.00758
DELAWARE	.00627
FLORIDA	.00050
GEORGIA	.00036
HAWAII	.00208
IDAHO	.00328
ILLINOIS	.00332
INDIANA	.00352
IOWA	.00930
KANSAS	.00434
KENTUCKY	.00618
LOUISIANA	.00332
MAINE	.01823
MARYLAND	.00232

MASSACHUSETTS	.00623
MICHIGAN	.00039
MINNESOTA	.00494
MISSISSIPPI	.00274
MISSOURI	.00268
MONTANA	.01001
NEBRASKA	.00085
NEVADA	.00000
NEW HAMPSHIRE	.01321
NEW JERSEY	.00472
NEW MEXICO	.00102
NEW YORK	.00296
NORTH CAROLINA	.00552
NORTH DAKOTA	.00225
OHIO	.00096
OKLAHOMA	.00847
OREGON	.01081
PENNSYLVANIA	.01004
RHODE ISLAND	.00391
SOUTH CAROLINA	.00129
SOUTH DAKOTA	.00499
TENNESSEE	.00679
TEXAS	.00185
UTAH	.00456
VERMONT	.01016
VIRGINIA	.00233
WASHINGTON	.00779
WEST VIRGINIA	.00615
WISCONSIN	.00943
WYOMING	.00209

Table D-19
Effective Rates of Taxation: Imported Taxes (Allocator-Consumption)

	$ 0- 1,999	2,000- 2,999	3,000- 3,999	4,000- 4,999	5,000- 5,999	6,000- 7,499	7,500- 9,999	10,000- 14,999	OVER 15,000
ALABAMA	.01970	.01762	.01736	.01536	.01486	.01380	.01297	.01192	.00839
ALASKA	.02119	.01573	.01508	.01340	.01227	.01226	.01107	.00986	.00706
ARIZONA	.02190	.01623	.01560	.01392	.01274	.01272	.01149	.01024	.00733
ARKANSAS	.01801	.01611	.01587	.01404	.01359	.01261	.01186	.01090	.00767
CALIFORNIA	.02152	.01595	.01534	.01369	.01252	.01251	.01130	.01007	.00721
COLORADO	.02170	.01607	.01546	.01379	.01262	.01261	.01139	.01014	.00726
CONNECTICUT	.01940	.01715	.01562	.01438	.01327	.01273	.01183	.01096	.00839
DELAWARE	.01536	.01373	.01353	.01196	.01158	.01075	.01011	.00929	.00653
FLORIDA	.01774	.01588	.01564	.01384	.01339	.01243	.01169	.01074	.00756
GEORGIA	.01822	.01630	.01605	.01420	.01374	.01276	.01200	.01102	.00776
HAWAII	.02144	.01590	.01529	.01365	.01248	.01247	.01126	.01003	.00718
IDAHO	.02515	.01865	.01792	.01599	.01463	.01461	.01320	.01176	.00842
ILLINOIS	.02039	.01690	.01495	.01417	.01302	.01218	.01153	.01056	.00754
INDIANA	.02130	.01765	.01562	.01481	.01361	.01273	.01204	.01104	.00788
IOWA	.02046	.01695	.01500	.01422	.01307	.01222	.01156	.01060	.00756
KANSAS	.02109	.01749	.01547	.01466	.01348	.01261	.01193	.01093	.00780
KENTUCKY	.01869	.01672	.01648	.01457	.01410	.01309	.01231	.01131	.00796
LOUISIANA	.01916	.01715	.01689	.01494	.01446	.01342	.01262	.01160	.00816
MAINE	.02020	.01783	.01624	.01495	.01380	.01324	.01229	.01140	.00872
MARYLAND	.01774	.01588	.01565	.01384	.01339	.01243	.01169	.01074	.00756

MASSACHUSETTS	.01953	.01726	.01573	.01448	.01336	.01282	.01191	.01104	.00845
MICHIGAN	.02140	.01773	.01569	.01487	.01367	.01279	.01210	.01143	.00791
MINNESOTA	.02059	.01707	.01511	.01432	.01316	.01231	.01165	.01067	.00762
MISSISSIPPI	.01837	.01643	.01619	.01433	.01386	.01287	.01210	.01112	.00782
MISSOURI	.01946	.01613	.01427	.01353	.01244	.01163	.01101	.01008	.00720
MONTANA	.02264	.01677	.01611	.01439	.01316	.01315	.01187	.01058	.00757
NEBRASKA	.01871	.01551	.01372	.01301	.01196	.01118	.01058	.00970	.00692
NEVADA	.01783	.01326	.01270	.01133	.01036	.01035	.00935	.00833	.00596
NEW HAMPSHIRE	.02078	.01835	.01667	.01535	.01416	.01359	.01262	.01170	.00896
NEW JERSEY	.02061	.01822	.01659	.01527	.01409	.01352	.01256	.01164	.00891
NEW MEXICO	.02508	.01859	.01786	.01595	.01459	.01457	.01316	.01173	.00840
NEW YORK	.01897	.01676	.01527	.01406	.01297	.01245	.01156	.01072	.00820
NORTH CAROLINA	.01697	.01519	.01497	.01324	.01281	.01189	.01118	.01028	.00723
NORTH DAKOTA	.01707	.01415	.01253	.01187	.01091	.01020	.00965	.00885	.00632
OHIO	.02125	.01761	.01558	.01477	.01358	.01270	.01202	.01101	.00786
OKLAHOMA	.01893	.01694	.01669	.01476	.01429	.01326	.01247	.01146	.00806
OREGON	.02444	.01812	.01742	.01555	.01422	.01421	.01284	.01144	.00819
PENNSYLVANIA	.02102	.01859	.01693	.01559	.01439	.01380	.01282	.01188	.00910
RHODE ISLAND	.01987	.01757	.01600	.01473	.01359	.01304	.01211	.01123	.00860
SOUTH CAROLINA	.01802	.01612	.01589	.01405	.01359	.01262	.01187	.01091	.00765
SOUTH DAKOTA	.01735	.01438	.01272	.01206	.01109	.01037	.00981	.00899	.00642
TENNESSEE	.01863	.01668	.01643	.01454	.01407	.01306	.01228	.01128	.00794
TEXAS	.01822	.01630	.01606	.01421	.01375	.01276	.01200	.01103	.00776
UTAH	.02388	.01768	.01701	.01518	.01388	.01386	.01252	.01116	.00799
VERMONT	.02022	.01782	.01626	.01496	.01379	.01323	.01229	.01140	.00873
VIRGINIA	.01808	.01618	.01594	.01410	.01364	.01266	.01203	.01094	.00770
WASHINGTON	.02360	.01749	.01682	.01502	.01374	.01372	.01240	.01105	.00791
WEST VIRGINIA	.01987	.01774	.01748	.01546	.01496	.01389	.01306	.01200	.00845
WISCONSIN	.02136	.01770	.01566	.01485	.01365	.01276	.01207	.01106	.00790
WYOMING	.02430	.01802	.01730	.01541	.01410	.01409	.01271	.01133	.00811

Table D-20
Effective Rates of Taxation: Total Taxes (Allocator-Consumption)

	$ 0- 1,999	2,000- 2,999	3,000- 3,999	4,000- 4,999	5,000- 5,999	6,000- 7,499	7,500- 9,999	10,000- 14,999	OVER 15,000
ALABAMA	.11951	.10688	.10534	.09317	.09016	.08371	.07872	.07234	.05091
ALASKA	.16343	.12132	.11630	.10339	.09465	.09460	.08537	.07604	.05444
ARIZONA	.19260	.14272	.13724	.12248	.11203	.11191	.10109	.09006	.06448
ARKANSAS	.12472	.11162	.10996	.09727	.09411	.08738	.08218	.07550	.05315
CALIFORNIA	.20612	.15278	.14690	.13116	.11996	.11985	.10825	.09645	.06906
COLORADO	.19262	.14265	.13722	.12247	.11203	.11193	.10110	.09007	.06449
CONNECTICUT	.14273	.12619	.11495	.10581	.09764	.09369	.08701	.08065	.06174
DELAWARE	.12143	.10862	.10698	.09463	.09159	.08499	.07994	.07344	.05169
FLORIDA	.14002	.12534	.12349	.10924	.10569	.09812	.09229	.08480	.05968
GEORGIA	.12645	.11314	.11145	.09859	.09539	.08857	.08329	.07654	.05387
HAWAII	.21543	.15975	.15358	.13714	.12541	.12528	.11311	.10078	.07216
IDAHO	.18155	.13465	.12938	.11545	.10558	.10550	.09527	.08488	.06080
ILLINOIS	.15466	.12815	.11338	.10746	.09879	.09239	.08742	.08011	.05719
INDIANA	.14891	.12336	.10919	.10350	.09512	.08898	.08419	.07715	.05508
IOWA	.17629	.14604	.12921	.12250	.11262	.10532	.09965	.09132	.06519
KANSAS	.17965	.14896	.13181	.12491	.11486	.10741	.10165	.09314	.06649
KENTUCKY	.12572	.11250	.11084	.09805	.09486	.08806	.08283	.07611	.05357
LOUISIANA	.16722	.14964	.14740	.13040	.12616	.11713	.11016	.10122	.07123
MAINE	.15509	.13688	.12466	.11479	.10596	.10164	.09439	.08751	.06699
MARYLAND	.13101	.11725	.11552	.10217	.09887	.09178	.08632	.07932	.05582

MASSACHUSETTS	.16270	.14383	.13105	.12062	.11132	.10681	.09921	.09196	.07040
MICHIGAN	.17325	.14356	.12702	.12041	.11068	.10353	.09796	.09252	.06408
MINNESOTA	.19339	.16035	.14188	.13449	.12364	.11563	.10942	.10027	.07159
MISSISSIPPI	.14775	.13214	.13023	.11523	.11146	.10350	.09731	.08943	.06295
MISSOURI	.13354	.11071	.09796	.09286	.08537	.07984	.07555	.06923	.04942
MONTANA	.18920	.14017	.13464	.12025	.11000	.10987	.09924	.08843	.06332
NEBRASKA	.13577	.11256	.09957	.09441	.08680	.08116	.07680	.07038	.05024
NEVADA	.16979	.12627	.12096	.10791	.09867	.09855	.08904	.07932	.05680
NEW HAMPSHIRE	.14179	.12520	.11376	.10472	.09663	.09272	.08612	.07981	.06112
NEW JERSEY	.13989	.12369	.11263	.10367	.09567	.09180	.08526	.07903	.06050
NEW MEXICO	.18275	.13549	.13018	.11626	.10634	.10619	.09594	.08547	.06121
NEW YORK	.17669	.15618	.14227	.13096	.12086	.11597	.10772	.09985	.07644
NORTH CAROLINA	.12689	.11361	.11195	.09901	.09580	.08894	.08366	.07687	.05410
NORTH DAKOTA	.15676	.12991	.11502	.10898	.10017	.09369	.08863	.08124	.05801
OHIO	.14408	.11944	.10566	.10016	.09208	.08611	.08148	.07467	.05330
OKLAHOMA	.14247	.12747	.12559	.11110	.10751	.09981	.09386	.08624	.06070
OREGON	.18021	.13359	.12842	.11467	.10486	.10478	.09464	.08432	.06037
PENNSYLVANIA	.13768	.12176	.11090	.10210	.09422	.09042	.08397	.07784	.05959
RHODE ISLAND	.14264	.12608	.11487	.10576	.09757	.09363	.08695	.08061	.06172
SOUTH CAROLINA	.12336	.11037	.10878	.09621	.09308	.08644	.08128	.07468	.05237
SOUTH DAKOTA	.16722	.13857	.12253	.11620	.10683	.09990	.09455	.08664	.06184
TENNESSEE	.12096	.10825	.10669	.09438	.09132	.08477	.07973	.07326	.05157
TEXAS	.13460	.12043	.11867	.10498	.10156	.09428	.08868	.08148	.05735
UTAH	.19068	.14117	.13579	.12118	.11083	.11070	.10001	.08910	.06379
VERMONT	.17743	.15637	.14267	.13127	.12108	.11614	.10787	.10005	.07662
VIRGINIA	.11066	.09900	.09753	.08628	.08348	.07750	.07365	.06698	.04714
WASHINGTON	.19384	.14367	.13819	.12340	.11287	.11274	.10183	.09074	.06496
WEST VIRGINIA	.13621	.12163	.11988	.10603	.10256	.09522	.08956	.08229	.05792
WISCONSIN	.18263	.15132	.13394	.12695	.11669	.10913	.10326	.09462	.06755
WYOMING	.18972	.14072	.13506	.12032	.11007	.10999	.09929	.08846	.06338

Table D-21
Effective Rates of Taxation: Total Taxes (Allocator-Sum of Effective Rates for Individual Taxes)

	$ 0- 1,999	2,000- 2,999	3,000- 3,999	4,000- 4,999	5,000- 5,999	6,000- 7,499	7,500- 9,999	10,000- 14,999	OVER 15,000
ALABAMA	.10209	.09367	.09498	.08518	.08283	.07989	.07626	.07525	.06426
ALASKA	.12548	.09690	.09721	.08912	.08335	.08257	.07811	.07300	.06465
ARIZONA	.16344	.12086	.11531	.10468	.09636	.09423	.08733	.07910	.06338
ARKANSAS	.10863	.09942	.10012	.08882	.08568	.08216	.07771	.07634	.07332
CALIFORNIA	.17619	.13027	.12505	.11318	.10384	.10230	.09451	.08693	.07937
COLORADO	.16008	.11894	.11572	.10552	.09825	.09756	.09196	.08614	.08497
CONNECTICUT	.13126	.11806	.10584	.09716	.09031	.08455	.07766	.07225	.06791
DELAWARE	.06470	.05937	.06266	.05815	.05833	.05559	.05945	.06134	.06534
FLORIDA	.12878	.11710	.11787	.10432	.09991	.09460	.08783	.08143	.05791
GEORGIA	.10759	.09825	.09927	.08815	.08493	.08154	.07869	.07870	.06904
HAWAII	.16289	.12250	.12146	.11051	.10343	.10250	.09717	.09083	.08034
IDAHO	.14781	.11163	.10991	.10106	.09478	.09542	.09241	.08842	.08332
ILLINOIS	.14797	.12213	.10759	.10125	.09274	.08688	.08043	.07219	.05389
INDIANA	.14402	.12024	.10729	.10178	.09315	.08700	.08118	.07281	.05421
IOWA	.15374	.12845	.11437	.10929	.10123	.09671	.09330	.08626	.07648
KANSAS	.15781	.13215	.11795	.11209	.10364	.09815	.09290	.08398	.07314
KENTUCKY	.09858	.09037	.09163	.08253	.08117	.07927	.07639	.08120	.08953
LOUISIANA	.13339	.12041	.12039	.10624	.10194	.09646	.09103	.08747	.07823
MAINE	.14595	.13273	.12114	.11196	.10456	.09851	.09021	.08312	.08245
MARYLAND	.10573	.09679	.10199	.08977	.08748	.08350	.07944	.07524	.06185

MASSACHUSETTS	.13781	.12402	.11404	.10713	.10211	.09727	.09153	.08782	.08754
MICHIGAN	.15977	.13503	.12089	.11374	.10427	.09769	.09075	.08447	.05829
MINNESOTA	.15564	.12928	.11574	.11094	.10381	.10042	.09778	.09521	.09730
MISSISSIPPI	.12701	.11607	.11658	.10327	.10002	.09331	.08653	.08320	.08509
MISSOURI	.11767	.09822	.08699	.08376	.07823	.07510	.07274	.06953	.06387
MONTANA	.15759	.11746	.11359	.10410	.09647	.09500	.08947	.08295	.08234
NEBRASKA	.13066	.10989	.09827	.09321	.08518	.07937	.07382	.06572	.04620
NEVADA	.15385	.11426	.11003	.09956	.09081	.08830	.08042	.07019	.04943
NEW HAMPSHIRE	.14038	.12662	.11400	.10478	.09788	.09204	.08402	.07708	.08159
NEW JERSEY	.13851	.12398	.11031	.10093	.09382	.08762	.07991	.07352	.06473
NEW MEXICO	.15641	.11553	.11545	.10621	.09783	.09508	.08893	.07898	.06269
NEW YORK	.14061	.12816	.11644	.10811	.10217	.09761	.09260	.09026	.09690
NORTH CAROLINA	.09673	.08836	.09165	.08391	.08293	.08064	.07811	.07971	.08569
NORTH DAKOTA	.13728	.11446	.10267	.09782	.09001	.08463	.08003	.07573	.07126
OHIO	.14575	.11975	.10539	.09907	.09016	.08391	.07784	.06948	.04904
OKLAHOMA	.11660	.10608	.10669	.09513	.09241	.08779	.08318	.08112	.07706
OREGON	.13767	.10485	.10365	.09573	.09082	.09159	.08915	.08512	.08736
PENNSYLVANIA	.12090	.11106	.10215	.09491	.08884	.08356	.07778	.07355	.07696
RHODE ISLAND	.13265	.12048	.10940	.10093	.09392	.08825	.08112	.07543	.06703
SOUTH CAROLINA	.10199	.09322	.09483	.08626	.08350	.08107	.07713	.07791	.07867
SOUTH DAKOTA	.15781	.13172	.11747	.11137	.10199	.09533	.08887	.07959	.06079
TENNESSEE	.10791	.09846	.09905	.08750	.08449	.07916	.07350	.06966	.06388
TEXAS	.11441	.10343	.10279	.09064	.08707	.08159	.07568	.06914	.04965
UTAH	.16354	.12148	.11853	.10740	.09918	.09800	.09282	.08521	.07404
VERMONT	.14569	.13519	.12453	.11824	.11242	.10843	.10355	.10608	.10627
VIRGINIA	.09375	.08554	.08838	.07845	.07650	.07387	.07351	.06958	.06139
WASHINGTON	.18844	.13873	.13251	.11992	.10979	.10612	.09654	.08464	.06706
WEST VIRGINIA	.12026	.10957	.11085	.09956	.09633	.09091	.08549	.07979	.06784
WISCONSIN	.14757	.12286	.11181	.10714	.09948	.09611	.09054	.08925	.10582
WYOMING	.17473	.12954	.12356	.11209	.10245	.09896	.09026	.07875	.05759

Table D-22
Effective Rates of Taxation: Total Taxes Net of Property Tax (Allocator-Sum of Effective Rates for Individual Taxes)

	$ 0- 1,999	2,000- 2,999	3,000- 3,999	4,000- 4,999	5,000- 5,999	6,000- 7,499	7,500- 9,999	10,000- 14,999	OVER 15,000
ALABAMA	.08382	.07736	.07893	.07128	.06936	.06730	.06431	.06425	.05617
ALASKA	.09001	.07043	.07397	.06775	.06358	.06331	.06102	.05819	.05382
ARIZONA	.09033	.06641	.06730	.06037	.05543	.05435	.05189	.04838	.04090
ARKANSAS	.07968	.07354	.07466	.06677	.06433	.06220	.05875	.05891	.06049
CALIFORNIA	.08177	.05994	.06307	.05593	.05096	.05078	.04874	.04727	.05034
COLORADO	.07726	.05729	.06135	.05532	.05189	.05239	.05182	.05135	.05950
CONNECTICUT	.05977	.05555	.05195	.04882	.04507	.04243	.03922	.03647	.03818
DELAWARE	.04413	.04100	.04459	.04250	.04316	.04142	.04599	.04897	.05625
FLORIDA	.07917	.07275	.07424	.06653	.06331	.06039	.05534	.05155	.03593
GEORGIA	.07372	.06798	.06950	.06236	.05995	.05820	.05652	.05831	.05404
HAWAII	.13044	.09831	.10015	.09083	.08525	.08480	.08145	.07720	.07036
IDAHO	.07384	.05650	.06133	.05622	.05338	.05507	.05656	.05735	.06057
ILLINOIS	.07724	.06425	.05736	.05405	.04945	.04600	.04323	.03867	.02994
INDIANA	.07303	.06215	.05686	.05437	.04968	.04594	.04382	.03914	.03015
IOWA	.06690	.05740	.05270	.05132	.04806	.04650	.04760	.04507	.04706
KANSAS	.07176	.06168	.05679	.05461	.05091	.04836	.04757	.04313	.04396
KENTUCKY	.06797	.06301	.06472	.05922	.05860	.05817	.05635	.06277	.07597
LOUISIANA	.10262	.09291	.09334	.08281	.07924	.07524	.07089	.06895	.06460
MAINE	.06756	.06431	.06213	.05899	.05498	.05235	.04809	.04390	.04988
MARYLAND	.06355	.05909	.06490	.05766	.05637	.05442	.05182	.04985	.04318

MASSACHUSETTS	.04303	.04114	.04257	.04302	.04212	.04140	.04055	.04035	.04810
MICHIGAN	.08703	.07549	.06923	.06517	.05973	.05563	.05248	.04893	.03365
MINNESOTA	.06224	.05280	.04936	.04854	.04658	.04638	.04859	.05088	.06563
MISSISSIPPI	.09036	.08333	.08436	.07536	.07299	.06804	.06253	.06113	.06886
MISSOURI	.06704	.05677	.05101	.04994	.04720	.04580	.04607	.04550	.04670
MONTANA	.06967	.05200	.05592	.05083	.04727	.04707	.04688	.04602	.05532
NEBRASKA	.04732	.04164	.03906	.03752	.03411	.03114	.02992	.02615	.01794
NEVADA	.10774	.07980	.07978	.07163	.06503	.06319	.05810	.05085	.03527
NEW HAMPSHIRE	.05336	.05062	.04863	.04614	.04300	.04093	.03739	.03367	.04551
NEW JERSEY	.05507	.05100	.04741	.04451	.04102	.03846	.03505	.03175	.03002
NEW MEXICO	.11723	.08634	.08973	.08245	.07589	.07371	.06994	.06252	.05064
NEW YORK	.06482	.06190	.05930	.05685	.05420	.05294	.05183	.05230	.06537
NORTH CAROLINA	.06699	.06177	.06549	.06125	.06098	.06012	.05863	.06180	.07251
NORTH DAKOTA	.06791	.05767	.05334	.05148	.04751	.04450	.04350	.04280	.04772
OHIO	.08046	.06630	.05901	.05547	.05017	.04615	.04347	.03852	.02692
OKLAHOMA	.07948	.07291	.07406	.06687	.06503	.06219	.05887	.05877	.06062
OREGON	.06133	.04798	.05352	.04943	.04807	.04993	.05213	.05303	.06388
PENNSYLVANIA	.07570	.07152	.06805	.06432	.06021	.05690	.05345	.05090	.05815
RHODE ISLAND	.06889	.06474	.06132	.05779	.05356	.05066	.04682	.04349	.04049
SOUTH CAROLINA	.07924	.07289	.07482	.06894	.06672	.06538	.06224	.06421	.06863
SOUTH DAKOTA	.07061	.06034	.05555	.05314	.04857	.04489	.04295	.03820	.03122
TENNESSEE	.07435	.06846	.06953	.06194	.05973	.05602	.05152	.04945	.04901
TEXAS	.06824	.06218	.06220	.05549	.05302	.04977	.04546	.04134	.02921
UTAH	.09190	.06818	.07152	.06401	.05910	.05896	.05812	.05514	.05204
VERMONT	.06853	.06792	.06641	.06611	.06367	.06304	.06213	.06749	.07422
VIRGINIA	.06025	.05561	.05894	.05295	.05180	.05078	.05135	.04942	.04656
WASHINGTON	.13470	.09870	.09722	.08731	.07968	.07679	.07047	.06205	.05052
WEST VIRGINIA	.09142	.08385	.08554	.07764	.07510	.07107	.06665	.06247	.05509
WISCONSIN	.05762	.04925	.04790	.04708	.04440	.04409	.04321	.04660	.07535
WYOMING	.09353	.06902	.07030	.06301	.05711	.05478	.05103	.04474	.03268

Notes

Notes

Chapter 1
Introduction: Purposes, Achievements, and Caveats

1. See, for example, Advisory Commission on Intergovernmental Relations, TAX OVERLAPPING IN THE UNITED STATES 1964 (Washington, D.C.: Advisory Commission, 1964); ACIR, STATE-LOCAL TAXATION AND INDUSTRIAL LOCATION (Washington, D.C.: Advisory Commission, 1967). Central to the recent literature on comparative local fiscal analysis is the work done on disparities, e.g., ACIR, FISCAL BALANCE IN THE AMERICAN FEDERAL SYSTEM, vol. 2, Metropolitan Fiscal Disparities (Washington, D.C.: Advisory Commission, 1967), Seymour Sacks, "Metropolitan Fiscal Disparities: Their Nature and Determinants," THE JOURNAL OF FINANCE, 23 (May 1968): 229-50 and Alan Campbell and Seymour Sacks, METROPOLITAN AMERICA (New York: Free Press, 1967).

2. See the study by W. Irwin Gillespie, "Effect of Public Expenditures on the Distribution of Income," in R.A. Musgrave (ed.) ESSAYS IN FISCAL FEDERALISM (Washington, D.C.: The Brookings Institution, 1965), pp. 122-186, and Harvey Brazer's review in JOURNAL OF POLITICAL ECONOMY, 74 (December 1966): 637.

3. The terms allocation, distribution and stabilization follow the convention established by R.A. Musgrave in THE THEORY OF PUBLIC FINANCE (New York: McGraw Hill, 1959).

Chapter 2
Who Pays State-Local Taxes?

1. This is not necessarily at variance with Milton Friedman's stance on the reality of economic assumptions since, while he is concerned with theoretical constructs, this study is focused upon the empirical implications of using such constructs. See Milton Friedman, "The Methodology of Positive Economics," in ESSAYS IN POSITIVE ECONOMICS (Chicago: University of Chicago Press, 1959), pp. 3-43.

2. Helen Tarasov, "Who Does Pay the Taxes?" SOCIAL RESEARCH, Supplement 4, 1942, p. 1.

3. On excess burden see Carl Shoup, PUBLIC FINANCE (Chicago: Aldine, 1969), pp. 28-31. On variations in the marginal utility of money see Henry Aaron, "Some Criticisms of Tax Burden Indices," and Richard Bird, "Comment," NATIONAL TAX JOURNAL, 18 (September 1965): 313-18.

4. Mabel Newcomer, "Estimate of the Tax Burden on Different Income

Classes," in STUDIES IN CURRENT TAX PROBLEMS (New York: Twentieth Century Fund, 1937), pp. 1-52.

5. An earlier study dealt with the burden of taxation but only for direct taxes. In addition, the analysis was based upon the assumption that impact and incidence were equivalent thus giving no recognition to incidence theory. See Maxine Yaple, "The Burden of Direct Taxes as Paid by Income Classes," AMERICAN ECONOMIC REVIEW, 26 (December 1936): 691-710.

6. Gerhard Colm and Helen Tarasov, WHO PAYS THE TAXES? Monograph no. 3 of the TNEC.

7. Tarasov, "Who Does Pay the Taxes?"

8. R.A. Musgrave, J.J. Carroll, L.D. Cook, and L. Frane, "Distribution of Tax Payments by Income Groups: A Case Study for 1948," NATIONAL TAX JOURNAL, 4 (March 1951): 1-53.

9. Ibid., p. 1.

10. Rufus Tucker, "Distribution of Tax Burdens in 1948," NATIONAL TAX JOURNAL, 5 (September 1952): 270.

11. Ibid., p. 274.

12. National Tax Association Third Round Table, "Who Pays the Taxes?" PROCEEDINGS OF THE FORTY-FIFTH ANNUAL CONFERENCE ON TAXATION (Toronto 1952), papers by Musgrave and Tucker, pp. 179-203.

13. George A. Bishop, "The Tax Burden by Income Class, 1958," NATIONAL TAX JOURNAL, 14 (March 1961): 42-43.

14. National Tax Association, "Who Pays the Taxes," p. 193.

15. John H. Adler, "The Fiscal System, the Distribution of Income and Public Welfare," in Kenyon Poole (ed.), FISCAL POLICIES AND THE AMERICAN ECONOMY (New York: Prentice Hall, 1951), pp. 359-409.

16. Ibid., pp. 366-67.

17. Ibid., p. 41 provides detailed data on the results and the net effect of the total budget. The statistical allocation techniques used by Adler are explained in Eugene Schlesinger, "The Statistical Allocation of Taxes and Expenditures in 1938/39 and 1946/47," in Poole's FISCAL POLICIES, pp. 410-421.

18. Rufus S. Tucker, "The Distribution of Government Burdens and Benefits," A.E.A. PAPERS AND PROCEEDINGS, 43 (May 1952): 518-43.

19. Ibid., p. 528.

20. Ibid., p. 529. The allocators are (1) population, (2) income, (3) consumption and (4) capital.

21. Ibid., p. 533.

22. See W. Irwin Gillespie, "The Effect of Public Expenditures on the Distribution of Income: An Empirical Investigation" (unpublished Ph.D. dissertation, Dept. of Economics, Johns Hopkins University, 1963). This is presented in summary form in "Effect of Public Expenditures on the Distribution of Income," in R.A. Musgrave (ed.), ESSAYS IN FISCAL FEDERALISM (Washington, D.C.: The Brookings Institution, 1965), pp. 122-86.

23. Ibid., p. 125.

24. See ibid., p. 128 for all ten budget experiments.

25. Harvey E. Brazer, Review of ESSAYS IN FISCAL FEDERALISM, R.A. Musgrave (ed.), JOURNAL OF POLITICAL ECONOMY, 74 (December 1966): 637.

26. Tax Foundation, TAX BURDENS AND BENEFITS OF GOVERNMENT EXPENDITURES BY INCOME CLASS, 1961 AND 1965 (New York: Tax Foundation, 1967).

27. United States Department of Labor, Bureau of Labor Statistics, SURVEY OF CONSUMER EXPENDITURES AND INCOME 1960-61, Reports 237-89, 90, 91, 92 and supplemental reports (Washington, D.C.: U.S. Government Printing Office, 1966). Past studies were forced to rely upon data from the Time-Life Survey and Survey Research Center, University of Michigan, SURVEY OF CONSUMER FINANCES (Ann Arbor: Survey Research Center, annual) and Time-Life, LIFE STUDY OF CONSUMER EXPENDITURES (New York: Time, 1957). For a discussion of the BLS data see Tax Foundation, "Tax Burdens," pp. 35-37.

28. It must be noted that intertemporal comparisons of this sort need to account for changes in the price level—acting as an implicit form of taxation—and the movement of persons from one income class to another. See Albert C. Neisser, "The Dynamics of Tax Burden Comparisons," NATIONAL TAX JOURNAL, 5 (March 1952): 351-64.

29. Tax Foundation, "Tax Burdens," p. 38. For a detailed discussion of the use of NNP and the imputation of indirect business taxes as income see George A. Bishop, "Income Redistribution in the Framework of the National Income Accounts," NATIONAL TAX JOURNAL, 19 (December 1966): 378-90.

30. See, for example, Minnesota Tax Study Committee, REPORT OF THE GOVERNOR'S MINNESOTA TAX STUDY COMMITTEE (Minneapolis: Tax Study Committee, 1956); Edwin W. Hanczaryk and James H. Thompson, THE ECONOMIC IMPACT OF STATE AND LOCAL TAXES IN WEST VIRGINIA (Morgantown, W.Va.: College of Commerce, West Virginia University, 1958) and Florida Legislative Council, FINANCING GOVERNMENT IN FLORIDA (Tallahassee, Fla.: Florida Legislative Council, 1962) to mention just a few. For a more inclusive list see Charles McLure, "An Analysis of Regional Tax Incidence, with Estimation of Interstate Incidence of State and Local Taxes" (unpublished Ph.D. dissertation, Department of Economics, Princeton University, 1966), pp. 369-70.

31. R.A. Musgrave and Darwin Daicoff, "Who Pays the Michigan Taxes?" in MICHIGAN TAX STUDY PAPERS (Lansing, Michigan: Michigan Tax Study Committee, 1958), pp. 131-183.

32. Ibid., p. 131.

33. Ibid., p. 138.

34. University of Wisconsin Tax Study Committee, WISCONSIN'S STATE

AND LOCAL TAX BURDEN (Madison, Wisconsin: University of Wisconsin, 1959).

35. See ibid., pp. 39-42. Chapter 4 will discuss the exporting of taxes and "closed" versus "open" economy assumptions for tax burdens studies.

36. Michigan Tax Study Committee, MICHIGAN TAX STUDY PAPERS, p. 134.

37. O.H. Brownlee, ESTIMATED DISTRIBUTION OF MINNESOTA TAXES AND PUBLIC EXPENDITURE BENEFITS (Minneapolis: University of Minnesota Press, 1960).

38. Ibid., p. 7.

Chapter 3
A Model for Estimating the Distribution of Tax Burdens

1. See R.A. Musgrave, "General Equilibrium Aspects of Incidence Theory," AMERICAN ECONOMIC ASSOCIATION PAPERS AND PROCEEDINGS, 43 (May 1953): 505.

2. See E.R.A. Seligman, "Introduction to the Shifting and Incidence of Taxation," in R.A. Musgrave and C.S. Shoup (eds.), A.E.A. READINGS IN THE ECONOMICS OF TAXATION (Homewood, Ill.: Richard D. Irwin, 1959), p. 202. Seligman also points out that there are other ways in which the burden of taxation can be avoided. They involve capitalization, transformation and evasion, either legal or illegal. For purposes of tax burden analysis, however, the distinction becomes empirically untenable, see Musgrave, et al., "Distribution of Tax Payments by Income Groups: A Case Study for 1948," NATIONAL TAX JOURNAL, 4 (March 1951): 5-6, 8-10.

3. R.A. Musgrave, THE THEORY OF PUBLIC FINANCE (New York: McGraw Hill, 1959), p. 223. See Chapter 10 for a complete discussion of this point of view.

4. Carl Shoup, PUBLIC FINANCE (Chicago: Aldine, 1969), p. 13.

5. For an enlightening discussion of the empirical content of incidence theory supplemented with a case study for a particular industry, see Robert P. Collier, "Some Empirical Evidence of Tax Incidence," NATIONAL TAX JOURNAL, 11 (March 1958): 35-55.

6. See Musgrave, et al., "Distribution of Tax Payments," p. 13, and George A. Bishop, "The Tax Burden by Income Class, 1958," NATIONAL TAX JOURNAL, 14 (March 1961): 48.

7. Data for these calculations are taken from the following sources:

Average family size	Bureau of Labor Statistics, SURVEY OF CONSUMER EXPENDITURES AND INCOME

	1960-61 (Washington, D.C.: GPO, 1966).
Personal and dependent exemptions	Advisory Commission on Intergovernmental Relations, TAX OVERLAPPING IN THE UNITED STATES 1961 (Washington, D.C.: Advisory Commission, 1961), p. 57.
Standard deduction	Ibid., p. 63.
State income tax rates	Ibid., pp. 58-62.

Adjustments were made in the calculations to account for factors such as (1) all income tax in Pennsylvania is local and (2) Tennessee and New Hampshire tax only interest and dividend income. This procedure was applied to each income class for each state.

8. See B.U. Ratchford and P.B. Han, "The Burden of the Corporate Income Tax," NATIONAL TAX JOURNAL, 10 (December 1957): 310-311.

9. See John G. Cragg, A.C. Harberger, and Peter Mieszkowski, "Empirical Evidence on the Incidence of the Corporation Income Tax," JOURNAL OF POLITICAL ECONOMY, 75 (December 1967): 811-21; A.C. Harberger, "The Incidence of the Corporation Income Tax," JOURNAL OF POLITICAL ECONOMY, 70 (June 1962): 215-40; Marion Krzyzaniak (ed.), EFFECTS OF THE CORPORATION INCOME TAX (Detroit: Wayne State University Press, 1966), which includes a series of papers discussing the corporate income tax; see especially the article by Slitor, "Corporate Tax Incidence: Economic Adjustments to Differentials under a Two-Tier Structure," pp. 136-206, and Marion Krzyzaniak and R.A. Musgrave, THE SHIFTING OF THE CORPORATION INCOME TAX (Baltimore: Johns Hopkins Univ. Press, 1963).

10. Cragg, et al., "Corporation Income Tax," p. 820.

11. SHIFTING OF THE CORPORATION INCOME TAX.

12. Ibid., pp. 46-49. K-M arrive at an estimated coefficient for the shifting parameter of 1.34. With a standard error for the cofficient of 0.1096, at the 0.05 level of significance, with 15 degrees of freedom, this gives a range between 1.11 and 1.57. At any rate, 0.0 percent shifting is clearly rejected. More surprisingly, shifting of less than 100 percent is rejected at the 0.01 level.

13. See Cragg, et al., "Corporation Income Tax," p. 812, and Richard E. Slitor, "Corporate Tax Incidence: Economic Adjustments to Differentials under a Two-Tier Tax Structure," in M. Krzyzaniak, EFFECTS OF THE CORPORATION INCOME TAX, p. 138.

14. Dick Netzer, ECONOMICS OF THE PROPERTY TAX (Washington, D.C.: Brookings Institution, 1966), p. 1.

15. George Bishop, "The Tax Burden by Income Class, 1958," NATIONAL TAX JOURNAL, 14 (March 1961): 48.

16. The argument of John Due, "Sales Taxation and the Consumer," AMERICAN ECONOMIC REVIEW, 53 (December 1963): 1078-84 applies here. In fact, it applies even more strongly since the tax is general in nature and is levied predominantly at the state level, making shifting much easier.

17. Tax Foundation, TAX BURDENS AND BENEFITS OF GOVERNMENT EXPENDITURES BY INCOME CLASS, 1961 AND 1965 (New York: Tax Foundation, 1967), p. 26, emphasis added.

18. Due, "Sales Taxation," p. 1078. The balance of the article presents a succinct summary of the "burden does not rest on the consumer" arguments.

19. See ibid., p. 1081.

20. Data for the allocators are derived from BLS, SURVEY OF CONSUMER EXPENDITURES.

21. Musgrave, et al., "Distribution of Tax Payments," p. 25.

22. United States Bureau of the Census, CENSUS OF GOVERNMENTS: 1962, vol. 4, COMPENDIUM OF GOVERNMENT FINANCES (Washington, D.C.: GPO, 1964), Table 28, p. 49.

23. See Ursula K. Hicks, "The Terminology of Tax Analysis," in R.A. Musgrave and C.S. Shoup (eds.), A.E.A. READINGS IN THE ECONOMICS OF TAXATION (Homewood, Ill.: Richard D. Irwin, 1959), pp. 215-221.

24. Rufus S. Tucker, "Distribution of Tax Burdens in 1948," NATIONAL TAX JOURNAL, 4 (September 1951): 270-71.

25. R.A. Musgrave, "Distribution of Tax Payments by Income Groups: A Review," National Tax Association, PROCEEDINGS OF FORTY-FIFTH ANNUAL CONFERENCE, (Toronto 1952), p. 191. Musgrave's approach is backed up by Joseph Pechman who states: " . . . once we go beyond the money income concept, it is difficult to determine where to stop." "Some Technical Problems in the Measurement of Tax Burdens," ibid., p. 205.

26. Gerhard Colm and Haskell P. Wald, "Some Comments on Tax Burden Comparisons," NATIONAL TAX JOURNAL, 5 (March 1952): 13. The resulting distortion would be much more serious for Tucker's results since he included a large component of nonmonetary and imputed income in his base. See also Pechman, "Measurement of Tax Burdens," pp. 206-209 for a numerical illustration of this problem and its potential effect upon effective rates.

27. Musgrave, "Tax Payments by Income Groups: A Review," p. 191.

28. An attempt to resolve this problem was made by examining urban families of the same size (four persons), see James Beaton, "Family Tax Burdens by Income Levels," NATIONAL TAX JOURNAL, 15 (March 1962): 14-25.

29. Bishop, "Tax Burden," pp. 42-46.

30. George Bishop, "Income Redistribution in the Framework of the National Income Accounts," NATIONAL TAX JOURNAL, 19 (December 1966): 390.

31. The best income data for states are published regularly by the Department of Commerce, see, e.g., "Personal Income by States and Regions in 1963," SURVEY OF CURRENT BUSINESS, 44 (August 1964): 16-23.

Chapter 4
Spatial Incidence and State-Local Taxation

1. Charles McLure, "Commodity Tax Incidence in Open Economies," NATIONAL TAX JOURNAL, 17 (June 1964): 187. The literature in this area is sparse. Each of the major state studies has dealt with the problem as it relates to a particular state. The only study dealing with the exporting phenomenon in its full context is C.E. McLure, "Tax Exporting in the United States: Estimates for 1962," NATIONAL TAX JOURNAL, 20 (March 1967): 49-77 and McLure's dissertation, "An Analysis of Regional Tax Incidence, with Estimation of Interstate Incidence of State and Local Taxes" (unpublished Ph.D. dissertation, Dept. of Economics, Princeton University, 1966).

2. A theoretical discussion of the implications of an open economy on the geographical incidence of taxation is presented in McLure, "Commodity Tax," pp. 187-204. The data on tax-exporting used in this study are derived from estimates made by McLure.

3. Richard Musgrave and Darwin Daicoff, "Who Pays the Michigan Taxes?" in MICHIGAN TAX STUDY PAPERS (Lansing, Mich.: Michigan Tax Study Committee, 1958), pp. 131-83.

4. University of Wisconsin, WISCONSIN'S STATE AND LOCAL TAX BURDEN (Madison: University of Wisconsin, School of Commerce, 1959).

5. O.H. Brownlee, ESTIMATED DISTRIBUTION OF MINNESOTA TAXES AND PUBLIC EXPENDITURE BENEFITS (Minneapolis: University of Minnesota, 1960), pp. 5-7. See Table III, col. 7, 17, and 18 for Brownlee's estimates of shifted Minnesota taxes.

6. Musgrave and Daicoff, "Michigan Taxes," p. 134.

7. University of Wisconsin, "Tax Burden," p. 45.

8. Ibid., p. 45.

9. Werner Z. Hirsch, Elbert Segelhorst, and Morton Marcus, SPILLOVER OF PUBLIC EDUCATION COSTS AND BENEFITS, 2nd ed. (Los Angeles: University of California, Institute of Government and Public Affairs, 1969).

10. It must be recognized that McLure's estimates are as good as his method. Acceptance of his data is a direct function of the credence given his methodology. His work remains, however, the only detailed empirical analysis of the geographical flow of state-local taxation and provides a tractable approximation to the magnitudes involved.

11. James Maxwell, TAX CREDITS AND INTERGOVERNMENTAL FISCAL RELATIONS (Washington, D.C.: The Brookings Institution, 1962). The same deductions hold for the study year, see Benjamin Bridges, Jr., "Deductibility of State and Local Nonbusiness Taxes under the Federal Individual Income Tax," NATIONAL TAX JOURNAL, 19 (March 1966): 1.

12. Bridges, "Deductibility," Table A, p. 17.

13. McLure, "An Analysis," pp. 256-59.

Chapter 5
The Nature of Individual State-Local Taxes

1. See Advisory Commission on Intergovernmental Relations, TAX OVERLAPPING IN THE UNITED STATES: 1964 (Washington, D.C.: Advisory Commission, 1964) for a detailed discussion of state-local tax systems.

2. See ibid., pp. 140-47, for the features of the tax by state.

3. See Jeffrey M. Schaefer, "The Regressivity of State-Local Taxation: A Case Study of New Jersey," THE QUARTERLY REVIEW OF ECONOMICS AND BUSINESS, 9 (Spring 1969): 15-17 for one such test.

4. The hypothetical exemption of items such as food from the general sales tax base does not necessarily imply that the total tax structure will be less regressive. The major determinant of the change in incidence of the entire structure in response to selected exemptions will be the distributional pattern of the tax(es) used to maintain constant yield, assuming constant yield.

For a study that examined in more detail the inclusion/exclusion of food from the general sales tax base, see David G. Davies, "An Empirical Test of Sales Tax Regressivity," JOURNAL OF POLITICAL ECONOMY, 67 (February 1959): 72-78. His conclusions coincide with those indicated here.

5. There is some empirical evidence that the exemption of clothing may actually serve to increase the regressivity of the general sales tax. See Schaefer, "Regressivity," p. 16.

6. David G. Davies, "The Significance of Taxation of Services for the Pattern of Distribution of Tax Burden by Income Class," National Tax Association, PROCEEDINGS OF THE SIXTY-SECOND ANNUAL CONFERENCE (Boston, Mass., 1969), p. 146.

7. There are, of course, valid questions to be raised concerning the sumptuary nature of these taxes. If the tax is indeed sumptuary, are the proceeds used to offset social costs or is the tax merely a convenient, institutionally accepted revenue source? Maxwell has stated that "in fact, in an affluent society the taxes are pushed not hard enough to secure much [if any] diminution but hard enough to secure a large revenue." James Maxwell, FINANCING STATE AND LOCAL GOVERNMENTS, rev. ed. (Washington, D.C.: Brookings Institution, 1969), p. 87.

8. John F. Due, GOVERNMENT FINANCE: ECONOMICS OF THE PUBLIC SECTOR (Homewood, Ill.: Richard D. Irwin, 1968), p. 372.

9. See Advisory Commission, TAX OVERLAPPING, Chapters 11-16 for state-by-state breakdown of selective sales tax provisions.

10. For a study involving the use of the assignment ratio in explaining fiscal behavior, see Alan K. Campbell and Seymour Sacks, METROPOLITAN AMERICA (New York: Free Press, 1967), especially Chapter 2.

11. Dick Netzer, ECONOMICS OF THE PROPERTY TAX (Washington, D.C.: Brookings Institution, 1966), pp. 40-46.

12. Dick Netzer, "Impact of the Property Tax: Its Economic Implications for Urban Problems," report to the National Commission on Urban Problems, (Washington, D.C.: U.S. Government Printing Office, 1968), p. 47.

13. Defined as the ratio of local taxes to total state-local taxes, see Campbell and Sacks, METROPOLITAN AMERICA.

14. In 1962, $309 million was locally raised income taxes. All of the income tax in Pennsylvania and Ohio and part of the yield in Kentucky, Missouri, and Alabama is local. The distributional pattern of the local component is proportional since all but a few units levy a flat rate tax on gross income with no exemptions or deductions. See Tax Foundation, CITY INCOME TAXES (New York: Tax Foundation, 1967), especially pp. 15-25 and 41. A detailed analysis of state personal income taxes is presented in Emanuel Melichar, STATE INDIVIDUAL INCOME TAXES (Storrs, Conn.: University of Connecticut, 1963).

15. See Advisory Commission, TAX OVERLAPPING, pp. 113-139, for a partial indication of the variation in provisions across states.

16. Ibid., p. 152.

Chapter 6
The Structure of the State-Local Tax System

1. James Maxwell, FINANCING STATE AND LOCAL GOVERNMENTS, rev. ed. (Washington, D.C.: Brookings Institution, 1969), p. 98.

2. Higher local tax assignment meaning, on the average, greater reliance on property taxation. See A.K. Campbell and S. Sacks, METROPOLITAN AMERICA (New York: Free Press, 1967) for a discussion and empirical implementation of the assignment variable.

3. The literature in this area is considerable; see, for example, R.A. Musgrave and Tun Thin, "Income Tax Progression, 1929-48," JOURNAL OF POLITICAL ECONOMY, 56 (December 1948): 498-514. For an excellent discussion, with numerical examples, of the problems inherent in measuring progression-regression, see Emanuel Melichar, STATE INDIVIDUAL INCOME TAXES (Storrs, Conn.: University of Conn., 1963).

4. See Musgrave and Thin, "Income Tax," p. 498. There are, unfortunately numerous other ways to measure the same phenomenon with little consensus as to the correct one.

5. An exception is a study done by A.S. Donnahoe, "Measuring State Tax Burden," JOURNAL OF POLITICAL ECONOMY, 55 (June 1947): 234-244. Donnahoe's analysis, however, does not deal with data by income class, as done here, but rather aggregate taxes and income.

6. See, for example, J.R. Lotz and E.R. Morss, "Measuring 'Tax Effort' in Developing Countries," INTERNATIONAL MONETARY FUND STAFF

PAPERS (November 1967), pp. 478-499 or R.A. Musgrave, FISCAL SYSTEMS (New Haven, Conn.: Yale University Press, 1969), especially Chapters 6 and 7.

7. Alan S. Donnahoe, "Measuring State Tax Burden," JOURNAL OF POLITICAL ECONOMY, 55 (June 1947): 236. See also, H.J. Frank, "Measuring State Tax Burdens," NATIONAL TAX JOURNAL, 12 (June 1959): 179-85.

8. See A.R. Jensen, "How Much Can We Boost IQ and Scholastic Achievement?" HARVARD EDUCATIONAL REVIEW, 39 (Winter 1969): 9.

9. An excellent summary of the philosophical-mathematical basis and differential applications of factor analysis is given in R.J. Rummel, "Understanding Factor Analysis," JOURNAL OF CONFLICT RESOLUTION, 11 (December 1967): 444-480. For a more detailed treatment see Paul Horst, FACTOR ANALYSIS OF DATA MATRICES (New York: Holt, Rinehart and Winston, 1965) or R.J. Rummel, APPLIED FACTOR ANALYSIS (Evanston, Ill.: Northwestern University Press, 1970).

10. The factor loadings (weights for the linear combination) used in calculating the scores in Table 6-5 are indicated below. The column number below refers to the column in Table 6-5; V1-V9 represent each of the nine income classes, treated as variables in the factor analysis.

	(1)	(2)	(3)	(4)
V1	–0.9417	–0.9492	–0.9513	–0.9691
V2	–0.9570	–0.9652	–0.9743	–0.9770
V3	–0.9560	–0.9736	–0.9584	–0.9645
V4	–0.9669	–0.9844	–0.9550	–0.9592
V5	–0.9241	–0.9513	–0.9144	–0.9223
V6	–0.8963	–0.9282	–0.8825	–0.8938
V7	–0.8107	–0.8390	–0.8103	–0.8212
V8	–0.5139	–0.5146	–0.6161	–0.6306
V9	–0.0079	+0.0921	–0.0399	–0.0504

The factor scores calculated from the above loadings have been multiplied by –1.0 for convenience of presentation, i.e., high burden-high score, low burden-low score. This has no effect on the absolute value of the scores and serves only to facilitate interpretation.

Chapter 7
Recent Developments in State-Local Tax Policy

1. Unless otherwise noted, the sources of information for this chapter are Advisory Commission on Intergovernmental Relations, STATE-LOCAL FINANCES: SIGNIFICANT FEATURES AND SUGGESTED LEGISLATION:

1972 (Washington, D.C.: ACIR, 1972)–hereinafter cited as ACIR, STATE-LOCAL FINANCES: 1972–and TAX OVERLAPPING IN THE UNITED STATES: 1961 (Washington, D.C.: ACIR, 1961).

2. ACIR, STATE-LOCAL FINANCES: 1972, pp. 235-37.

3. In four states, the tax is only on capital gains (Connecticut), commuter income (New Jersey) or interest and dividend income (New Hampshire and Tennessee). Local income taxes are now levied in nine states and raise about $1.1 billion.

4. It must again be noted that these are nominal changes in the *marginal*, not effective, rates of taxation. See ibid., pp. 201-207.

5. Ibid., p. 5.

6. Ibid., p. 5.

7. Ibid.

Chapter 8
Conclusions, Implications, and Future Research

1. See George Break, INTERGOVERNMENTAL FISCAL RELATIONS IN THE UNITED STATES (Washington, D.C.: Brookings, 1967), pp. 128-29.

2. See S.E. Lile and D.M. Soule, "Interstate Differences in Family Tax Burdens," NATIONAL TAX JOURNAL, 22 (December 1969): 433-45 for an attempt to refine the tax effort index in aid formulae.

3. See K.E. Quindry and B.D. Cook, "Humanization of the Property Tax for Low Income Households," NATIONAL TAX JOURNAL, 22 (September 1969): 357-67.

4. RESHAPING GOVERNMET IN METROPOLITAN AREAS (New York: Committee for Economic Development, 1970), p. 50.

Appendixes

1. Bureau of Labor Statistics, SURVEY OF CONSUMER EXPENDITURES AND INCOME 1960-61 (Washington, D.C.: GPO, 1966).

2. For a discussion of some alternative measures see Mary Jean Bowman, "A Graphical Analysis of Personal Income Distribution in the United States," in R.A. Musgrave and C.S. Shoup (eds.) A.E.A. READINGS IN THE THEORY OF INCOME DISTRIBUTION (Philadelphia: The Blakiston Co., 1946), pp. 72-99 and Dwight Yntema, "Measures of the Inequality in the Personal Distribution of Wealth or Income," JOURNAL OF THE AMERICAN STATISTICAL ASSOCIATION, 28 (December 1933): 423-33.

3. Yntema, "Measures," p. 428. See also W.I. Greenwald, STATISTICS FOR ECONOMICS (Columbus, Ohio: C.E. Merrill, 1963), p. 26.

Bibliography

Bibliography

Books

Black, Duncan. THE INCIDENCE OF INCOME TAXES. London: MacMillan and Co. Ltd., 1939.

Brownlee, O.H. ESTIMATED DISTRIBUTION OF MINNESOTA TAXES AND PUBLIC EXPENDITURE BENEFITS. Minneapolis: University of Wisconsin Press, 1960.

Buchanan, James. COST AND CHOICE. Chicago: Markham, 1969.

Fox, Karl. INTERMEDIATE ECONOMIC STATISTICS. New York: Wiley, 1968.

Fruchter, B. INTRODUCTION TO FACTOR ANALYSIS. Princeton, N.J.: D. Van Nostrand Co., Inc., 1954.

Gillespie, W. Irwin. THE INCIDENCE OF TAXES AND PUBLIC EXPENDITURES IN THE CANADIAN ECONOMY. (Report no. 61, for the Royal Commission on Taxation) Ottawa: Queen's Printers, 1965.

Goode, Richard. THE INDIVIDUAL INCOME TAX. Washington, D.C.: Brookings Institution, 1964.

Greenwald, William I. STATISTICS FOR ECONOMICS. Columbus, Ohio: C.E. Merrill Books, 1963.

Hanczaryk, Edwin W. and James H. Thompson. THE ECONOMIC IMPACT OF STATE AND LOCAL TAXES IN WEST VIRGINIA. Morgantown, W. Va.: College of Commerce, West Virginia University, 1958.

Harman, Harry S. MODERN FACTOR ANALYSIS. Chicago: University of Chicago Press, 1960.

Herber, Bernard P. MODERN PUBLIC FINANCE. Rev. ed. Homewood, Ill.: Richard D. Irwin, 1967.

Hirsch, Werner Z., Elbert Segelhorst and Morton Marcus. SPILLOVER OF PUBLIC EDUCATION COSTS AND BENEFITS. 2nd ed., Los Angeles: University of California, Institute of Government and Public Affairs, 1969.

Kendall, M.G. A COURSE IN MULTIVARIATE ANALYSIS. London: Charles Griffin, 1965.

Krzyaniak, Marion (ed.). EFFECTS OF CORPORATION INCOME TAX. Detroit: Wayne State University Press, 1966.

Krzyaniak, Marion and R.A. Musgrave. THE SHIFTING OF THE CORPORATION INCOME TAX. Baltimore: Johns Hopkins University Press, 1963.

Lawley, D.M. and A.E. Maxwell. FACTOR ANALYSIS AS A STATISTICAL METHOD. London: Butterworth's, 1963.

Maxwell, James A. TAX CREDITS AND INTERGOVERNMENTAL FISCAL RELATIONS. Washington, D.C.: Brookings Institution, 1962.

_______. FINANCING STATE AND LOCAL GOVERNMENTS. Rev. ed. Washington, D.C.: Brookings Institution, 1969.

Melichar, Emanuel. STATE INDIVIDUAL INCOME TAXES. Storrs, Conn.: University of Connecticut, 1963.

Minnesota Tax Study Committee. REPORT OF THE GOVERNOR'S MINNESOTA TAX STUDY. Minneapolis: Minnesota Tax Study Committee, 1956.

Musgrave, Richard A. THE THEORY OF PUBLIC FINANCE. New York: McGraw Hill, 1959.

_______. FISCAL SYSTEMS. New Haven, Connecticut: Yale University Press, 1969.

Mushkin, Selma and John F. Cotton. FUNCTIONAL FEDERALISM: GRANTS-IN-AID AND PPB SYSTEMS. Washington, D.C.: State-Local Finances Project of the George Washington University, 1968.

Netzer, Dick. THE ECONOMICS OF THE PROPERTY TAX. Washington, D.C.: Brookings Institution, 1966.

Okner, Benjamin. INCOME DISTRIBUTION AND THE FEDERAL INCOME TAX. Ann Arbor, Mich.: Institute of Public Administration, University of Michigan, 1966.

Rummel, R.J. APPLIED FACTOR ANALYSIS. Evanston, Ill.: Northwestern University Press, 1970.

Seltzer, Lawrence H. THE PERSONAL EXEMPTION IN THE INCOME TAX. New York: National Bureau of Economic Research, 1968.

Sharkansky, Ira. THE POLITICS OF TAXING AND SPENDING. New York: Bobbs-Merrill, 1969.

Shoup, Carl. PUBLIC FINANCE. Chicago: Aldine, 1969.

Soltow, Lee, (ed.) SIX PAPERS ON THE SIZE DISTRIBUTION OF WEALTH AND INCOME. New York: National Bureau of Economic Research, 1969.

Tarasov, H. and Gerhard Colm. WHO PAYS THE TAXES? Monograph no. 3 of the Temporary National Economic Committee (1942).

Tax Foundation. TAX BURDENS AND BENEFITS OF GOVERNMENT EXPENDITURES BY INCOME CLASS, 1961 AND 1965. New York: The Tax Foundation, 1967.

_______. THE CORPORATION INCOME TAX. New York: The Tax Foundation, 1968.

_______. ALLOCATING THE FEDERAL TAX BURDEN BY STATE. New York: Tax Foundation, 1964.

_______. STATE TAX STUDIES: 1959-1967. New York: Tax Foundation, 1967.

_______. RETAIL SALES AND INDIVIDUAL INCOME TAXES IN STATE TAX STRUCTURES. Project note no. 48. New York: Tax Foundation, 1962.

_______. FACTS AND FIGURES ON GOVERNMENT FINANCE. 12th edition, 1962-63. New York: Tax Foundation, 1963.

_______. THE TAX BURDEN IN RELATION TO NATIONAL INCOME AND PRODUCT. New York: Tax Foundation, 1957.

_______. ALLOCATION OF THE TAX BURDEN BY INCOME CLASS. Project note no. 45. New York: Tax Foundation, 1960.

_______. PROPERTY TAXATION: ECONOMIC ASPECTS. Government finance brief no. 13. New York: Tax Foundation, 1968.

_______. CITY INCOME TAXES. New York: Tax Foundation, 1967.

University of Michigan, Survey Research Center. SURVEY OF CONSUMER FINANCES. Ann Arbor: University of Michigan Press, annual.

University of Wisconsin. WISCONSIN'S STATE AND LOCAL TAX BURDEN. Madison: University of Wisconsin, School of Commerce, 1959.

Weisbrod, Burton A. EXTERNAL BENEFITS OF PUBLIC EDUCATION. Princeton, New Jersey: Department of Economics, Industrial Relations Section, Princeton University, 1964.

Articles and Periodicals

Aaron, H. "Some Criticisms of Tax Burden Indices." NATIONAL TAX JOURNAL 18 (September 1965): 313-18.

Adler, John H. "The Fiscal System, the Distribution of Income and Public Welfare." In Kenyon Poole (ed.) FISCAL POLICIES AND THE AMERICAN ECONOMY. New York: Prentice Hall, 1951, pp. 359-409.

Allen, H.K. and R.F. Fryman. "Comparison of Revenues and Expenditures in Income and Non-income Tax States in 1962." NATIONAL TAX JOURNAL 17 (December 1964): 357-64.

Bannink, R. "The Incidence of Taxes and Premiums for Social Insurance on Family Budgets." PUBLIC FINANCE 15, no. 1: 72-91.

Beaton, J.R. "Family Tax Burdens by Income Levels." NATIONAL TAX JOURNAL 15 (March 1962): 14-25.

Bird, R.A. "A Note on Tax 'Sacrifice' Comparisons." NATIONAL TAX JOURNAL 17 (September 1964): 303-308.

Bishop, G.A. "The Tax Burden by Income Class, 1958." NATIONAL TAX JOURNAL 14 (March 1961): 41-57.

_______. "Income Redistribution in the Framework of the National Income Accounts." NATIONAL TAX JOURNAL 19 (December 1966): 378-90.

Bowman, Mary Jean. "A Graphical Analysis of Personal Income Distribution in the United States." In R.A. Musgrave and C.S. Shoup (eds.). A.E.A. READINGS IN THE THEORY OF INCOME DISTRIBUTION. Homewood, Ill.: Richard D. Irwin, 1951, pp. 72-99.

Bridges, Benjamin, Jr. "Deductibility of State and Local Nonbusiness Taxes under the Federal Individual Income Tax." NATIONAL TAX JOURNAL 19 (March 1966): 1-17.

Colberg, Marshall R. "Shifting of a Specific Excise Tax." PUBLIC FINANCE 9, no. 2 (1954): 168-73.

Collier, R.P. "Some Empirical Evidence of Tax Incidence." NATIONAL TAX JOURNAL 11 (March 1958): 35-55.

Colm, G. and H.P. Wald. "Some Comments on Tax Burden Comparisons." NATIONAL TAX JOURNAL 5 (March 1952): 1-14.

Conrad, Alfred. "On the Calculation of Tax Burdens." ECONOMICA (N.S.) 22 (November 1955): 342-48.

Cragg, John G., A.C. Harberger, and Peter Mieszkowski. "Empirical Evidence on the Incidence of the Corporation Income Tax." JOURNAL OF POLITICAL ECONOMY 75 (December 1967): 811-21.

Davies, David G. "An Empirical Test of Sales Tax Regressivity." JOURNAL OF POLITICAL ECONOMY 67 (February 1959): 72-78.

_______. "The Significance of Taxation of Services for the Pattern of Distribution of Tax Burden by Income Class." NATIONAL TAX ASSOCIATION PROCEEDINGS OF THE SIXTY-SECOND ANNUAL CONFERENCE (Boston 1969), pp. 138-46.

Donnahoe, Alan S. "Measuring State Tax Burden." JOURNAL OF POLITICAL ECONOMY 55 (June 1947): 234-44.

Due, John. "Sales Taxation and the Consumer." AMERICAN ECONOMIC REVIEW 53 (December 1963): 1078-84.

_______. "The Value Added Tax." WESTERN ECONOMIC JOURNAL 3 (Spring 1965): 165-71.

Frank, Henry. "Measuring State Tax Burdens." NATIONAL TAX JOURNAL 12 (June 1959): 179-85.

Gillespie, W. Irwin. "Effect of Public Expenditures on the Distribution of Income." In R.A. Musgrave (ed.). ESSAYS IN FISCAL FEDERALISM. Washington, D.C.: Brookings Institution, 1965, pp. 122-86.

Gordon, R.J. "The Incidence of the Corporation Income Tax in U.S. Manufacturing, 1925-62." AMERICAN ECONOMIC REVIEW 57 (September 1967): 731-58.

Harberger, A.C. "The Incidence of the Corporation Income Tax." JOURNAL OF POLITICAL ECONOMY 70 (June 1962): 215-40.

Hendricks, H.G. "The Incidence of the Gasoline Tax." AMERICAN ECONOMIC REVIEW 21 (March 1931): 88-89.

Hicks, Ursula K. "The Terminology of Tax Analysis." In R.A. Musgrave and C.S. Shoup (eds.). A.E.A. READINGS IN THE ECONOMICS OF TAXATION. Homewood, Ill.: Richard D. Irwin, 1959, pp. 214-26.

Hoffman, R.F. "Some Analysis Concerning the Regressivity of Hawaii's General Excise Tax." NATIONAL TAX JOURNAL 18 (June 1965): 219-21.

Kilpatrick, R.W. "The Short-Run Forward Shifting of the Corporation Income Tax." YALE ECONOMIC ESSAYS 5, no. 2: 355-420.

Liebenberg, M., and J.M. Fitzwilliams. "Size Distribution of Personal Income, 1957-60." SURVEY OF CURRENT BUSINESS 41 (May 1961): 11-21.

Lotz, Jørgen R., and Elliot Morss. "Measuring 'Tax Effort' in Developing Countries." I.M.F. STAFF PAPERS (November 1967): 478-99.

Maynes, E.S. and J.N. Morgan. "The Effective Rate of Real Estate Taxation: An Empirical Investigation." REVIEW OF ECONOMICS AND STATISTICS 39 (February 1957): 14-22.

McLure, Charles. "Commodity Tax Incidence in Open Economies." NATIONAL TAX JOURNAL 17 (June 1964): 187-204.

_______. "Tax Exporting in the United States: Estimates for 1962." NATIONAL TAX JOURNAL 20 (March 1967): 49-77.

Megee, Mary. "On Economic Growth and the Factor Analysis Method." SOUTHERN ECONOMIC JOURNAL 31 (January 1965): 215-28.

Mieszkowski, Peter. "On the Theory of Tax Incidence." JOURNAL OF POLITICAL ECONOMY 75 (June 1967): 250-62.

Morag, A. "Is the 'Economic Efficiency' of Taxation Important?" ECONOMIC JOURNAL 69 (March 1959): 87-94.

Musgrave, R.A. "Distribution of Tax Payments by Income Groups: A Review." PROCEEDINGS OF THE FORTY-FIFTH ANNUAL CONFERENCE OF THE NATIONAL TAX ASSOCIATION (Toronto 1952), pp. 179-95.

_______. "On Incidence." JOURNAL OF POLITICAL ECONOMY 61 (August 1953): 306-23.

_______. "General Equilibrium Aspects of Incidence Theory." A.E.A. PAPERS AND PROCEEDINGS 43 (May 1953): 504-17.

Musgrave, R.A., J.J. Carroll, L.D. Cook, and L. Frane. "Distribution of Tax Payments by Income Groups: A Case Study for 1948." NATIONAL TAX JOURNAL 4 (March 1951): 1-53.

Musgrave, R.A., and Darwin Daicoff. "Who Pays the Michigan Taxes?" In MICHIGAN TAX STUDY STAFF PAPERS. Lansing: Secretary of Finance, 1958, pp. 131-83.

Musgrave, R.A., and Tun Thin. "Income Tax Progression, 1929-48." JOURNAL OF POLITICAL ECONOMY 56 (December 1948): 498-514.

Musgrave, R.A. and L. Frane. "Rejoinder to Dr. Tucker." NATIONAL TAX JOURNAL 5 (March 1952): 15-35.

Neisser, Albert C. "The Dynamics of Tax Burden Comparisons." NATIONAL TAX JOURNAL 5 (March 1952): 351-64.

Newcomer, Mabel. "Estimate of the Tax Burden on Different Income Classes." In STUDIES IN CURRENT TAX PROBLEMS. New York: Twentieth Century Fund, 1937, pp. 1-52.

Pechman, Joseph. "Some Technical Problems in the Measurement of Tax Burdens." PROCEEDINGS OF THE FORTY-FIFTH ANNUAL CONFERENCE OF THE NATIONAL TAX ASSOCIATION (Toronto 1952), pp. 204-12.

Pettengill, Robert B. "The Tax Burden Among Income Groups in the United States in 1936." AMERICAN ECONOMIC REVIEW 30 (March 1940): 60-71.

Prest, A.R. "Statistical Calculation of Tax Burdens." ECONOMICA (N.S.), 22 (August 1955): 234-45.

_______ . "On the Calculation of Tax Burdens: A Rejoinder." ECONOMICA (N.S.) 23 (August 1956): 270-72.

Ratchford, B.U., and P.B. Han. "The Burden of the Corporate Income Tax." NATIONAL TAX JOURNAL 10 (December 1957): 310-24.

Rummel, R.J. "Understanding Factor Analysis." JOURNAL OF CONFLICT RESOLUTION 11 (December 1967): 444-80.

Sacks, Seymour. "State and Local Finances and Economic Development." In STATE AND LOCAL TAXES ON BUSINESS. Princeton: Tax Institute of America, 1965, pp. 209-24.

_______ . "Metropolitan Fiscal Disparities: Their Nature and Determinants." THE JOURNAL OF FINANCE 23 (May 1968):229-50.

Schaefer, Jeffrey. "The Regressivity of State-Local Taxation: A Case Study of New Jersey." THE QUARTERLY REVIEW OF ECONOMICS AND BUSINESS 9 (Spring 1969): 7-18.

Schlesinger, Eugene. "The Statistical Allocation of Taxes and Expenditures in 1938/39 and 1946/47." In K.E. Poole (ed.), FISCAL POLICIES AND THE AMERICAN ECONOMY. New York: Prentice Hall, 1951, pp. 410-21.

Seligman, E.R.A. "Introduction to the Shifting and Incidence of Taxation." In R.A. Musgrave and C.S. Shoup (eds.). A.E.A. READINGS IN THE ECONOMICS OF TAXATION. Homewood, Ill.: Ricahrd D. Irwin, 1959, pp. 202-13.

Tarasov, Helen. "Who Does Pay the Taxes?" SOCIAL RESEARCH. Supplement 4, 1942.

Tiebout, Charles M. "A Pure Theory of Local Expenditures." JOURNAL OF POLITICAL ECONOMY 64 (October 1956): 416-24.

Tucker, Rufus. "The Distribution of Government Burdens and Benefits." A.E.A. PAPERS AND PROCEEDINGS 43 (May 1953): 518-43.

_______ . "Distribution of Tax Burdens in 1948." NATIONAL TAX JOURNAL 4 (September 1951): 269-85.

_______ . "Rebuttal." NATIONAL TAX JOURNAL 5 (March 1952): 36-38.

_______ . "Distribution of Tax Burdens in 1948." PROCEEDINGS OF THE FORTY-FIFTH ANNUAL CONFERENCE OF THE NATIONAL TAX ASSOCIATION (Toronto 1952), pp. 195-203.

Wales, T.J. "Analysis of the Constancy of the Effective Tax Rate." REVIEW OF ECONOMICS AND STATISTICS 50 (February 1968): 103-10.

Worcester, D.A. "A Graphic General Equilibrium Analysis of the Burden of Taxes." WESTERN ECONOMIC JOURNAL 2 (Summer 1964): 267-82.

Yaple, Maxine. "The Burden of Direct Taxes as Paid by Income Classes." AMERICAN ECONOMIC REVIEW 26 (December 1936): 691-710.

Yntema, Dwight. "Measures of the Inequality in the Personal Distribution of Wealth or Income." JOURNAL OF THE AMERICAN STATISTICAL ASSOCIATION 28 (1933): 423-33.

Government Documents

Advisory Commission on Intergovernmental Relations. FEDERAL-STATE COORDINATION OF PERSONAL INCOME TAXES. Washington, D.C.: Advisory Commission, 1965.

_______. TAX OVERLAPPING IN THE UNITED STATES 1961. Washington, D.C.: Advisory Commission, 1961.

_______. STATE AND LOCAL TAXES: SIGNIFICANT FEATURES 1968. Washington, D.C.: Advisory Commission, 1968.

_______. TAX OVERLAPPING IN THE UNITED STATES 1964. Washington, D.C.: Advisory Commission, 1964.

_______. STATE-LOCAL TAXATION AND INDUSTRIAL LOCATION. Washington, D.C.: Advisory Commission, 1967.

_______. STATE AND LOCAL FINANCES: SIGNIFICANT FEATURES 1966 TO 1969. Washington, D.C.: Advisory Commission, 1968.

United States Bureau of the Census. CENSUS OF GOVERNMENTS: 1962, vol. 2, TAXABLE PROPERTY VALUES. Washington, D.C.: U.S. Government Printing Office, 1963.

_______. CENSUS OF GOVERNMENTS: 1962, vol. 5, LOCAL GOVERNMENT IN METROPOLITAN AREAS. Washington, D.C.: U.S. Government Printing Office, 1964.

_______. CENSUS OF GOVERNMENTS: 1962, vol. 4, COMPENDIUM OF GOVERNMENT FINANCES. Washington, D.C.: U.S. Government Printing Office, 1964.

United States Department of Commerce. "Personal Income by States and Regions in 1963," SURVEY OF CURRENT BUSINESS, vol. 44 (August 1964), pp. 16-23.

United States Department of Labor, Bureau of Labor Statistics. SURVEY OF CONSUMER EXPENDITURES AND INCOME 1960-61. Reports 237-89, 90, 91, 92 and supplemental reports. Washington, D.C.: U.S. Government Printing Office, 1966.

United States Treasury Department. STATISTICS OF INCOME: INDIVIDUAL INCOME TAX RETURNS 1963. Washington, D.C.: U.S. Government Printing Office, 1966.

Unpublished Material

Campbell, Alan K. "The Tax Burden of Three Hypothetical Detroit Families." Unpublished Master's thesis, Department of Public Affairs, Wayne University, 1948.

Lemale, Helen H. "Uses of Family Expenditure Data." Paper, annual meeting American Home Economics Association, Atlantic City, New Jersey, June 22, 1965.

McLure, C.E. "An Analysis of Regional Tax Incidence, with Estimation of Interstate Incidence of State and Local Taxes." Unpublished Ph.D. dissertation, Department of Economics, Princeton University, 1966.

Tax Foundation. "Allocation of the Tax Burden and Expenditure Benefits by Income Class." Research Bibliography no. 15, revised April 1966.

Index

Index

About the Author

Donald Phares is currently a Fellow of the Center of Community and Metropolitan Studies and Assistant Professor of Economics at the University of Missouri-St. Louis. He did his undergraduate work at Northeastern University, graduating in 1965. He subsequently earned both masters and doctoral degrees from Syracuse University. He has been a consultant to numerous organizations, including the Department of Housing and Urban Development, the Urban Institute, RAND Corporation, Advisory Commission on Intergovernmental Relations and the Temporary State Commission to Make a Study of the Governmental Operations of the City of New York. He is a member of the American Economics Association, National Tax Association, American Real Estate and Urban Economics Association and other organizations. His publications have appeared in *Social Science Quarterly, Proceedings of the National Tax Association, Economic Geography, The Annals of Regional Science, Journal of Regional Science* and sections in three books. In addition to state and local finance, his research interests and publications deal with housing and racial transition and the economics of drug abuse.

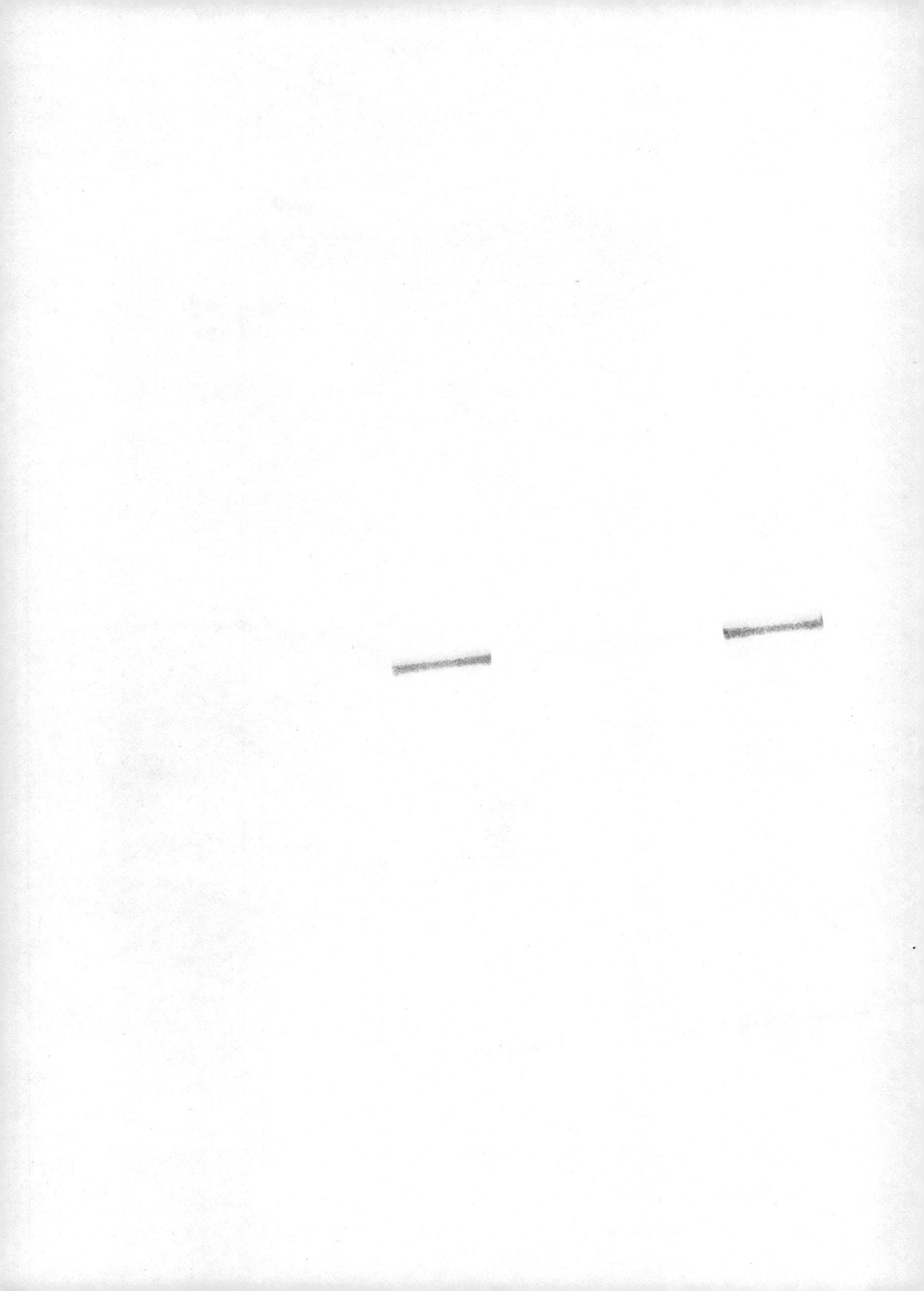